# WRITING GATSBY

# WRITING GATSBY

*The Real Story of the Writing of the Greatest
American Novel*

## WILLIAM ELLIOTT HAZELGROVE

Essex, Connecticut

An imprint of Globe Pequot, the trade division of
The Rowman & Littlefield Publishing Group, Inc.
4501 Forbes Blvd., Ste. 200
Lanham, MD 20706
www.rowman.com

Distributed by NATIONAL BOOK NETWORK

British Library Cataloguing in Publication Information available

**Library of Congress Cataloging-in-Publication Data**
Names: Hazelgrove, William, 1959– author.
Title: Writing Gatsby : the real story of the writing of the greatest American novel / William
   Elliott Hazelgrove.
Description: Essex, Connecticut : Lyons Press, [2022] | Includes bibliographical references and
   index.
Identifiers: LCCN 2022011989 (print) | LCCN 2022011990 (ebook) | ISBN 9781493068036
   (cloth) | ISBN 9781493070145 (epub)
Subjects: LCSH: Fitzgerald, F. Scott (Francis Scott), 1896–1940. Great Gatsby. | Fitzgerald, F.
   Scott (Francis Scott), 1896–1940. | American fiction—20th century—History and criticism. |
   Novelists, American—20th century—Biography.
Classification: LCC PS3511.I9 G8466 2022  (print) | LCC PS3511.I9  (ebook) | DDC 813/.52
   [B]—dc23/eng/20220415
LC record available at https://lccn.loc.gov/2022011989
LC ebook record available at https://lccn.loc.gov/2022011990

*The past is never dead. It's not even past.*

—WILLIAM FAULKNER

*No amount of fire or freshness can challenge what a man can store up in his ghostly heart.*

—F. SCOTT FITZGERALD, *THE GREAT GATSBY*

*Once Again For
Kitty, Clay, Callie,
and Careen*

# Contents

# PREFACE

They all turned against him in the end. Hemingway, the critics, the reading public. Only Max Perkins, his editor at Scribner's, and Harold Ober, his agent, stuck with him. Even the church turned on him, refusing to let him be buried in a Catholic cemetery. "The only reason I agreed to give the service, was to get the body in the ground," said the Episcopalian rector later. "He was a no-good drunken bum and the world was well rid of him."[1] Sheila Graham, the Hollywood gossip hound, his companion/girlfriend of his final years, would publish a tell-all book in the fifties, *Beloved Infidel*, that portrayed F. Scott Fitzgerald as a gin-soaked lunatic who Gregory Peck would famously play in the movie adaptation. There would be a scene where Sheila Graham and Scott wrestled over a loaded gun until Graham screamed, "Shoot yourself you son of a bitch! See if I care! . . . I didn't pull myself out of the gutter to waste my life on a drunk like you!"[2]

In his final years, Scott was reduced to telling people he was a famous author. Scott would get drunk on flights and buttonhole the stewardess, inquiring, "Do you know who I am?" The stewardess smiled. "No sir . . . I don't have my passenger list with me." He spread his arms, "I'm F. Scott Fitzgerald the very well-known writer. . . . "[3] The stewardess smiled and then moved on before he turned to the man across the aisle. "Do you know me?" he demanded. The man threw him a tolerant glance. "Nope. Who are you?" Scott paused. "I'm F. Scott Fitzgerald. You've read my books. You've read *The Great Gatsby*, haven't you? Remember?" The other looked surprised. "I've heard of you,"[4] he said grinning . . . a note of respect in his voice.

Years before, Scott and Sheila Graham had walked into the largest bookstore in Hollywood. He was faded, though just a touch over forty.

Grayish-blond hair, blue eyes, a scarf around his neck. Scott dressed like a dandy from the twenties with a pack of Chesterfields bulging from his pocket. Smoking and heavy drinking for twenty years had taken years off his life by now. The book clerk had a pencil behind his ear with a Mickey Rooney pompadour and had no time for the soft-spoken man and the younger, pretty woman. Scott asked him, "Have you any books by F. Scott Fitzgerald?" The clerk replied, "Sorry—none in stock." The scene gets worse as Scott pursues the clerk. "Do you have any calls for them?"

"Oh once in a while . . . but not for some time now."[5]

So Scott and Sheila go looking for his books in other stores only to be met with the same indifference. Finally, a small bookstore is their salvation. "I believe I can get hold of a title or two . . . which ones are you interested in?" The owner asked him. Scott wrote down *This Side of Paradise, The Great Gatsby, Tender is the Night*. The gray-haired man said, "I'll do my best to find these for you." Scott pauses. "I'm Mr. Fitzgerald." The owner put out his hand. "I'm happy to meet you Mr. Fitzgerald," he said. "I've enjoyed your books very much."[6]

So it came down to an old bookseller in a small bookstore in a rundown part of Hollywood to recognize the man who had written *The Great Gatsby*. F. Scott Fitzgerald would never fully realize his achievement, written in a villa off the beaches of the French Riviera. When he died in 1940, there were copies of *The Great Gatsby* in the Scribner warehouses. These copies were from the original print run in 1925. The book had not gone out of print; worse, it just didn't sell. The final royalty statement sent to Scott in 1940 was for $2.10 for the sale of seven copies of *The Great Gatsby* and nine copies of *Tender is the Night*. The reviews on *The Great Gatsby* had been mixed, and many had dismissed the book as nothing more than a sensational story. The publication of *The Great Gatsby* did not change the author's life in a significant way, but in the end, the fifty-thousand-word novel became a triumph of the artist over the philistine, the brilliant light over the darkness.

The story of the writing of *The Great Gatsby* is a story in itself. Fitzgerald had descended into an alcoholic run of parties on Great Neck, Long Island, where he and Zelda had taken a home. His main source of income was writing for the "slicks" or magazines of the day, with the main market being the *Saturday Evening Post*, where Fitzgerald's name on a story got him as high as $4,000. But the grind of writing the stories after the failure of his play *The Vegetable*, along with the incessant parties, drinking, keeping his twenty-four-year-old wife entertained, had all foiled any progress on a third novel that would settle his debts and fulfill the promise of his early work. Scott decided then to abandon Long Island for the South of France, the French Riviera, where he would put his stake in the sand and create his greatest work.

The story of the writing of *The Great Gatsby* begins here in the hot sands of the Riviera in that summer of 1924 and would end eleven months later on April 10, 1925, when the book would be published. What happened between the two dates is what produced the greatest work of American fiction the world has ever known.

# The Riviera

### September 1925

THE RENAULT HAD STALLED ON THE TROLLEY TRACKS. THEY WERE still young, even though they had already been to heaven and hell and back. She was just twenty-five, and he was just touching thirty. Blond and tan and gin drunk, they might have been mistaken for brother and sister. She had passed out long ago from the "1,000 parties and no work," and he had been nodding on and off. It was sometime in the morning. Maybe 3:00 a.m. They had acted badly at a party, and he had thrown ashtrays and insulted people, but he always did that. If a radio had been in the car, it might have been playing "Ain't We Got Fun," but all that was in the car were empty gin bottles, cigarettes, and streamers from some party they had long forgotten about. He wore knickers and a tie and looked like his character in the last novel he had written. They had been on a five-year tear, which was how long they had been married. He was the most famous author in America.

But now the car had stopped on the trolley tracks. He tried the starter, but it didn't work. They had never put oil or water in the car, and the top was missing. They had it cut off when it was damaged after being shipped from Italy to France. The mechanic told them they should take better care of the car, but they didn't care. His wife had driven their last car off the dock in Long Island during a party and that was a used Rolls-Royce. So, they didn't care about the Renault that sounded like it had seized up, but of course, he had never touched an engine before. Besides, he was drunk as drunk could be. Gin drunk. He drank gin to write, to get up, and to go to bed. He drank gin to breathe. He was still young, so it didn't matter yet the way it didn't matter that the car had stalled on the trolley tracks in the middle of the night. He looked at his sleeping wife. She was not the same anymore to him, but he was not the same to her. His last novel cost them plenty; really, it cost them their marriage.

But that was not what he was thinking about. In fact, he wasn't thinking. He had slumped down in the seat and laid his head back and passed out. He passed out everywhere. On lawns. In restaurants. In bars. On sidewalks in Manhattan. So, passing out was nothing. Why not? They were two young drunk Americans who had passed out in a small town on the Riviera in the middle of the biggest party the world had ever seen. People could have danced the Charleston around the couple. They could have poured champagne all over them, and no one would have thought it odd. Besides, they had invented jazz, the flapper, and they even invented the youth culture. But none of this mattered now.

They snored lightly. A breeze picked up and tousled his hair, picked at her hair. They looked absurdly young. Asleep, they looked like children to the Europeans. America was still a child, and nobody was quite sure how to define what constituted an American or what the American Dream was. They snored lightly, a purr, really. Down the trolley tracks, a whistle shrieked in the distance. Then a light turned the corner, and the trolley train lined up with the Renault. The light reflected in the side mirror and crept onto the windshield and the fender. The author and his wife slept on.

# CHAPTER I

# Myrtle Wilson

## *1924*

THE BANGING ON THE DOOR MIXED WITH HIS OWN PROSE. THE SHRIEKS. Yes, he had locked his wife into her own bedroom. Yes, he had. *BANG! BANG! BANG!* Scott kept one hand on his forehead, concentrating on the penciled words on the page. *BANG! BANG! BANG!* He could hear her pacing from one side of the bedroom to the other. Some would say later he kept her locked in the bedroom for a month. He had to do it. He had to keep his characters in front of him. One could not just have a character run away with another man and leave him. He owned his characters. So, he locked Zelda up and continued to write.

Scott took a swallow of gin and lit another cigarette. He wiped his forehead. It was damn hot on the Riviera and sweat darkened his page. *BANG! BANG! BANG!* Scott concentrated on the page in front of him. His pencil formed words, and the words formed monuments. The monuments created a world. The moonlight drenched the balcony. It was quiet now. The curtains twisted and blew in. A good image. The scratch of the pencil. Labored breath. The banging on the door had faded with the gin. What did he expect? You couldn't lock your wife up forever, but he had to. No, they were not going to divorce.

Scott sucked on his Chesterfield. The cigarettes would kill him one day. He chain-smoked when he wrote. He chain-smoked when he didn't write. He had written his first novel, *This Side of Paradise*, in his parents' attic on cigarettes and Coca-Cola. This novel had been fueled by black coffee and cigarettes and then . . . gin. The scent of the surf came in through the open window. Scott breathed in the Mediterranean air, along with a slight tang of a fish market. The pencil had gone cold in his hand. There was no more gas in the tank. He had to work to get back into the scene. It was like this now. It was her fault. The carnival could never stop, and he was the ringmaster. Not anymore. He had planted his flag in the Riviera sand. Here he put his writing first. Zelda would have to entertain herself. That was the problem. She *had* entertained herself.

Scott looked again at the door to the bedroom. She might have fallen asleep. He had heard nothing for hours. He lit another cigarette and eyed the glass of gin. He sipped it again. Well, he needed to lubricate the machine with something, and it was the end of the day. Sometimes it gave the world cover, uncovered nuance, loosened up the saddle just enough. It was the door into the other world, and once he was there, it was fine, but he found it harder and harder to keep the other world out. Zelda was no help, and he felt many times she was trying to purposely stop him, and many times, he felt she was jealous he had a purpose, a *raison d'être*, and she was left to her own devices. She had been doing just that, and at first, the days at the beach with the young aviators seemed harmless. But she had been coming back later and later. More intoxicated. Wilder. Then the fights. Her drinking. His drinking. None of it helped. It was gasoline during the fights. Many times, they bordered on violence where he had to hold her from running into the hallway and then into the street. She would go shrieking down the street like a madwoman if he didn't stop her. Alright, it was time.

Scott stood up and felt slightly dizzy. Maybe too much gin. He walked to the door and was about to knock and then unlocked the door. He walked in and saw Zelda sprawled facedown on the bed with her short, bobbed hair up over her cheek. Scott paused, then walked slowly to the bed. He was about to speak when he saw the glass bottle of DIAL, a sedative. It was on the left side, slightly under the bed, a white buoy against the dark African teak. Scott leaned down and recognized the vial. They both had trouble sleeping. Writing tied him up in knots, and between the gin and the coffee, he spent half the night tossing and turning. Zelda, too, had the same problems and had taken the sleeping pills before. Scott shook the bottle. Nothing. *Nothing.*

He turned the top, and the cap rolled away. *Empty.* There had been at least six in the vial before. Scott stared at Zelda's body, then dropped the vial and shouted. Zelda didn't move. He pulled her over and put his hand over her mouth. *Faint. Faint.* Scott felt the panic rise over him, running to the door then running back, putting his ear to her chest, his hand over her mouth. She was almost dead. He ran and tore open the door to their room and ran into the hallway, screaming for help like a madman.

# CHAPTER 2

# Ain't We Got Fun

## *1920*

SCOTT WAS HOLDING ONTO THE TOP OF THE YELLOW CHECKER TAXICAB going down Fifth Avenue in the bright spring sunshine. The wind was watering his eyes, and the buildings were flying by like the picture shows where everything is in fast motion. Zelda was in the taxi, and they had done this trick before with his tie flying back and his short yellow hair flattened against his head. It was the twenties, after all. Scott was flying as his book, *This Side of Paradise*, was flying off Scribner's shelves. Scott and Zelda had stumbled into the youth culture and taken the city by storm. They lived in the Plaza Hotel just off Central Park and drank until they dropped at a time when liquor was illegal. Zelda plunged into the fountain at the Plaza with her clothes on. Scott remembered the way the sun lit the water with Zelda swimming like a mermaid. People just stared. It was all too much to be believed, and even Scott was having a hard time with it.

" . . . from the confusion of the year 1920 I remember riding on top of a taxicab along deserted Fifth Avenue on a hot Sunday night, and a luncheon in the cool Japanese gardens at the Ritz with the wistful Kay Laurel and George Jean Nathan, and writing all night again and again and paying too much for minute apartments and buying magnificent but broken down cars. The first speakeasies had arrived, the toddle was passe, the Montmartre was the smart place to dance and Lillian Tashman's hair weaved around the floor among the liquored college boys."[1]

There had been no youth culture until the Fitzgeralds arrived. None. People just got old. Not anymore. Scott and Zelda looked like children, absurdly young. If you were young, you were gin-soaked and immortal. That was how Scott felt. Immortal. *Clink. Clink.* That was why he took off his clothes at the show, *George White's Scandals.* They escorted him out by the time he got down to his underwear. "In between time in the meantime. Ain't we got fun?" This decade was theirs. He and Zelda knew that. They flew around in the revolving doors for a half-hour at the Commodore to prove it. He was flying down Fifth Avenue on top of the taxi to prove it. "We felt like small children in a great bright unexplored barn . . . I remember riding in a taxi one afternoon between very tall buildings under a mauve and rosy sky; I began to bawl because I had everything I wanted and I knew I would never be so happy again."[2]

There is a picture in his scrapbook. Scott was a freak about lists and scrapbooks and ledgers and notebooks. He was a walking scribe. In the photo, they are all there in the Great Neck house on Long Island. He is lying on the floor in a tuxedo. The women have the sack dresses and long beads with the bobbed hair, and the men are all in suits. He's drunk as hell. The Victorians had given up the ghosts, but they all still dressed like young, elegant accountants. What did the new younger generation wear now? The men still wore three-piece suits, but the women had started to break convention with short hair and shorter skirts. They smoked, drank, and had lots of sex. They were in some sort of middle ground. That's why the press was so damn interested.

"What A Flapper Novelist Thinks of His Wife":[3] "The reporter from the *Brooklyn Eagle* appeared on Sunday in their home in Great Neck, Long Island to interview Scott and Zelda. Scott had just begun to sober up. This was when Long Island still reverted to the small fishing village. It was a lazy warm day. The reporter was star stuck. 'Obediently Scott Fitzgerald left his study, scene of the creation of those brilliant tales to which the American flappers thrill en masse. Tall, blonde, broad shouldered, he towers above his petite wife whose blue eyes and yellow hair match his own.'"[4]

Zelda loved that. They played their roles perfectly. The successful author and his wife whom he made famous through his fiction. "Asked to use his much-lauded gift for description in composing a word picture of his wife, he replied laconically and readily, 'She is the most charming person in the world.' 'Thank you dear,' was the gracious response. Asked to continue the description thus commenced so auspiciously he said, 'that's all I refuse to amplify. Except she's perfect.' 'But you don't think that,' came the protest from the overstuffed armchair. 'You think I'm a lazy woman.' 'No judicially I like it. I think you're perfect. You're always ready to listen to my manuscripts at any hour day or night. You're charming—beautiful. You do, I believe clean the ice box once a week.'"[5]

Zelda then leaned in and summed up their lives in a paragraph.

"'We were married on April Fool's Day, 1920,' Mrs. Fitzgerald continued, 'then came a trip abroad—I loved England and hated Italy—then came Patricia Scott Fitzgerald, known popularly as Scotty, 1922, then Great Neck, Long Island 1923. In the interim were lots of short stories from my husband's pen and two books, *This Side of Paradise* and *The Beautiful and the Damned.*'"

The reporter asks Zelda what constituted her perfect day. "'Peaches for breakfast . . . then golf, then a swim. Then just being lazy. Not eating or reading but being quiet and hearing pleasant sounds—rather a total vacuity. The evening? A large, brilliant gathering, I believe . . . am I ambitious? Not especially, but I've plenty of hope.'"[6]

What the reporter didn't see was the way it really was. The way it was now. One large, brilliant gathering after another. One party after another. That photo in Scott's scrapbook was just a glimmer of their life. Their life had become a whirl since Scott became famous and Zelda, his heroine, his flapper creation, became just as famous. His ledger entries from 1920 tell stories. "Started South on 15th. Parties in Montgomery. Sold Car. Biggs. Beginning novel. Zelda hides 500. Uncle Legrand and his honey. Sleeping upright. Grand Central Station, Longacre Drugstore John Williams Dance. Hot evenings in New York."[7]

There are photos of Zelda in a fur coat, and both of them in knickers. Scott in a suit with a pencil bent over a desk. Zelda and Scott in a 1918 Marmon. If they were movie stills from the twenties, they would be no different. It is hard to believe two young, attractive people had found fame at the same time the country had found the roaring twenties. But the fairytale of fame and fortune tapped them both on the forehead, and both were astounded with the ride that was just beginning. As Scott would later write, "I who knew less of New York than any reporter of six months standing and less of its society than any hall room boy in a Ritz Stag line, was pushed into the position not only of spokesman for the time but of the typical product of that same moment. I or rather it was 'we' now did not know exactly what New York expected of us and found it rather confusing."[8]

The reporter was last Sunday, and now there was another party, and Scott stood outside his home in Great Neck staring at the sun. *Riotous*. The swirl of clouds over the sound. Or maybe that was the gin. But it was *riotous*. Scott watched the flappers, the dancers, the drunks. Yes. It was a party. *The Charleston*. Now that was a complicated dance he could never get the hang of. The music blared. *Charleston Charleston . . . Charleston . . . Charleston . . .* But women seemed to have no problem. He watched two women kicking up their heels, with beads, pearls, necklaces swinging. "In between time . . . ain't we got fun." Another party among parties. When did this one start, and how did it start? How they all started.

Someone stopped in from New York. Then someone else stopped in from New York. Then someone just wandered up the road. Then people just appeared out of thin air, and suddenly their living room, their kitchen, their portico, their lawn was wall-to-wall people. Champagne popped. Whiskey was poured. Gin was tickled with ice. And there you were. Another party at the Fitzgerald's at the "nifty little Babbitt home,"[9] as Zelda described the white country home in Great Neck, complete with the room over the garage where Scott could write, complete with a short walk to the sound where they could swim, though they rarely did, no, scratch that, they *never swam*. Well, Zelda did, sometimes, but they did enjoy the view.

And now the riotous clouds. God, he loved that word. Scott dropped the match, then his drink. He lit the cigarette and picked up the glass. Some gin had survived. A cold, clean swallow. Gin was cold and clean. He stared at the room over the garage where he had been grinding out stories for the *Saturday Evening Post*. Always the pull between money and art. He could never just write. The stories paid the bills, and the novels paid his soul. The riotous swirling pink and orange clouds were in the windows of his office where he should be working on his third novel, but this celebration might be the one that was worth having instead of the other parties of dissipation that characterized the two and half years they had been out on Long Island.

They were celebrating with friends his play, *The Vegetable*, that was due to open tomorrow in Atlantic City, New Jersey. The Ring Lardner's were going with them to the opening, and word had gotten around this was a send-off for the opening, and the party had grown from that . . . although one thing people did not need in the twenties was a reason to have a party. *Pop, Pop, Pop. Fizz, Fizz, Fizz. Charleston, Charleston, Charleston . . . In the morning . . . in the evening . . . ain't we got fun . . .* The champagne exploded while someone started dancing, and people staggered into each other and discovered the famous among the drunkards and laggards who came to populate the Fitzgerald lawn on weekends, weekdays, and even holidays. His neighbors were celebrities from show business. "Sam Goldwyn, Eddie Cantor, Ed Wynn, the actress Mae Murray and the songwriter Gene Buck as well as General John Pershing."[10] Scott was really not sure where one party started and another ended, but wasn't that what the whole decade was about anyway? He had published a collection of short stories, *Tales of the Jazz Age*, although he could not have cared less and known less about jazz. Whatever it was, the age was one big, long party that had to end someday, but no one really wanted to know when that day was because . . . *then what?*

No. Better to just keep the party going, and to that end, Scott swallowed some more gin, lit another cigarette, and toasted the coming success of his play that would give him the financial independence he craved so he could settle down and write the third novel that had eluded him for the last few years and liberate him from writing for the magazines that paid the rent, bought the groceries, and kept the empty gin bottles that he put out every morning clinking on his back porch. It had been a hell of a party. Ring Lardner, friend, journalist, and drinking company, lived just a stone's throw away, and he and Ring had gotten drunk many nights, and one night, they ended up on the Doubleday Estate looking for Joseph Conrad by performing a dance on the lawn but were then thrown off the property. Lardner was a sportswriter, humorist, short story writer who had moved east to establish himself as a syndicated writer of humor with his own column and was the perfect foil for the younger, wilder, and more accomplished F. Scott Fitzgerald, all of twenty-seven now. Or was he twenty-eight? He forgot . . . time sloshed into time then into gin.

They were only fifteen miles from New York, and this kept a steady stream of revelers going to and from the Big Apple with the way-stop if not destination of the Fitzgerald's being part amusement park, part watering hole, and then part celebrity row. Great Neck was also "favored by business types. Among the residents were Herbert Bayard Swoop, Tom Meighan, Gene Buck, and Lew Fields." The Fitzgeralds were added to the list of celebrities with a "live in servant couple 160 a month, a nurse for their new baby Scottie, 90 a month, a part-time laundress at 36 a month."[11] So, what was not to like? Their life was a social whirl that kept them spending, drinking, sleeping until noon or even later until it all started over. Scott was twenty-seven, yes twenty-seven . . . no, wait a minute, in 1920, he was twenty-four. It was now 1924, that was right, he was *twenty-eight* and Zelda was *twenty-four*, and the world was their oyster . . . and there were pearls. He had just given Zelda an expensive string of pearls he had bought on a bender in Manhattan.

Scott looked up at the room over the garage again and breathed deeply from his Chesterfield nonfilter. If only he could get some work done. If only he could spend less. He seemed incapable of either. But no matter. *The Vegetable*, his play, would be a success. He had just written his editor, Max Perkins, for another $1,000 to be deposited, following up the request with a prediction. "After my play is produced, I'll be rich forever and never have to bother you again." But the drinking would continue. They drank when they made love. They drank when they ate. They drank when they walked. Talked. Slept. Ate breakfast, lunch, and dinner. They drank with company or without company. It didn't matter. Zelda drank when she went golfing with Helen Buck at the Sound View Golf Club where "they finished a shaker of orange blossoms (gin and orange juice)" and had to be fetched back by Ring Lardner after another thermos of gin and orange juice.

Scott recorded a typical day in his ledger of July 1923. "Tootsie (Rosalind) arrived. Intermittent work on novel. Constant drinking. Some golf. Baby begins to talk. Parties at Allen Dwans. Gloria Swanson and the movie crowd. Our party of Tootsie The Perkins (Max Perkins the famous Scribner editor) arrives. I drive into the lake."[12] It was all madness, and yet that third eye was always present. There was a neighbor named Von Gerlach who had an odd way of talking. A speech tag, if you will. "How are you and the family, old sport?"[13] A newspaper referred to him as a yachtsman.

> *"That's a great expression of yours isn't it" Tom said sharply.*
> *"What is?"*
> *"All this old sport business. Where'd you pick that up?"[14]*

Zelda would later say Gerlach was "in trouble over bootlegging."[15] Even at Scott's drunkest, most inebriated, one eye was always open. Recording. Recording. Recording. Neighbor Robert Kerr, a Great Neck resident who was a "jeweler, singer, piano player, philanthropist"[16] who Scott drank and swapped stories with, told Scott a story about when he was fourteen that Scott would use to create his greatest character. "One day I was out in the bay (Sheepshead Bay Brooklyn) when I noticed a handsome big yacht had come into the harbor—one of the finest I'd ever seen, and with a kid's curiosity, I made for it. I'd noticed they'd run in so the stern was up, and I realized that when the tide ran out as it was sure to do, the yacht would tilt more and more and probably break in two."[17]

> *It was James Gatz who had been loafing along the beach that afternoon in a torn green jersey and a pair of canvas pants, but it was already Jay Gatsby who borrowed a rowboat, pulled out to the Tuolomee and informed Cody that a wind might catch him and break him up in half an hour . . . To young Gatz, resting on his oars and looking up at the railed deck, that yacht represented all the beauty and glamour in the world.[18]*

"So I rowed alongside and yelled to one of the crew, 'hey mister, you're going to break your boat!' The captain waved the boy away, but the owner told the boy to come on board 'What do you do,' he asked and I told him. 'How'd you like to work for me?' He next asked. 'I'll give you twenty-five dollars a week.' I was barefoot and in old clothes, tanned and dirty . . . I had only old clothes at the beach. So he took me to Jim Bells and had me outfitted completely, with blue coat with brass buttons and white flannels. O it was great!"[19]

Tommy Hitchcock was at the party somewhere. Where was he? He was Scott's other close friend in Great Neck and would people the novel he was still gestating. A wealthy polo player and war hero who won the *Croix de Guerre* for escaping from German territory after being shot down and jumping from a train to elude his captors. He went to Harvard and then attended Oxford briefly before marrying a steel heiress and becoming a successful investment banker with Lehmann Brothers. " . . . *a national figure in a way, one of these men who reach such an acute limited excellence at twenty-one that everything afterwards savors of anticlimax. . . . He'd brought down a string of polo ponies from Lake Forest. It was hard to realize that a man in my own generation was wealthy enough to do that. . . . "*[20] He was Scott's ideal as a man and dominated the international polo scene as a ten-goal player from 1919 to 1939. A biographer later wrote of Hitchcock, "He was deficient in the graces as country aristocrats often are, sloppy in dress and awkward in manner, but he possessed in full measure the virtues valued by his class, modesty, loyalty, and magnanimity . . . "[21]

Then there were the New York trips that turned into New York weekends. Booze-sloshed weekends in warm hotel rooms at the Plaza, more dives into fountains, cars wrecked, chauffeurs fired. A used Rolls-Royce driven into the bay by Zelda with mud up to the axles. The story of Arnold Rothstein, who fixed the 1919 World Series, told to him by Ring Lardner who had inside information.

*"Meyer Wolfshiem? No., he's a gambler." Gatsby hesitated, then added coolly; "He's the man who fixed the World Series back in 1919."*[22]

Rothstein lived in Great Neck, and Scott met him at one of his parties. Edward M. Fuller had an estate in Great Neck, and he appeared on their kitchen table in the morning papers. Bleary hungover breakfasts with coffee and cigarettes and the Fuller McGee stock fraud case front-page news on the newspapers. Easy money all around. Corruption all around.

Through all this, Scott's drinking "had progressed from a party drinker to a steady drinker with increasingly erratic behavior."[23] Really, his drinking started in college at Princeton. "Occasionally I was conscious of his stumbling down the corridor when he came in or dropping his pencil," recalled Dale Warren, a freshman during Fitzgerald's junior year who lived across the hall from him. "His first few hours seldom refreshed him and I began to suspect the morning haze might well be due to a berry night at the Nass . . . Once or twice I found him lying fully or partly clothed on top of the rumpled bedspread. One morning when he was not there at all . . . he had spent the small hours of the night on the dewy grass somewhere out behind the Peacock Inn."[24]

Scott was no longer a social drinker, just a drinker. Later, many psychologists, doctors, and authors would try to explain his drinking. Scott himself took a crack at it in his fourth novel, *Tender is the Night*. "The drink made past happy things contemporary with the present, as if they were still going on, contemporary with the future as if they were about to happen again."[25] His preferred drink was straight gin. Maybe a textbook definition of alcoholism was better.

"A chronic behavioral disorder manifested by an undue preoccupation with alcohol and it's use to the detriment of physical and mental health, by loss of control when drinking is begun and by a self-destructive attitude in dealing with personal relationships and life situations."[26] Maybe. How about, it was *really fun*? At least in the twenties, it was when Scott and Zelda were in their twenties. Being blasted was *really fun*. But no matter. After the success of his play, all this would end. He would be able to concentrate on his . . . his . . . his *novel* (he stuttered sometimes when he was really lit). He would later make a list of the sources for his *Gatsby* chapters in 1938 and to prove to himself that the two and half years in Great Neck were not a total waste.

1. Glamor of Rumsies and Hitchcock

2. Ash heaps. Memory of 125th Great Neck

3. Goodards Dwannis Swopes

4. Vegetable days in New York (the play rehearsals) Memory of Guinevere's wedding

5. The meeting all an invention. Mary

6. Bob Kerr's story. The second party

7. The day in New York

8. The murder

9. Funeral an invention. [27]

So even when he was plastered as he was now, he was still *working*. He had already taken a shot at his third novel, but it petered out. So now, he was gathering information for the novel he would produce right after the play. *The play*. Everything depended on *the play*. The Vegetable . . . Vege . . . *Vegetable*. Yes. That would do it for him . . . *damn*. He had sloshed gin on his tie. *One things surer and nothings surer . . . the rich get richer and the poor get children*. Riotous . . . yes . . . it was all riotous . . . *riotous*. . . . riotous. . . . those pink clouds in the windows . . . *in the meantime in between time, Ain't we got fun* . . .

Scott dropped his drink again the way he did in the living room with the reporter still scribbling. It was a pastoral day on Long Island. A sailboat was a white triangle out on the sound against brilliant blue. Their daughter was playing in the yard. A rare moment of peace. Zelda repeated the question and looked at Scott. "Am I ambitious?" He had put a record on the phonograph. " . . . not especially, but I've plenty of hope. I don't want to belong to clubs. No committees. I'm not a joiner. Just be myself and enjoy living. . . . Home is the place to do things you want to do. Here, we eat, just when we want to. Breakfast and luncheons are extremely movable feasts. It's terrible to allow conventional habits to gain a hold on a whole household, to eat, sleep and live by clock ticks. . . . "[28]

Scott later wrote an article for the magazines, "How to Live on $36,000 a Year," and wrote down his monthly household expenses in 1923. Income Tax $198; Food $202; Rent $300; Coal, wood, ice, gas, light, phone and water $114.50; Servants $295; Golf clubs $105; Clothes $158; Doctor and dentist $42.50; Drugs and cigarettes $32.50; Automobile $25; Books $14.50; Other household expenses $112.50. Total $1,600. It wasn't enough. They spent $36,000 when Scott made $28,759. The room over the garage was there again. He drank some more gin. The play. It was all on the play. That would take him out of the drudgery of writing for the magazines, and he could finally get going on his third novel. It was all on the play now. He drank some more. Hummed along. The record played on, "In the meantime in between time . . . ain't we got fun. . . . "

## CHAPTER 3

# Flat as One of Aunt Jemima's Pancakes

## *1923*

SCOTT SUNK LOWER IN HIS CHAIR. HE WAS DRUNK, BUT THAT DIDN'T help. The heat slipped up his neck and centered in a throbbing between his eyes. The Ring Lardners were staring straight ahead. Zelda glanced at him and then turned back to the stage. It was as if they were all in straitjackets, forced to watch an execution. The execution was the death of his play, *The Vegetable*, and like an execution, it was not pretty. The people standing up during the second act was becoming a rout. Not quite a stampede but a steady stream of hard shoes heading for the exits.

The author of the play sank lower and pulled out his silver flask, took a hit of gin, then handed it to Ring Lardner, who took a long swallow and handed it back. They needed that now because this play was stinking up the theatre. People were holding their noses; Scott was sure he saw that. He took another hit and offered it to Ring, but he waved Scott off. Well, he really didn't need it; it wasn't *his play* bleeding all over the stage. It really wasn't Scott's fault. He had pulled off brilliant musical comedies at Princeton and had produced two well-received novels. Why shouldn't he be able to write a play with the premise of a young man falling asleep and dreaming he had become president. But plays were different. Scott knew nothing of plot and stage direction. He wrote by ear. "Perhaps it is too obvious to say that the play suffered for not being a novel, Fitzgerald's best work relied on a strong authorial voice creating mood, tension, and presence. The atmosphere he wove into his books required the kind of subtle imagery and foreshadowing that was not easily transferred from page to stage."[1]

Whatever the problem was, the play was sinking like the *Titanic* that had plunged to the bottom of the Atlantic just ten years before. Scott glanced at Zelda in her new dress, him in his new suit, new shoes, handkerchief, the flag of his success now the skull and crossbones of his pirate ship looking to skulk away. Scott wasn't sure if she was talking about the play or the people leaving. He really didn't want to know. But it was awful. He had tried his hand in theatre with *The Vegetable* and worked on it with the cast and crew, and here they were on opening night in Atlantic City and there had been a pre-party at their home in Great Neck, then a long, inebriated drive to Atlantic City and the introduction of the author to the audience and then the lights had gone down, and then the hemorrhaging began.

The title Scott had taken from a magazine quote. "Any man who does not want to get on in the world, to make a million dollars, and maybe even park his toothbrush in the White House hasn't got much good to him as a good dog has—he's nothing more or less than a vegetable."[2] It was a slow bleed at first, and Scott thought it might correct itself the way books suddenly found their rhythm, but this play went the other way. The lines were terrible suddenly. Wooden. Hackneyed. There was no coherence to the plot. No real order to the scenes. The play had self-immolated, and Act Two brought the coup de grâce with the fantasy scene. It was here the few people who might be going to the bathrooms turned into the stampede for the doors out of the theatre. It was here the hope of a financial payday from a successful play withered then vanished in the floodlights now illuminating this still-born creation.

Scott had been in debt before the play, and on November 5, he had to appeal to his brilliant editor, Max Perkins at Scribner's, to loan him money. The crash of the play is even worse as Fitzgerald promises repayment from the proceeds of *The Vegetable*.

"Dear Max, I have got myself into a terrible mess. As you know for the past month I have been coming every day to the city to rehearsals and then at night writing and making changes on the last act and even on the first two. It's in shape at last and everybody around the theatre who has seen it says it's a great hit. I put aside the novel (an unfinished beginning of *Gatsby*) and wrote a short story but it was done under such pressure that it shows it and Hovey doesn't want it. . . . I went up to the American Play Company yesterday and tried to get some money on the grounds that the show was in rehearsal. They sighed and moaned a little but said firmly it was against their rules. I'm at the end of my rope as the immortal phrase goes. I owe the Scribner Company something over $3500 even after deducting the reprint money from *The Beautiful and Damned* . . . could I assign the first royalty payments on the play to you to be paid until the full amount be cleared up? . . . What I need to extricate myself from the present hole is $650.00 which will carry me to the 15th . . . if I don't in some way get $650 in the bank by Wednesday morning I'll have to pawn the furniture . . ."[3]

Scott went on to predict all indebtedness would be paid to Scribner by January 15 with the play's success. But this was not to be. Zelda would later write a friend, pulling no punches. "In brief the show flopped as flat as one of Aunt Jemima's famous pancakes—Scott, Truex, and Harris were terribly disappointed and so was I. I had already spent the first weeks NY royalty for a dress to wear to the opening night that could not be exchanged. . . . "[4]

The question now was how to get out of the theatre and not be seen as one of the many abandoning the sinking ship. Scott looked longingly to the aisles, daring not to catch the eye of anyone in the theatre. He could feel their stares boring into the back of his head. He was tired. He had just had to pound out another *Saturday Evening Post* story that was just awful, and he had hoped his play might be the ticket away from the pulpy stories he had to keep pumping out to keep the lights on and the liquor flowing.

"The first act went fine but Ernest says he never had an experience on the stage like the second. I heard one woman hit the roof when the bible was mentioned," Zelda continued in her letter. "They seemed to think it was sacrilegious or something. People were so obviously bored. And it was all so very well done, so there was no use trying to fix it up.

The idea was what people didn't like—Just hopeless! . . . It is too terrible to contemplate."[5]

Scott could contemplate how terrible it was. He wrote it. "It was a colossal frost," he wrote later. "People left their seats and walked out, people rustled their programs and talked audibly in bored impatient whispers. After the second act I wanted to stop the show and say it was all a mistake but the actors struggled heroically on."[6] Somehow, they got out of the theatre that night. Scott even made some efforts to fiddle with the play for a week, but every night, it just seemed to get worse. No, the play was dead. The reviews were not kind. "Mr. Fitzgerald would better stick to his modernistic realism and leave fantasy to those of lighter touch and whim."[7] Scott had even had the play bound and published by Scribner's, but it fizzled after one printing.

In his ledger, he recorded the arc of the play. "Rehearsal. Short of money. Excitement. More Rumsey parties. Atlantic City. The Failure and dismal return. On the wagon. Writing story in one day. . . . "[8]

A week later, he was back over his garage in Great Neck, Long Island, writing another story to pay the bills. It wasn't that he wasn't making good money. He was. It's just he had no idea where it all went. In the *Saturday Evening Post* story "How to Live on $36,000 a Year," which had paid him a thousand for that story, he ruminated on where all the money had gone. "Over our garage is a large bare room wither I now retired with pencil and paper and oil stove, emerging the next afternoon at five o'clock with a 7,000-word story. That was something; it would pay the rent and last months overdue bills. It took twelve hours a day for five weeks to rise from abject poverty back into the middle class, but within that time we had paid our debts and the cause for immediate worry was over."[9]

But the worry was not over. There was another party. Another trip into New York. The parties had not really stopped since 1920. Scott's ledger for 1922 read, "a comfortable but dangerous and deteriorating year at Great Neck. No ground under our feet . . . more drinking."[10] The newspapers tracked the Fitzgeralds' every move, every party. "In the Sunday section of the *Morning Telegraph* it was reported that 'F. Scott Fitzgerald prefers piquant hors d'oeuvre's to a hearty meal. He is also fond of Charlie Chaplin, Booth Tarkington, real Scotch, old fashioned hansom riding in Central Park and the Ziegfeld Follies. He admires Mencken and Nathan, Park and Tilford, Lord and Taylor, Lea and Perrins, the Smith Brothers, and Mrs. Gibson the pig lady and her Jenny mule.'"[11] Another clipping commented on the celebrity the Fitzgeralds generated: "We are accustomed enough to this kind of rumor in regard to stage stars but it is fairly new in relation to authors. The great drinking bouts, the petting may be what the public expects of Fitzgerald whose books told so much of this kind of life."[12]

Another entry in the ledger: "Both sick. Drinking . . . struggling with money. Work all night on Baby Party."[13] Zelda and Scott had been in the home in Great Neck for two years now, and the drive into New York or people coming from New York was a steady train of revelers only too glad to drink with the fabulously young and successful Fitzgeralds. Scott and Zelda had just appeared in *Hearst International* in a full-page photograph of the young author and his wife. "They were the apotheosis of the twenties: The F. Scott Fitzgeralds; Scott sitting behind Zelda, leaning slightly forward, his right hand casually holding her fingers, both of them pouting a little, dramatically; Zelda in a dress trimmed with white fur, wearing a long strand of pearls, with her hair parted uncharacteristically in the middle and falling back from her brow in deeply marcelled waves."[14] The photo was picked up by newspapers all over the country and put Scott and Zelda on the same level as movie stars. They came to parties at midnight, passed out in each other's arms, fought, went on three-day binges in New York, and ended up in strange apartments.

But the pulp for the magazines had to keep pace, and after *The Vegetable* implosion, Scott churned out stories over his garage. *"Why Blame it on the Poor Kiss if the Girl Veteran of Many Petting Parties is Prone to Affairs After Marriage? What Kind of Husbands Do Jimmies Make? Does A Moment of Revolt Come Sometime to Every Married Man? Wait till you Have Children of Your Own!"*[15] These were horrible stories that made Scott pull up the dredge from his soul to hit the deadlines. Six months later, he would write, "I no longer cough and itch and roll from one side of the bed to the other all night and have a hollow black ache in my stomach after two cups of black coffee. I really worked hard as hell last winter but it was all trash and it nearly broke my heart as well as my iron constitution."[16]

Scott had gone on a tear after the fenestration of his play but had managed to stash away some cash. He had to do something because he had no idea how the very good money he had made had vanished. "I wanted to find out where the $36,000 had gone. Thirty-six thousand is not very wealthy, not yacht and Palm Beach wealthy, but it sounds to me as though it should buy a roomy house full of furniture, a trip to Europe once a year, and a bond or two besides. But our $36,000 had bought nothing."[17] In today's money, the Fitzgeralds had blown a quarter-million dollars with nothing to show but extravagant parties and more extravagant nights into New York. So, Scott was right to be concerned because he could not keep up pace with the magazines. And worse, his literary career would slide unless he could get another novel out the door.

The decision had been made. They would go to the South of France, and there he could plant his flag in the sand and write the elusive third novel. By March, Scott had earned $16,500 from his magazine stories. By April, he wrote in his ledger, "Out of the woods at last and starting novel. Decision on the 15th to go to Europe."[18] But then comes the list of parties that prevented any real work on his third novel. "Gloria Swanson's party. Kauffman's party. Miss Comyn, William and Sally. Bunny and Ring talk all night. The 'one day' story again. Leland Hayward and Connie Bennet. Esther Murphy's party."[19] A final letter to Max Perkins on April 10 before he sails: "While I have every hope and plan of finishing my novel in June you know how these things often come out. And even if takes me ten times that long I cannot let it go out unless it has the very best I am capable of. Much of what I wrote last summer was good (a start on *Gatsby*) but it was so interrupted that it was ragged and in approaching it from a new angle I've had to discard a lot of it . . . it is only in the last four months that I've realized how much I've, well, almost deteriorated in the three years since I finished *The Beautiful and Damned*. The last four months of course I've worked but in the two years—over two years—before that, I produced exactly one play, half a dozen short stories, and three or four articles—an average of about one hundred words a day. If I'd spent this time reading or traveling or doing anything even staying healthy—it be different but I spent it uselessly, neither in study or contemplation but only in drinking and raising hell generally. . . . I feel

I have an enormous power in me now, more than I've ever had in a way but it works so fitfully and with so many bogeys because I've talked so much . . . I don't know anyone who has used up so much personal experience as I have at twenty-eight . . . This book will be a consciously artistic achievement and must depend on that as the first books did not . . . please believe me when I say that now I'm doing the best I can."[20]

Scott turned off the light of his office one last time and walked down the stairs into the garage, then plunged into the warm evening air outside. The close night was there. He stopped and cupped another Chesterfield nonfilter, tossing the match into the sand. The crickets were in the high reeds down by the sound. He walked down the driveway and across the road toward the beach. Across the Long Island Sound were the glittering palaces of the mega-rich. They came to his parties sometimes. Barons. Industrialists. Movie stars. They came and drank and then vanished. They, too, were riding the wave of easy money that the twenties had become with prohibition booze, speakeasies, champagne, sex, parties, an overheated stock market, a rapidly growing credit market.

The tranquil darkness closed in around Scott as he walked further onto the sand. Zelda was in New York, and he hadn't eaten all day. Cigarettes, booze, and coffee did that to him. No appetite at all. But now, he was just tired, and he looked out onto the sound where a few boats slit the night with their green-and-red running lights. Scott put his hands in his flannels and scratched his chin. What had he done? A lot, actually. His first novel, *This Side of Paradise*, had been a surprise success. Then *The Beautiful and the Damned* had followed. His second was not reviewed as well, but it had sold decently, and there had been movie rights sales on both novels. But the money slipped away, and he had to keep writing stories so they could just buy groceries sometimes. Scott had borrowed a lot of money from his agent and his publisher, but now he had managed to get some put away.

Scott breathed in the air, his eyes drifting to the lighthouse on the far side of the sound. The flash of the green light always made him feel better. Possibility. That is what the light said to him. Something about the way it crossed the sound. "*Involuntarily I glanced seaward—and distinguished nothing except a single green light, minute and far away, that might have been at the end of a dock.*"[21] The century was still young. He was just a little older. And yet he felt strangely used up. He had written in his ledger: "A comfortable but dangerous and deteriorating year at Great Neck. No ground under our feet." Then "—another fight. Tearing Drunk." Then "A bad year. No work. Slow deteriorating repression with outbreak just around the corner."[22] But it was still out there. They said he didn't know what to do with his talent. They said he was like an old woman with a diamond. Someone with a gift who didn't have the intellectual framework to use it. They were wrong. He just needed time. He saw something out there. It was in the people who came to his home. They were all riding a wave. America was riding a wave, but there was something else behind it.

Scott stared at the flashing green light, listening to a gull, a lanyard slapping a mast out in the darkness. The breeze fanned his blond hair. It was there, some glimmer, but he would have to leave to find it. This he knew. And that was why they were leaving. He, Zelda, Scottie. They were leaving under the cover of night. Slipping away to the French Riviera, where he could finally write the novel that he was destined to write. It was to be something different. Something magnificent. It had to be. The summer was coming, and the revelers would come only to find the empty house. But he was taking with him the memories, the moments, the raw material he would pound into form, then break apart and put back together in an entirely new way. He was leaving to get a view. A fresh view of the country. Of the carnival of America. He would sack away some more money, and then they would go.

Scott stood in the warm darkness and watched the green eye of the Long Island lighthouse wink across the sound again. He raised his hand up. Then he mouthed the cigarette and held up his other hand. He liked the gesture. " . . . *he stretched out his arms toward the dark water in a curious way, and, far as I was from him, I could have sworn he was trembling.*"[23] What did it say? It said he had come far; a Midwestern boy who had come East to find his destiny. A good premise.

# CHAPTER 4

# Rich Girls Don't Marry Poor Boys

## *1911*

SCOTT FITZGERALD LEAPFROGGED OVER THE FIRE HYDRANT ON SUM-
mit Avenue. He was fifteen and headed East in the fall to school. All was
going well for him. He walked past the Victorian mansions that stood
haughtily at attention and counted off the families he knew. They were all
rich: E. L. Hersey, the lumberman; Charles W. Ames of the West Publishing Company; C. Milton Greggs, the wholesaler. Summit Avenue of
St. Paul, Minnesota, was the same as the Millionaires Row of Cleveland,
and Scott thought that by going East to school, he might rise up and be
a man like the millionaire James J. Hill. James J. Hill was a leading figure
in St. Paul who had organized the Great Northern and Northern Pacific
railroad.

> *He had a big future before him you know. He was only a young man,*
> *but he had a lot of brain power here. . . . If he of lived he'd have been*
> *a great man. A man like James J Hill. He'd of helped build up the*
> *country.[1]*

And as Scott walked, he immortalized the moment in the short story,
*A Night at the Fair*, written years later. And in that story, the Van Schellinger limousine pulls up and Gladys Van Schellinger, future debutante,
local rich girl who also was going away to school in the East, gives him

a ride in her limousine. He climbs into the limousine and settles in the back with Gladys and her parents, the chauffer driving in front. Basil (Scott) is excited, she whom he had pinned after for a year had finally recognized him as a potential suitor. "Gladys Van Schellinger had never been his girl, not anyone's girl, but the fact that they were starting away to school at the same time gave him a feeling of kinship for her—as if they had been selected for the glamorous adventure of the East, chosen together for a high destiny that transcended the fact that she was rich and he was only comfortable."[2]

But Scott Fitzgerald is, in fact, an interloper. A spy among the rich. His father actually guided Confederate spies in the Civil War. Edward Fitzgerald in photos is a dapper man with shined shoes, a dark, well-trimmed beard, and a retiring reticence already in place by thirty. "Courtly, deferential, and distinguished by a neatly sculpted Vandyke beard, Edward fairly trailed clouds of faded Southern glory . . . stubbornly proud of his inability to make money."[3]

When Scott was nine, he would go downtown with his father with a little cane to get his shoes shined. Edward went through a series of jobs, finally ending up as a salesman for Procter & Gamble until he lost his job in 1908. In an interview years later, Scott recalled the day the family fortunes changed. "One afternoon I was ten or eleven the phone rang and my mother answered it. I didn't understand what she said but I felt that disaster had come to us. My mother, a little while before, had given me a quarter to go swimming. I gave the money back to her. I knew something terrible had happened and I thought she could not spare the money now. Then I began to pray, 'Dear God,' I prayed, 'please don't let us go to the poorhouse.' A little later my father came home. I had been right. He had lost his job."[4]

Edward was fifty-five, and his prescient son later remarked, "that morning he had gone out a comparatively young man, a man full of strength, full of confidence. He come home that evening, an old man, a completely broken man. He had lost his essential drive, his immaculateness of purpose. He was a failure the rest of his days."[5]

But, in fact, Scott later held his father's standards as a bulwark against the world. A failure in the mercantile world making money, he was a patrician who was honorable, polite, reserved, his Old World values that vanished with the nineteenth century informing Scott's frame of reference for judging the modern world of the East.

*In my younger and more vulnerable years my father gave me some advice that I've been turning over in my mind ever since. Whenever you feel like criticizing anyone, he told me, just remember that all the people haven't had the advantages you've had.*[6]

Francis Scott Fitzgerald, twice removed from the famous Francis Scott Key who wrote "The Star-Spangled Banner," was born on September 24, 1896, to a doting if eccentric mother, Mary Mollie McQuillan, who held the purse strings of her inheritance from her father, Philip F. McQuillan, a prosperous wholesale grocer in St. Paul, Minnesota, who died at forty-four of Bright's disease complicated by tuberculosis. Scott's mother spoiled him and, at the same time, didn't understand why her son would become a writer. In one story, Scott refers to the character's mother, "the books by her son were not vivid to her and while she was proud of him in a way, and was always glad when a librarian mentioned him or when someone asked her if she was his mother, her secret opinion was that such a profession was risky and eccentric."[7]

Scott's grandfather would become the reference of a Horatio Alger story Scott would carry all his life. When Philip McQuillan died, St. Paul mourned their prosperous son in the local paper. "He came here a poor boy with but a few dollars in his pocket, depending solely on a clear head, sound judgement, good habits, strict honesty and willing hands with strict integrity his guiding motive. How these qualities have aided him is shown in the immense business he has built up, the acquisitions of large property outside and the universal respect felt for him by the businessmen of the country . . . he leaves as his immediate family a wife and four children."[8]

Two daughters preceded Scott who died. One daughter followed who died. A sister, Annabel survived. Infant mortality in the late nineteenth century was disastrously high. After Scott's fathers lost a series of jobs the family settled permanently in the Summit Hill Area of St. Paul.

It was in these twelve blocks of mansions at the eastern end of Summit Avenue above downtown St. Paul that the Fitzgeralds lived, in rented houses or apartments. A middleclass boy among the rich; F. Scott Fitzgerald would never live in a home owned by his parents nor as an adult would he ever purchase a home. America's greatest author would remain a renter his entire life.

But Scott was "Mollie McQuillan's boy." Even though his family is essentially living on his mother's inheritance and living in apartments, Scott is allowed to associate with the rich children of Summit Avenue, casting his view of the world as the Cinderella among the one percent. He would later write, "I am half black Irish and half old American stock with the usual exaggerated ancestral pretensions. The black Irish half of the family had the money and looked down upon the Maryland side of the family who had, and really had, that certain series of reticence and obligations that form under that poor old, shattered world "breeding. So being born in that atmosphere of crack, wisecrack and counter crack, I developed a two-cycle inferiority complex . . . "[9]

In the story *Forging Ahead* his middle-class status is painfully revealed when Basil Duke Lee realizes he cannot go to college because his mother has lost a great deal of money. "His ideas of money were vague and somewhat debonair, but he had noticed the family dinners and immemorial discussions as to whether the third block would be sold to the railroads had given place to anxious talk of Western Pacific Utilities. At half past six his mother telephoned for him to have his dinner and with growing uneasiness he sat alone at the table, . . . she came in at seven, distraught and miserable and dropping down at the table, gave him his first information about finance—she and her father and her brother Everett had lost something more than eighty thousand dollars."[10]

Scott's father Edward imaginatively ceases to exist and rarely pops in to stories. With a mother who often wore her hat backwards and sometimes two different shoes, Scott would have to create his own family. *His parents were shiftless and unsuccessful farm people—his imagination had never really accepted them as his parents at all. The truth was that Jay Gatsby of West Egg Long Island sprang from his Platonic conception of himself. He was a son of God—a phrase which if it means anything, means just that and*

*he must be about his father's business, the service of a vast, vulgar and mere-
tricious beauty.*[11] Scott admired his father for his sense of Southern honor
and the stories he told him about the Civil War, but beyond a spiritual
totem pole he felt his father's failure keenly. At one point later in life
Scott would refer to his father as "a moron."

It is here Scott creates the fantasy he was a foundling "placed on the
Fitzgerald doorstep wrapped in a blanket with the Stuart coat of arms."[12]
In the short story *Absolution* the young protagonist Rudolf Miller is
the son of a local freight agent who disowns his lower middle-class
family and his abusive father and creates a new identity, Blatchford Sarnemington. "When he became Blatchford Sarnemington a suave nobility
flowed from him. Blatchford Sarnemington lived in great sweeping triumphs. When Rudolf half closed his eyes it meant that Blatchford had
established dominance over him and as he went by, there were envious
mutters in the air: "Blatchford Sarnemington! There goes Blatchford
Sarnemington."[13]

Scott might be able to even pin his alcoholism on his father. In his
ledger in 1905, he noted, "Father used to drink too much and then play
baseball in the back yard."[14] Scott grew up disowning his own parents
and seeing the man he would become in the East. At the same time Scott
carries the Midwestern stability with him.

*I am part of that, a little solemn with the feel of those long winters,
a little complacent from growing up in the Carraway house in a city
where dwellings are still called through decades by a family's name.*[15]

Walking the sidewalks of Summit Avenue, he would be the boy peering in the keyholes of the mansions at the rich. The grandson of Mollie
McQuillan's father was allowed to associate with the rich but never be
the rich. Estimates of Mollie's eventual inheritance range up to $125,000,
but she would not receive this until Scott is ready to go to college. In
contemplating going East to school "beyond the dreary railroad stations
of Chicago and the night fires of Pittsburgh, back in the old states,
something went on that made his heart beat fast with excitement."[16] The
dreamy fifteen-year-old plays with future debutantes and is shamefully

aware of his circumstances (it seems the shame comes primarily from his father's loss of job and earning power) and in *Forging Ahead*, after his mother loses her money through bad investments going to Yale (Princeton) vanishes over the next hill. Scott realizes it is not just school he is losing, but the dream of the East.

"Yale (Princeton) was the far away East that he loved with a vast nostalgia since he had first read books about great cities. Beyond the railway setations of Chicago and the night fires of Pittsburgh, back in the old states, something went on that made his heartbeat fast with excitement. He was attuned to the vast breathless bustle of New York, to the metropolitan days and nights that were tense as singing wires. Nothing needed to be imagined there, for it was the very stuff of romance, life was as vivid and satisfactory as in books and dreams."[17]

In the story, Basil Duke Lee then takes a job with his rich uncle who is standing in for grandfather McQuillan to "work his way through Yale,"[18] He grovels in front of his uncle and his younger wife. His uncle looks down on Scott's side of the family and scoffs at his idea of going to Yale. "It might be different if you wanted a permanent place, but you say you want to go to Yale." He said this with some irony of his own and glanced at his wife. "Why yes," said Basil. That's why I really want the job." "Your mother can't afford to send you eh?" The note of pleasure in his voice was unmistakable. "Spent all her money?"[19]

Basil gets the job with the promise to escort the daughter of his uncle's wife Rhoda to dances. But he loses it just as quickly when he doesn't take Rhoda to a dance, and just when all seems lost he registers at the community college. Basil (Scott) was losing his portal to the bigger life in the East where Yale "evoked the memory of a heroic team backed up against its own impassable goal in the crisp November twilight and later of a half dozen immaculate noblemen with opera hats and canes standing in the Manhattan hotel bar. And tangled up with its triumphs and rewards, its struggles and glories, the vision of the inevitable, incomparable girl."[20]

Miss Reilly then telephones his mother to find out why Basil has stood up her daughter and Basil hears his mother say, "very well Mrs. Reilly. I'll tell my son. But his going to Yale is scarcely a matter I care to discuss with you. In any case he no longer needs anyone's assistance. Uncle Ben might be interested to know that this afternoon we sold the Third Street Block to the Union Depot Company for four hundred thousand dollars."[21] Basil (Scott) is saved from the fate of community college, in reality, by the death of his grandmother McQuillan and he heads for Princeton on his mother's inheritance, but it shows how precarious Scott's position is and that without his mother's money, he would lose his tenuous spot as observer of the rich.

Before Princeton though, Scott heads off to the Newman School prep school at fifteen in 1911 where he is unpopular because of his conceit and braggadocio manner. Later in *This Side of Paradise* he would write, "Miserable, confined to bounds, unpopular with both faculty and students—that was Amory s first term. But at Christmas he had returned to Minneapolis, tight lipped and strangely jubilant. 'Oh I was sort of fresh at first,' he told Froggy Parker patronizingly. 'But I got along fine—lightest man on the squad. You ought to go away to school, Froggie, its great stuff."[22]

It is here Scott begins to experiment with alcohol. He and his friends drank drugstore Sherry in St Paul. In 1913 he began to try stronger liquors at Newman. In his ledger he notes that he was "tight at Susquehanna."[23] His grades were abysmal and he failed four courses in the two years. But Fitzgerald profited at Newman by his association with the best and brightest who were barreling toward Ivy League colleges. "I was at prep school in New Jersey with Pulitzer Prizeman Herbert Agar and novelist Cyril Hume and Edward Hope Coffey. Hope and I were destined to follow a similar pattern—to write librettos at Princeton, 'drool' for the college comic and later college novels. But I remember him best when he was center and I was the college quarterback on the second team at school. We were both fifteen and awful . . . were the laziest and lowest ranking boys in school."[24]

Scott comes to know Ginevra King a rich debutante from Lake Forest Illinois whom he tries to court. Ginevra has grown up among the Swifts, the Armors, and the McCormicks. It is a doomed two-year romance where Scott writes thirty-page letters to the debutante who is engaged to multiple men. He overhears someone at a party in a North

Shore visit in 1916 say that poor boys shouldn't think of marrying rich girls. *That was it. I'd never understood it before. It was full of money—that was the inexhaustible charm that rose and fell in it, the jingle of it, the cymbals song of it . . . High in a white palace lived the king's daughter, the golden girl.*[25]

In his ledger there are clues as to where Scott was given the low-down. "Lake Forest. Peg Carry Petting Party. Ginevra. Party. The bad day at the McCormicks. The dinner at Pegs. Disappointment. Mary Buford Pierce. Little Marjorie King and her smile. Beautiful Billy Mitchell. Peg Cary stands straight. "Poor boys shouldn't think of marrying rich girls."[26]

In his first novel *This Side of Paradise* he turns Ginevra into Rosalind and Scott is Amory as he asks her to marry him. She shakes her head tragically. "I can't Amory. I can't be shut away from the trees and flowers cooped up in a little flat, waiting for you. You'd hate me in a narrow atmosphere. I'd made you hate me. . . . I don't want to think about pots and kitchens and brooms. I want to worry about whether my legs will get slick and brown when I swim in the summer."[27]

How Ginevra really viewed Scott was revealed when he asked for his letters back at the end of their two-year romance. She responds in a letter, "I have destroyed your letters—so you needn't be afraid that they will be held up as incriminating evidence. They were harmless—have you a guilty conscience? I'm sorry you think that I would hold them up to you as I never did think they meant anything. If it isn't too much trouble you might destroy mine too."[28] While Ginevra had destroyed Scott's letters, he had hers copied and bound. He was never really in the running . . . a boy of moderate means competing with the uber-rich.

And now we are back in the Van Schellinger limousine where Basil (Scott) believes he has made it. The richest girl of Summit Avenue has found favor with him. "Sitting beside Gladys in the little seats he loved her suddenly. His hand swung gently against hers from time to time and he felt the warm bond that they were both going away to school tighten around them and pulling them together. 'Can't you come and see me tomorrow?' She urged him swiftly. 'Basil . . .' He waited. Her breath was warm on his cheek. He wanted her to hurry or when the engine stopped, her parents dozing in the back, might hear what she said. She seemed beautiful to him then, that vague unexciting quality about her was more than compensated for by her exquisite delicacy, the fine luxury of her life. 'Basil . . . Basil when you come tomorrow, will you bring that Hubert Blair?' The chauffeur opened the door and Mr. and Mrs. Van Schellinger woke up with a start. When the car had driven off, Basil stood looking after it thoughtfully until it turned the corner of the street."[29]

Hubert Blair is a rich, popular boy. Poor boys don't marry rich girls. Scott would carry this view with him to the East, where he would become the dispassionate narrator, sitting in judgment on the rich. For the rest of his life, no matter how much money Scott made or spent, he was forever the poor boy in the thrall of the rich and, especially, the rich girl. He would take this thought with him to the Riviera and build a monument.

# CHAPTER 5

# The Rough Crossing

## *1924*

ON MAY 1, 1924, F. SCOTT FITZGERALD, HIS WIFE ZELDA, BABY SCOT-tie Fitzgerald, seventeen pieces of luggage, a hundred feet of copper screen for mosquitoes, and an *Encyclopedia Britannica* boarded the steamer *SS Minnewaska* and sneaked away from New York. The *Minnewaska* was a dry ship, reflecting the famous author's desire to separate himself from his gin-soaked residence in Great Neck, New York, on Long Island Sound. He wanted to dry out and escape the continual parties that left him hungover, exhausted, and unable to get anywhere on his third novel. They were sailing for Paris and then the Riviera, where Fitzgerald would plant his flag to write his elusive third novel that would pull him out of the grind of writing *Saturday Evening Post* stories for needed cash and resuscitate his literary career after the disastrous flop of his play, *The Vegetable.*

Smelling of gin, cigarettes, faintly hurried, hungover from the night before, Scott squinted against the blazing sun reflecting off the water of New York Harbor. He and his family had marched up the gangplank and poured themselves onto the *Minnewaska.* "The ship's brochure promised "richly decorated public rooms and staterooms and a full orchestra, some cabins came with private sitting room and bath."[1] They had done it. They were escaping from the constant parties, drinking, carousing, lost days, hungover mornings. Maybe it was when Zelda rushed into the room of

Scott's good friend, John Peale Bishop, and asked to sleep with him or when she invited Townsend Martin into the bathroom and asked him to give her a bath, or kissing Scott's friends in public, or when Scott passed out on the lawn, pulled the table cloth off the table at dinner, had a party with a guest of honor he forgot to invite because he was too drunk, or gave Zelda a black eye when he busted down the bathroom door in their home, but the drinking had spiraled out of control over the last few years. So, they were going.

Scott turned and stared at the mélange of people; brand-new, shining black Model Ts; the smell of burned anthracite coal in the air from the three funnels belching black smoke; heating the steam for the boilers that would send the reciprocating engines churning and moving the great ship out toward sea. Scott had already had a bracer, just one to knock back the hangover, but this was to be the moment of drying out. It was a dry ship, but they would find champagne cocktails on board and keep an old lady awake whom they would have to apologize to.

But he was off to write his novel. A letter to his editor, Max Perkins, in 1922 was the first clue as to what his new book would be about. "It's locale will be in the middle west and New York of 1885 I think. It will concern less superlative beauties than I run to usually and will be centered on a smaller period of time. It will have a catholic element."[2] This book never got off the ground, and by April 1924, Scott wrote Perkins, "Much of what I wrote last summer was good but it was so interrupted that it was ragged and in approaching it from a new angle I've had to discard a lot of it."[3] So, he was starting over, a clean slate in every way, and this was very much in line with leaving America.

Traveling on a steamship across the ocean in 1924 was glamorous, cosmopolitan, and, usually, very expensive. As Scott would later write in his third novel, *Tender is the Night*, "up the gangplank and the vision of the world adjusts itself, narrows. One is a citizen of a Commonwealth smaller than Andorra. One is no longer sure of anything. Curiously unmoved the men at the pursuers desk, cell like the cabin, disdainful the eyes of voyagers and their friends, solemn the officer who stands on the deserted promenade deck thinking something of his own as he stares at the crowd below. . . . then the loud mournful whistles and the thing—certainly not the boat, but rather a human idea, a frame of mind—pushes forth into the dark night."[4]

Scott lights a Chesterfield and stares at the dull gray skyline of Manhattan. He and Zelda had taken a lot of blood out of the turnip, and now it was time to be free "from extravagance and clamor and from all the wild extremes among which we had dealt with for the last five hectic years, from the tradesmen who laid for us, and the nurse who bullied us, and the couple who kept our house for us and knew us all too well. We were going to the Old World to find a new rhythm for our lives with the true conviction we had left our old selves behind . . ."[5]

Scott had pulled them back from the abyss after the failure of the play. But he was now a true alcoholic. No matter. This would be a new start. He wanted to write something no one else had ever written. He wanted to set American literature on its head and free him from the grind of the magazine stories. He had squirreled away $7,000 after a brutal run of *Post* stories, and now he was going to focus solely on his new novel. He was giving himself the luxury of the summer. He had a daughter and a wife to support now. This was where he would turn it all around by resuscitating his literary career, solving his financial instability and living up to his talent once and for all. "So in my new novel I'm thrown directly on purely creative work—not trashy imaginings as in my stories," he had written Maxwell Perkins at Scribner before he left. "But the sustained imagination of a sincere and yet radiant world. So I tread slowly and carefully and at times in considerable distress. This book will be a consciously artistic achievement and must depend on that as the first books did not."[6]

They were sneaking away and envisioned people driving to their home from New York with bottles of champagne in hand, only to sulk away, wondering where the Fitzgeralds had gone. But their getaway was not so clandestine. Fitzgerald was the equivalent of a midlevel rock star today, with authors enjoying a type of fame now reserved for actors and sports figures. An article in the *New York Daily News* with a drawn picture of Zelda dated May 11, 1924, let readers know they could no longer find the famous author on Long Island. It was ten days after they left and who knows how the reporter deduced their plans, but the Fitzgeralds were great copy and just about anything they did was news.

"No one can say the Scott Fitzgeralds ever do things by halves. Not that anyone has ever so intimated. But one day last week Scott arose early. The sky was divinely blue. Poetic thoughts surged into his writer's mind. He called Zelda, his fetching and pretty wife. 'Let's go to the Riviera,' suggested he. Zelda, being only twenty-three and quite as romantic as her brilliant young husband, took no chances. She reached for the telephone. Within five minutes they had advertised their rambling colonial home on Great Neck drive for rent. Within five more minutes they had reserved passage for themselves, the baby and her nurse for Europe. And on Saturday morning, unencumbered by home servants, possessions or social obligations, they sailed for sunny Italy. One of Scott's friends suggested that he write his books contrariwise. He used to live in Minneapolis but came to New York to write a novel about that city. Then he moved to Great Neck and wrote 'The Beautiful and the Damned' a novel about New York. Now he's gone to Europe to write a novel about Long Island."[7]

The crossing would take a week, and Scott, five years later, would write in "The Rough Crossing" about a couple who escapes New York to find peace. It is a thinly veiled story of him and Zelda and a composite of their crossings. "Adrian Smith, one of the celebrities on board, not a very great celebrity, but important enough to be bathed in flashlight by a photographer who had been given his name but wasn't sure what his subject did . . . 'We're going,' he cried presently, and they both laughed in ecstasy. 'We've escaped. They can't get us now.' 'Who?' 'All those people out there. They'll come with their posses and their warrants and list of crimes we've committed and ring the bell at our door on Park Avenue and ask for the Adrian Smiths, but what ho, the Adrian Smiths and their children and nurse are off for France.'"[8]

During the crossing, Adrian has an affair with a beautiful young woman while his wife is seasick down in her cabin. The short story is a study of infidelity as Adrian tastes the forbidden fruit of another: "He could not remember when anything had felt so young and fresh as her lips. The rain like tears shed for him, upon the softly shining porcelain cheeks. She was all new and immaculate and her eyes wild."[9] Eva finds out about the affair as a hurricane engulfs the ship and demands a divorce, going to the wireless room with Adrian following her. She throws her pearls into the sea, mirroring the pearls Scott bought Zelda in Manhattan. Then a wave crashes against the side of the ship, and all seems lost.

"There was another shuddering crash and high over his head, over the very boat, he saw a gigantic, glittering white wave, and in the split second that it balanced there he became conscious of Eva, standing beside a ventilator twenty feet away. Pushing out from the stanchion, he lunged desperately toward her, just as the wave broke with a smashing roar. For a moment the rushing water was five foot deep, sweeping with enormous force towards the side, and then a human body was washed against him and frantically he clutched it and was swept with it back towards the rail. He felt his body bump against it, but desperately he held onto his burden; then, as the ship rocked slowly back, the two of them, still joined by his fierce grip, were rolled out exhausted on the wet planks. For a moment he knew no more."[10]

For Scott, the ship is taking him away from many things, but he "*wanted to recover something, some idea of himself perhaps, that had gone into loving Daisy. His life had been confused and disordered since then, but if he could return to a certain starting place and go over it slowly, he could find out what that thing was.*"[11] And now the ship is leaving. Scott and Zelda feel the ocean breeze and listen to the shouts of "Visitors Ashore, please!" The stevedores start to work the ropes, and "the pier with its faces commenced to slide by, and for a moment the boat was just a piece accidently split off from it, then the faces became remote, voiceless . . . now the harbor flowed swiftly toward the sea."[12]

Scott and Zelda watched Manhattan become small, and like Adrian and Eva in "The Rough Crossing," they had to wonder if they could really escape the two people who had created so much carnage on the island now behind them. The ship is clearing the red buoys flashing in the harbor, warning of shallow waters and shoals. For now, Scott, leaning against the railing, flicks his spiraling cigarette into the fast white water, betting an unwritten novel would prove his talent, straighten out his finances, and bring him and Zelda back from the cliff they had been dancing on. Nothing less than his salvation.

# CHAPTER 6

# Last of the Belles

## *1917*

ZELDA SAYRE STOOD AT THE TOP OF THE DIVING BOARD. HER flesh-colored, tight-fitting suit was giving her trouble. She had climbed to the highest board that even the boys would not attempt. The pool was a small blue rectangle beneath. Zelda felt the wind, a strong Southern gust of super-heated air that started in the cotton fields, streaked across the sharecropper shacks, past the ruins of the plantations Zelda had explored as a girl, then blew red dust down the riveted dirt and bricked roads of Montgomery and across the dusty wagon-wheel-rimmed roads that bordered the old swimming pool.

The Old South was still out there in the abandoned plantations and the grizzled Confederate veterans who gathered in the park to swap stories on Gettysburg or Pickett's Charge. But the New South was out there, too, with slick new Model-Ts and lanky young men who drank moonshine and hung around girls like Zelda Sayre, who made a point of breaking all the rules for young Southern belles, which included not letting your back touch the chair, making sure your white gloves were buttoned, and being flirtatious but never sexual. And a Southern belle would never wear a bathing suit that looked like she had on nothing at all.

Of course, her mother bathed her and her sisters on the back porch in a washtub. Soon the neighborhood boys were peeking over the fence and through the hedges. The neighborhood women paid a call on Minnie

Sayre, wife of Judge Sayre, a man who came home at the same time every day, had a sandwich for dinner, then retired at eight o'clock every night. The judge was stability incarnate, and Zelda could use this fortress of respectability to flap her butterfly wings of rebellion, giving rise to a much fiercer wind than her friends who couldn't fall back on "that's Judge Sayre's daughter." This refrain was heard when she called the fire department and said a girl was stranded on the roof then climbed up on her own roof to be rescued. Her mother Minnie was an artist before she met Anthony Sayre and was known in the neighborhood as a bit of an eccentric with her strange clothes and permissive attitude toward her children, especially her youngest, Zelda, named for a gypsy queen in a novel. Minnie met the neighborhood women who told her young men were spying on her naked children when she gave them a bath and that they should bathe somewhere else.

"Why should they? God gave them beautiful bodies," Minnie retorted.[1]

So the judge's daughter could bathe on the back porch or anywhere else she damned well pleased. Montgomery was still a sleepy Southern town that Zelda recalled years later. "Lawns were drenched with arcs of water thrown from hoses, and everything, even time seemed to stand still before the onslaught of the heat. The drug stores are bright at night with the organdie balloons of girl's dresses under the big electric fans. Automobiles stand along the curbs in front of the open frame houses at dusk and sounds of supper being prepared drift through the soft splotches of darkness to the young world that moves every evening out of doors. Telephones ring and the lacy blackness under the trees disgorges young girls in white and pink, leaping over the squares of warm light toward the tinkling sound with an expectancy that people have only in places where any event is a pleasant one. Nothing ever seems to happen. . . . "[2]

Her mother, Minnie, gave her youngest free rein, and because they lived in "The Hill," a gentrified area of Montgomery reserved for only the oldest and most distinguished families with roots going back before the Civil War, Zelda was beyond reproach. "Certainly most of the families in the Sayres' neighborhood knew each other. They tacitly considered themselves 'thoroughbreds' of the genteel South . . . for in Montgomery it was never simply wealth that counted socially, but family. There were very definite lines of social distinction; one was not invited to parties on 'the Hill' if one was in trade, Catholic, Italian, or Shanty Irish . . . young ladies of these families were expected to behave themselves, to be decorative and charming."[3]

But that respectability just gave Zelda a license to do what she wanted. Even when she took her friend's new brougham (horse and carriage) for a ride by climbing up into the driver's seat and giving the matching bays a slap and shooting down the driveway toward the street while the carriage careened side to side out of control. Just when it looked like the carriage might tip over, the hub of a rear wheel hooked itself in the gate and like an emergency brake pulled the carriage to a halt. Zelda merely laughed and scampered off to play with her friends. Judge Sayre's daughter was already beautiful with golden curls, a small bow mouth, piercing blue eyes, and a long husky drawl that pulled in every boy she talked to. She could not have cared less what the town thought of her.

When she recalled her childhood years later, Zelda said she was "independent, courageous, without thought for anyone else . . . I was a very active child and never tired, always running with no hat or coat even in the Negro district and far from my house. I liked houses under construction and often I walked on the open roofs. I liked to jump from high places . . . I liked to dive and climb in the tops of trees, I liked taking long walks far from town, sometimes going to a country churchyard where I often went all by myself . . . I did not have a single feeling of inferiority, or shyness, or doubt, and no moral principles."[4]

Zelda was wild, fearless, and unconventional. She was already becoming the most popular belle of Montgomery, and her notoriety only added to her mystique and the legend growing up around her. When she was sixteen, she came out in 1916 at a ballet recital where people sat mesmerized by the young woman in the stiff, pink organdy dress made by Minnie with flowers at her waist. The crowd quieted and watched the ringlets swing from the blond-haired girl who moved with grace and supreme self-confidence. A newspaper, *The Advertiser*, posted a story that summer with a picture of Zelda. "You may keep an eye open for the possessor of this classic profile about a year from now when she advances just a little further beyond the sweet sixteen stage. Already she is in the crowd at the Country Club every Saturday night and at the script dances every other night of the week. She has the straightest nose, the most determined little chin and the bluest eyes in Montgomery. She might dance like Pavlova if her nimble feet were not so busy keeping up with the pace of young but ardent admirers set for her."[5]

Zelda took it all in stride. She smoked. She drank gin. She drank corn liquor cut with Coca-Cola. She went to Boodlers Bend and necked. Once, at a dance, she got so hot she slipped out of her petticoat and asked the shocked young man to hold it for her. This story would repeat itself with panties inserted for the petticoat. By fifteen, Zelda's skin was "flawless and creamy and her hair golden as a child's. Other girls began secretly to use blondine on their hair but Zelda didn't need to. She borrowed rouge and lipstick from her older sisters to heighten her coloring and her powder was the whitest she could find . . . Zelda was on the verge of becoming the most spectacular belle Montgomery would ever know."[6]

She had dates every night of the week, and each date became a billboard for another outrageous act. As one young man put it years later to a reporter, "She lived on the cream at the top of the bottle."[7] And that cream put her up on the diving board looking down at her friends who were squinting up toward her. No one else would climb up to the rickety diving board, and Zelda stood out toward the end, staring down at the pool of blue water that looked smaller and smaller. She raised her hands and felt the pull of her suit. It was a nuisance, and she was hot, and one couldn't blame her for wanting to be free of it. Besides, the war had just begun, and there were rumors the town was about to be overrun with young soldiers who were training at the camp just outside of town. The truth was she had become bored with Montgomery. She was at the top of the pyramid as the most popular Southern belle, and she could do as she pleased. She wanted more. She wanted the world beyond the stifling constraints of Southern decorum that, even though she galloped fast, was always nipping at her heels. The truth was she wasn't going away to college, and she saw no profession that interested her. She wanted something big, something glamorous, famous, that she couldn't even articulate yet. Her personality was simply too big for the quiet, restrained Old South or even the New South.

One thinks of a young Madonna with ambition so outsized it stripped others of all their defenses. Pictures don't do Zelda justice. Her beauty was a sleight of hand of coloring, size, personality, a husky Southern accent, a cupid mouth, and eyes that looked directly at someone like a hawk. She was a wild child. She was ahead of her time. And so, without a thought, she dropped the straps of her suit and kicked it off the board. The young men and women far below stared up, mouths agape at the young, perfectly formed body of Southern femininity. Zelda felt much better, but more than that, she felt free. She had just kicked off the last restraints of her provincial Southern world, and the world was now coming to her.

Thousands and thousands of soldiers, potential suitors, were even now taking trains and buses down to Montgomery, Alabama. They were coming to camps set up outside of town, but they would also see Zelda Sayre, who now was bouncing on the diving board, feeling the air on her breasts and between her legs as she jumped once, twice, then arced in the hot sunshine and dove down toward the earth like a missile of reckless abandon.

Zelda hit the water, plunging down, down, down into the cool blue brilliance before emerging as a sea nymph to the cheers and claps of her awed friends who could only shake their heads and say later to anyone who listened, and they all listened, "You wouldn't believe what Zelda Sayre did!"

# CHAPTER 7

# The Left Bank

## *1924*

GIN-SMASHED AGAIN. LIFE WAS SO MUCH BETTER THIS WAY. THOUGH the sink looked strange, it was France, and what did you expect. There was decadence here, and Scott had the same feeling of a world in decay that he had in 1921. Too much gin and too many bars in Paris. Too many friends. They were on their way to the Riviera, but they had stopped off in Paris, and now he was in the bathroom trying to get his head cleared before dinner. The porcelain bowl in the hotel bathroom looked inviting, and it had a nozzle that, when he pumped it, the side spout splashed water up on his face. Much better. Yes. He was getting clear now. Too damn low, though.

The author of *This Side of Paradise, The Beautiful and the Damned*, and many short stories, one failed play, countless magazine stories, got down on his knees and began to pump water over his face. These French were on to something. He immediately felt refreshed and walked out of the bathroom toweling his face, telling Zelda they really had to get one of those sinks with the nozzle for washing their face. It really did refresh you. Zelda stared at Scott dully and told him he had just washed his face in the bidet. He had given his daughter a bath in the bidet before but kept that to himself.

The City of Light had emerged from the fog as their ship reached port in May. The Fitzgeralds disembarked and greeted the city that had welcomed them several years earlier on a sightseeing trip. Then, Scott was the newly successful author, and he and his new bride tasted the fruits of Europe and found it wanting. In 1921, from May to July, they visited England, France, and Italy. The black-and-white pictures are of a couple not quite sure what to do with their newfound leisure, money, or fame. They are tourist photos, and in many, the Fitzgeralds' boredom comes through. Zelda would years later describe the trip to her daughter: "We went to London to see a fog and saw Tallulah Bankhead, which was, perhaps about the same effect. Then the fog blew up and we reconstituted Arnold Bennett's *The Pretty Lady* and the works of Compton Mackenzie which daddy loved so, and we had a curious nocturnal bottle of champagne with members of the British polo team. We dined with Galsworthy and lunched with Lady Randolph Churchill and had tea in the mellow remembrances of Shane Leslie's house who later took us to see the pickpockets pick in Wopping."[1]

But there were no adoring crowds and no photographers taking their pictures. New York was nowhere to be found, and the Fitzgeralds were too young, too new to their celebrity to enjoy the trip. They met Gertrude Stein and Edith Wharton and sampled the food and returned to America, with Scott writing Edmund Wilson, "Goddamn the continent of Europe. It is only of merely antiquarian interest. Rome is only a few years behind Tyree and Babylon. . . . I think it's a shame that England and America didn't let Germany conquer Europe. It's the only thing that would have saved the fleet of tottering old wrecks."[2]

On this trip, after Scottie had drunk gin fizz they had mistaken for lemonade and "ruined the luncheon the next day,"[3] they started to look for a nurse and hired one at $26 a month. "My God," Fitzgerald told a friend, "We paid $90 in New York."[4] Fitzgerald would later immortalize the trip in the article "On How to Live on Practically Nothing a Year": "The sun coming through the high French windows woke us one week later. Outside we could hear the high clear honk of strange auto horns and we remembered we were in Paris. The baby was already sitting up in her cot ringing bells which summoned the different functionaries of the hotel as though she had determined to start the day immediately. It was indeed her day, for we were in Paris for no other reason than to get a nurse."[5]

Artists flocked from all over the world to Paris, especially from America. Paris was the place to be in the twenties. "Cubist force had given way to Dadas crazy inspirations and erotic surrealism. Intellectuals had fallen for le jazz hot, popular movies and the circus. Diverse arts were excitingly linked to one another."[6] The great disaffection of the post–World War I world was centered in Paris, and the writers who would cross-pollinate there included Ezra Pound, Ernest Hemingway, William Faulkner, Gertrude Stein, and James Joyce and among the painters were Picasso, Renoir, and Monet. It was a mecca for the creative artist and would spawn novels, films, legends, biographies, studies. It would be seen as the great efflorescence after the great catastrophe of World War I. As Gertrude Stein said, "Paris was where the twentieth century was."[7]

So, the Fitzgeralds, with their seventeen pieces of luggage, booked into the Hotel des Deux Mondes. They strolled down the Champs-Élysées, a photographer took their picture with Scott in an immaculate suit and Zelda in a blue dress with Scottie in a double-breasted blue coat. Scott was an immensely successful author and was coming to Paris to pull something out of himself that only by leaving America could he glimmer. But the parties began anew in Paris, and they were pulled into the social whirl of the Left Bank.

They had hired as Scottie's nurse Lillian Maddock, an English woman who had a military bearing and brought order to Scottie's world at least. Then a cook and a maid. They were collecting servants for the summer, and during their nine days, they made the most significant discovery in the Murphys. A rich expatriate couple, Gerald and Sara Murphy, believed in the motto "living well is the best revenge." Gerald was heir to the New York leather goods store Mark Cross and had taken his wife, two sons, and daughter to Europe to escape family pressure and to take advantage of the rate of exchange in Paris. The Fitzgeralds and Murphys bonded over a sense of escaping something oppressive in America.

As Gerald would later write, "there was something depressing to the young married people about a country that could pass the eighteenth amendment. The country was tightening up and it was so unbecoming. You really resented being herded into the basements of old sandstone houses. It was I suppose the tone of life in America that we found all so uncongenial."[8]

So, Gerald came to Europe to paint and lead a renaissance life with his family. They adored the young famous couple (there was a seventeen-year difference in age between the couples), with daughter Scottie playing with their daughter Honoria. They were patrons of the arts and collected artists around them the way someone else might collect exotic cars. They came to know Picasso, Miro, and Juan Gris and, eventually, would be boosters of a young unknown writer, Ernest Hemingway. The biggest difference between the two couples was that Gerald, while professing to be a painter, was an amateur at best, and after that, it was a matter of simple economics; the Murphys were extremely wealthy while Scott and Zelda had $7,000 to their name, which was already shrinking. Sara Murphy was one of three Wibor sisters, who claimed as their father a rich ink manufacturer. Sara was a free spirit who ran her family with a steady hand and posed nude for Picasso with a strand of pearls around her neck. She would later describe Paris as a place "where everybody was young and you loved your friends and wanted to see them every day."[9]

Money was not an issue, and they told the Fitzgeralds about the beaches on the Riviera that they had discovered through Cole Porter, a friend of Gerald. They were building a villa at Antibes and recommended the small beach at Garoupe. Plans were quickly made to meet at the Riviera that summer, and for Scott, this made sense as already the gin-soaked revelries of Paris were making it clear he could not write there. They had been seeing the writers Dorothy Parker, Alexander Woollcott, and Robert Benchley, poet Archibald MacLeish, playwright Philip Barry, and songwriter Cole Porter. One would like to think Scott could hold himself back, but the lure of interesting people, Paris, gin, and the demand by Zelda that entertainment be given top priority was too much. This put the Riviera as the place where he could finally buckle down.

Another couple they were introduced to by the Murphys was Dick and Alice Lee Meyers. Dick was a part-time musician who had been in the war and now, with his wife, was wrestling the good times from the famous and near-great in Paris. Their daughter, Fanny, who played with Scottie, remembers Scott coming to their Paris apartment and ringing the doorbell while intoxicated. She finished her dinner and went to her room and found the author in her bed, her mother Alice sitting next to him. He was asleep, and Fanny's mother explained that "he was having a little lie down."[10] Scott later woke up and told the young girl she was very pretty, which she later reported turned her three shades of red.

It was an amazing time to be in Paris, but Scott and Zelda were just passing through and never really partook of the Left Bank experience of the struggling author. Scott was too successful for that, and they frequented bars, restaurants, and hotels that many on the Left Bank could not afford. Still, they were there and added their bit of glamour to the frenetic cross-pollination that was Paris in the early twenties. As Sara Murphy said much later when looking back, "You see most of us had given up something to come to France. Archie for instance a law career, it took courage to simply chuck it and come to France to write. Now Hemingway was without a penny."[11] It was not clear yet what Scott and Zelda gave up coming to France that summer, but it would be much more than Hemingway's vaunted literary poverty that was cushioned by his wife Hadley's trust fund he often failed to mention. The year before, Scott had written an article entitled "Making Monogamy Work Utilizing Jealousy as the Greatest Prop to Love." It is a lighthearted article, but it had an eerie prescience. "If ever a marriage seemed bound for the rocks this one did. We gave them six months—a year at the outside. It was too bad, we felt, because fundamentally they loved each other, but circumstances had undoubtedly doomed them . . ."[12]

# CHAPTER 8

# An Oxford Man

## *1910*

IT IS CRISP FALL. THE LEAVES ARE FALLING. SCOTT IS RUNNING AROUND the end with the football clutched tightly under his arm. This is his moment to make a name for himself as the opposing tackler runs straight for him. The Newman prep school had become his home in New Jersey, and now he could establish himself during this autumnal twilight with the few people in the stands and the mud up under his eyes and caked on his cleats. The tackler is big and thundering toward him, and Scott is running out of field. The sidelines are approaching, and what happens next sets the tone for his life; certain victory, and then . . . disaster.

Let's leave Scott on the field for a moment and catch up. After attending the St. Paul Academy, Scott finally went East to the Newman School. "A Catholic Andover emphasized as a lay education that prepared students for entrée to Princeton or Yale."[1] With no more than sixty students, Newman gave Fitzgerald his first introduction to the East with access to New York, Broadway, and the "hazy sense that an imminent, if not yet defined, glory there awaited his arrival."[2] The reality was much different than what Scott expected. "'He was unpopular starting out,' recalled his classmate Charles Donahue, 'partly because his good looks promoted classification as a sissy which was reinforced by a lack of physical courage.'"[3] Hold that thought while we go into the future where Scott takes the admission exam for Princeton but flunks the admission tests. In his ledger, he writes, "Grandmother dies. Her last gift. Studying for Princeton."[4] But her last gift, which was the inheritance to his mother that allowed him to attend an Ivy League college, was not enough. Nor was his studying. He pleads his case to an admissions board, pointing out that it was his birthday and that they should let him in. And amazingly . . . they did! At Princeton, he immediately is cut from the football team and proceeds to flunk three out of five of his classes each year but excels in writing plays and musicals for the Princeton dramatic group, the Triangle Club. "I spent my entire freshman year writing an operetta for the Triangle Club. I failed in algebra, trigonometry, coordinate geometry and hygiene, but the Triangle Club accepted my show and by tutoring all through a stuffy August I managed to come back a sophomore and act in it as a chorus girl. A little later I left college to spend the rest of the year recuperating in the West."[5]

This did not come out of the blue. Scott had found he had a literary talent in St. Paul when, at sixteen, he produced, starred, and wrote a play that was performed by the local dramatic club. The play was *The Coward*, and he would later immortalize the experience in "The Captured Shadow" that gave him a taste of impending literary fame. "There was a second and a third act scene that was very similar. In each of them, the Shadow, alone on the stage, was interrupted by Miss Saunders. Mayall De Bec, having had but ten days of rehearsal, was inclined to confuse the two, but Basil [Scott] was totally unprepared for what happened. Upon Connie's entrance, Mayall spoke his third-act line and involuntarily Connie answered in kind. . . . In a moment things righted themselves. Someone brought water for Miss Halliburton, who was in a stage of collapse, and as the act ended they all took a curtain call once more. Twenty minutes later it was all over. . . . An old man whom Basil didn't know came up to him and shook his hand saying, 'You're a young man that's going to be heard from some day,' and a reporter from the paper asked him if he was really only fifteen."[6]

Scott's sense of dramatic lyricism, his use of dialogue, was developed further by writing the plays and short stories and poems for the literary magazine *The Tiger* at Princeton. But Scott's real education was rubbing shoulders with the future leaders of the country in politics, business, and literature. "In college I was luckier. I knew the future presidents of many banks and oil companies, the Governor of Tennessee, and among the intellectuals encountered John Peale Bishop, warbird Elliott Springs, Judge John Biggs, and Hamilton Fish Armstrong. Of course I had no idea who they were and neither did they or I could have started an autographed tablecloth."[7]

Scott's dreams of literary fame died right there along with his academic career at Princeton, where he just couldn't buckle down between the drinking and the writing of plays and musicals to the point where, in his junior year, he was banned from holding any class offices. He had become absorbed in the production of the musicals to the detriment of everything else. He would capture the moment later in *This Side of Paradise*. "Every night for the last week they had rehearsed 'Ha Ha Hortense!' in the Casino, from two in the afternoon until eight in the morning, sustained by dark and powerful coffee, and sleeping in lectures through the interim.... A big barnlike auditorium, dotted with boys as girls, boys as pirates, boys as babies, the scenery in course of being violently set up, the spotlight man rehearsing by throwing weird shafts into angry eyes; over all the contestant tuning of the orchestra . . . the boy who writes the lyrics stands in the corner, biting a pencil, with twenty minutes to think of an encore, the business manager argues with the secretary. The old graduate, president in ninety-eight, perches on a box and thinks how much simpler it was in his day."[8]

Scott flunked out in his junior year but would forever refer to himself as a Princeton man.

*"By the way Mr. Gatsby, I understand you're an Oxford man."*

*"Not exactly."*

*"Oh yes, I understand you went to Oxford."*

*"Yes I went there."*

*"You must have gone there about the time Biloxi went to New Haven."*

*"I told you I went there," said Gatsby. "It was in nineteen nineteen, I only stayed five months. That's why I really can't call myself an Oxford man."*[9]

Scott was so sensitive about not graduating that he procured a letter from the Dean of the school saying he had dropped out because of ill health. "This is for your sensitive feelings, I hope you find it soothing,"[10] Dean Howard McClennan wrote dryly. But the truth was Scott had flunked out of college and would never get a degree. Scott would cling to the fantasy he had lost Princeton due to his health but later admitted it was the loss of prestige brought on by his failure to pass his courses. "I left Princeton in junior year with a complaint diagnosed as malaria. It transpired through an x-ray taken a dozen years later, that it had been tuberculosis, a mild case and after a few months of rest I went back to college. But I had lost certain offices, the chief one was the Presidency of the Triangle Club, a musical comedy idea, and also I dropped back a class. There were to be no badges of pride, no medals, after all. It seemed one March afternoon that I had lost all that I had wanted."[11]

And so, this, too, was very much in line with running straight into the tackler headed straight for him on the dusky field at Newman School . . . so why not join the army? World War I broke out and rescued Scott from the ignominious fate of a college dropout who essentially had just written plays and musicals and drank gin for three years and was looking at returning to the rented homes of his mother and father in St. Paul. So it was off to Brooks Brothers for a uniform and then off to Montgomery, Alabama, for training camp, where he decided to write a novel.

Among the crackle of newspapers and smoke, Scott hid his pad of paper behind *Small Problems for Infantry* and wrote line after line while the other young soldiers sat with legs crossed, cigarettes clipped between fingers, yawning, stretching, watching the sun retreat behind the far trees. Scott was writing furiously, beginning with a paragraph to himself. He would never learn to type, and so his long hand lent itself well to his furtive campaign to write a 120,000-word novel of his life up this point before he went over to France and was killed. He believed he would not survive World War I, and this was to be his last testament for himself and his generation. The trick was being able to mine the depths of his life under the watchful eyes of the commanding officer who knew already Scott was not really a good soldier. Scott believed the training camp was his last shot to set down his life into a form that would give him literary fame, even if it was postmortem.

But it was not smooth going.

"A week has gone here in the aviation school just hurried by with early rising by the November moon and here I am with not one chapter finished—scrawling pages with no form or style—just full of detail and petty history. I intended so much when I started and I'm realizing how impossible it all is. I can't rewire and all I do is form the vague notes for chapters that I have here beside me and the uncertain channels of an uneven memory. I don't even seem to be able to trace the skeins of development as I ought. I'm trying to set down the story part of my generation in America and put myself in the middle as a sort of observer and conscious factor. But I've got to write now for when the war's over I won't be able to see these things as important; even now they are fading out against the background of the map of Europe. I'll never be able to do it again, well done or poorly. So I'm writing almost desperately and so futilely . . ."[12]

The CO cleared his throat and looked over. Scott stared at the book in front of him with the pad on the hard walnut table. His commanding officer pulled on his cigarette with his shined boots catching the dim overhead light, then looked back at his paper. Scott returned to his narrative. He had already described the years in St. Paul with his eccentric mother, the rented homes, his father who lost his job and his "immaculate sense of purpose,"[13] his rich grandfather and aunt who gave their family money and made his mother say more than once "if it were not for your grandfather McQuillan, where would we be now?"[14]

His mind drifted back to going away to the Newman School in Hackensack, New Jersey, where he was still running with the football with the tackler bearing down on him. At five feet six inches and 130 pounds, Scott was no bruiser, but he had decided to make a name for himself on the football field. One observer noticed that Scott had "a desperate, bent forward, short legged scuttling way of running with the ball, but somehow it conveyed emotion and when he was good, it was thrilling and when he was bad you had to look away from his visible shame."[15] Now we can pick up there again with Scott staring at the tackler who was charging straight for him. He did not want to be hit. So he did it. Scott turned away from the tackler, and in full line with his life . . . *he ran the other way; he ran backward away from the opposing player.* His teammates stared open-mouthed, his coach was shocked, and the people in the stands groaned as he was cut down by another tackler far behind the line. Later, he wrote, "I remember the desolate ride in the bus back to the train and the desolate ride back to school with everybody thinking I had been yellow on the occasion, when actually I was just distracted and sorry for the opposing end. That's the truth. I have been afraid plenty of times but that wasn't one of the times."[16]

In the story "The Freshest Boy," Scott is called into the headmaster's office of the prep school. "Doctor Bacon was at his desk. He hesitated. Beneath the cynical incrustations of many years an instinct stirred to look into the unusual case of this boy and find out what made him the most detested boy in school. Among boys and masters there seemed to exist an extraordinary hostility toward him, and though Doctor Bacon had dealt with many sorts of schoolboy crimes, he had neither by himself nor with the aid of trusted sixth formers been able to lay his hands on its underlying cause."[17]

Scott wanted to go to New York, and no one would go with him except a wayward teacher named Mr. Rooney. His roommate had deserted him, and he had been backed down in a fight by a boy younger than him. On the train, Mr. Rooney turns on him. "Lee," he (Mr. Rooney) said suddenly, with a thin assumed air of interest. "Why don't you get wise to yourself?"

"What sir?"

"I said why don't you get wise to yourself? Do you want to be the butt of the school all your time here?"

"No, I don't."

"You oughtn't get so fresh all the time. A couple times in history class I could have broken your neck . . . then out playing football . . . you didn't have any nerve. You could play better than a lot of them when you wanted, like that day against the Pomfret seconds, but you lost your nerve."[18]

Then Mr. Rooney left him in New York and got drunk, and Scott (Lee) found him later in a saloon. By then, Scott had made up his mind to leave the school after he received a letter from his mother encouraging him to go to Europe with her. Scott doesn't leave, though, and finds himself in a basketball game months later with a boy, Brick Wales, who had previously hated him.

"Basil had dribbled down the court and Brick Wales, free, was crying for it. 'Here yar! Lee! Lee-y!' Basil flushed and made a poor pass. He had been called by a nickname. It was a poor makeshift, but it was something more than the stark bareness of his surname or a term of derision. Brick Wales went on playing, unconscious that he had done anything in particular or that he had contributed to the events by which another boy was saved from the army of the bitter, the selfish, the neurasthenic and the unhappy. It isn't given to us to know these rare moments when people are wide open and the lightest touch can wither or heal. A moment too late and we can never reach them any more in this world. They will not be cured by our most efficacious drugs or slain without sharpest words."[19]

So now Scott is essentially writing his last will and testament in the form of a novel. He is sitting among the smoke and crackling papers in the training camp. Scott stared at his pad. What had he done, really? Nothing. He had gone to a rich man's prep school and college and flunked out. He had learned to drink, and he had a literary education by meeting Edmund Wilson and John Bishop, and he dressed in drag for one of the musicals, written poetry and a smattering of short stories, and he met Monsignor Darcy, a colorful priest who loved him and wrote him tender letters and, from the vantage point of history, might have been gay, but really, what did it all amount to . . . not much.

Scott was now in training camp at Fort Leavenworth with a captain named Dwight D. Eisenhower. Scott was a bad soldier. He had almost gotten everyone killed when a live mortar round got stuck in the muzzle of the mortar. He had even gone AWOL once up to New York and gotten drunk. None of it was commendable. He wrote his mother from the camp and gave his view on the army and patriotism in general. "About the army, please let's not have either tragedy or heroics because they are equally distasteful to me. I went into this perfectly cold bloodedly and don't sympathize with the 'give my son to the country' or 'hero stuff' because I just went and purely for social reasons. If you want to pray, pray for my soul and not that I won't get killed—the last doesn't seem to matter particularly and if you are a good Catholic the first ought to . . ."[20]

Then a slow progression South began for F. Scott Fitzgerald. On March 15, he was assigned to the 45th Infantry Regiment at Camp Zachary Taylor close to Louisville, Kentucky. Scott should have received a platoon to command but was appointed as an assistant to the regimental school officer. The 45th was then transferred in April to Camp Gordon in Georgia, and finally, in June, Scott's regiment joined the 67th Infantry Regiment of the Ninth Division at Camp Sheridan near Montgomery, Alabama. Here is where the army would be built up for eventual deployment overseas. He was promoted to first lieutenant and began to explore this strange new land.

Scott was intrigued by the South. "Poetry is a Northern man's dream of the South."[21] He had written that much later in a *Saturday Evening Post* story, "The Last of the Belles." But to the young lieutenant prowling the streets of Montgomery, the South did speak to him. "It was a little hotter than anywhere we'd been—a dozen rookies collapsed the first day in the Georgia sun—and when you saw herds of cows drifting through the business streets, hi yayed by colored drovers, a trance stole down over you out of the hot light you wanted to move a hand or a foot to be sure you were alive."[22]

In the evenings on the weekends, Scott began to notice the Southern girls. He might have flunked out of Princeton, run from an opposing tackler in prep school, had an ineffectual father and an eccentric mother, and lived in rented houses his whole life, but he was probably the best-looking first lieutenant in the US Army in his Brooks Brothers uniform. So, while he completed his first novel, *This Side of Paradise*, of 120,000 words among the murmurs, smoke, and snaps of the newspapers, he heard of a dance at the local country club where the most popular Southern belles would be in attendance.

Really, all Scott had to offer at this point was ambition and a strange sense of destiny. He arrived in the close, smoky air of the country club with the throngs of other young soldiers looking for young Southern belles to dance with and saw a girl dancing out on the floor by herself. Scott felt his breath leave as he watched her twirl with her long blond ringlets flowing out. Later, he would write, "There was the eternally kissable mouth, small, slightly sensual, and utterly disturbing. There were gray eyes and an unimpeachable skin with two spots of vanishing color. She was slender and athletic, without underdevelopment, and it was a delight to watch her move about a room. . . . "[23]

To Scott, she looked like an angel. In his ledger, August 1918, Scott recorded, " . . . Zelda. . . . "[24]

## CHAPTER 9

# How To Live on Practically Nothing

## *1924*

IF THERE WAS AN IDYLLIC MOMENT IN SCOTT'S LIFE, IT BEGAN IN MAY of 1924 with the train ride to the South of France. He and Zelda and Scottie rode the train into the French countryside with the world behind them. The Fitzgeralds reached Grimms Park Hotel in Hyères. It was unbelievably hot, and they found it was primarily a resort for the elderly taking the "cure." This was at a time when medical science sent people out to beaches or dry climates to take the "rest cure," a sort of catchall for tubercular or heart patients with the thought that change of climate, usually a warm one, might cure whatever ailments the person might have. The heat and the people there for medicinal purposes pushed the Fitzgeralds on, but not before Scott sent a letter off to Thomas Boyd.

"Your letter was the first to reach me after I arrived here. This is the loveliest piece of earth I've ever seen without excepting Oxford or Venice or Princeton or anywhere. Zelda and I are sitting in the café L' Universe writing letters (it's 10:30 p.m.) and the moon is absolutely *au fait* Mediterranean moon with a blurred silver linen cap and we're both a little tight and very happily drunk if you can use that term for the less nervous, less violent reactions of that side. . . . Well, I shall write a novel better than any novel ever written in America and become par excellence the best second-rater in the world."[1]

Zelda, years later, would write in the novel *Save Me the Waltz* a description of their journey from France: "The train bore them down through the pink carnival of Normandy, past the delicate tracery of Paris and the high terraces of Lyon, the belfries of Dijon and the white romance of Avignon into the scent of lemon, the rustle of black foliage, clouds of moths whipping the heliotropic dusk—into Provence where people do not need to see unless they are looking for the nightingale."[2]

The heat the Fitzgeralds were experiencing was because the Riviera was a winter resort and experienced more excessive heat during summer. Still, they were enchanted and continued on and, in June, came to St. Raphael, where they came upon the town on the Mediterranean. In an essay written in July titled "How to Live on Practically Nothing a Year," Scott recorded his first impression. "When your eyes fall upon the Mediterranean, you know at once why it was here that man stood erect and stretched out his arms toward the sun. It is a blue sea . . . blue like blue books, blue oil, blue eyes, and in the shadow of the mountains a green belt of land runs along the coast for a hundred miles . . . The Riviera!"[3]

Scott immediately saw St. Raphael as the spot to write his third novel. "It was a little reed town built close to the sea," he later wrote, "with gay red roofed houses and an air of a repressed carnival about it . . ." The stated goal was to economize in France, but then they saw the very elegant Villa Marie. "Within an hour we had seen our home, a clean cool villa set in a large garden on a hill above town. It was what we had been looking for all along. There was a summerhouse and a sand pile and two bathrooms and roses for breakfast and a gardener who called me 'milord.' When we had paid the rent . . . thirty-five hundred dollars, only half our capitol remained."[4]

If there was an Eden, a place to write a masterpiece, then it was certainly Villa Marie. The villa was high above the cobalt-blue sea with "terraced gardens of lemon, palm, pine and silver olive trees with a winding gravel drive leading to its entrance and with Moorish balconies of brilliant white and blue tiles and faced the Mediterranean like an exotic fortress."[5] Zelda later wrote that Scott was revealing "the most romantic proclivities" and that he might drown in the Riviera. "I shall be obligated to snatch a heart from a burning body—which I should hate."[6]

A movie director could expect no better from his set designer. Here is where you will write brilliantly with the most beautiful landscape in the world below. Yes, it was expensive, but after the bestselling third novel that would not only be a strong seller but brilliant, their financial problems would be all solved. Everything else had come true when they became the toast of New York . . . why not have the fairy tale give them a little more ether? They bought an old Renault for $750. "It had the power of six horses . . . and it was so small that we loomed out of it like giants . . . no lock, no speedometer, no gauge."[7]

They had the English nanny Lillian Maddock, who cost $26 a month, and while the villa was expensive, it still was doable, and the cook and the maid were $16 and $13 a month. The unexpected costs would be the drain; restaurants, cafes, and shady local merchants . . . but for now, they were settling in for a long hot summer on the Riviera. Life did begin as in a dream. The Murphys visited them with their children while they were having their villa, "The American," built. The children played, and Sara Murphy remembered one day where Scott and Zelda staged a crusaders battle. "Zelda must have spent days making the intricate cardboard battlements and castle. There were lead soldiers (from Scott's collection) and Scott had fashioned a series of interconnecting moats that flooded at the proper time in the siege. The children loved it."[8]

Then they all went to the beach, where Gerald Murphy cleared the sand in a sort of hedonistic ritual of the rich doing manual labor. " . . . The man in the jockey cap was giving a quiet little performance for this group; he moved gravely about with a rake, ostensibly removing gravel and meanwhile developing some esoteric burlesque held in suspension by his grave face. Its faintest ramification had become hilarious, until whatever he said released a burst of laughter."[9] The Fitzgeralds were at the center of the world along with writers, painters, film stars, and the Murphys. There is a grainy film that has survived of Fitzgerald smoking under an umbrella with Zelda nearby. They are both in striped shirts, and one can almost smell the sea and feel the hot sand.

Scott would capture the mood on the Riviera in his essay "How To Live On Practically Nothing." "From Charles Dickens to Catherine de Medici from Prince Edward of Wales in the height of his popularity to

Oscar Wilde in the depth of his disgrace, the whole world had come here to forget or rejoice, to hide its face or have its fling, to build white palaces out of the spoils of oppression or to write the books which sometimes batter those places down. Under striped awnings beside the sea, grand dukes and gamblers and diplomats and noble courtesans and Balkan czars smoked their slow cigarettes while 1913 drifted into 1914 . . . and the fury gathered in the north that was to sweep three fourths of them away."[10]

And in the evening, they could drive down the 2.5 kilometers to St. Raphael and enjoy the cafes, the casino, or the restaurants or walk in the warm sand and warm themselves with gin or champagne or whiskey. There was no prohibition, and the young couple enjoyed the freedom of drinking in the open in an exotic setting. For Zelda, the weather of Provence felt like home with the nourishing warmth of Alabama, but it was a foreign, exciting landscape of a crystal-blue sea with amazing food, drinks, and the urbane French, who made sure the Americans had all they needed. The Eucalyptus trees perfumed the air from the burning of fires behind the beaches, and Zelda gushed in a letter home, "Oh we are going to be so happy from all the things that almost got us but couldn't quite because we were too smart for them."[11] They immediately bought new, brightly colored suits and beach umbrellas and espadrilles in Cannes, and with their new friends the Murphys, they readied themselves for the best life had to offer.

At night, when Zelda had gone to bed, Scott looked off the balcony toward the great blue globe hovering over the Mediterranean and contemplated how far he had come. "It is twilight as I write this and out my window darkening banks of trees, set one clump behind another in many greens, slope down to the evening sea. The flaming sun has collapsed behind the perks of the Esterels and the moon already hovers over the Roman aqueducts for Fréjus five miles away."[12]

Scott smoked a Chesterfield and stared out over the Mediterranean. He was twenty-eight and at the peak of his powers, and he had managed to extricate himself from the freeform debauchery of New York and Paris and now had an incredible bird's-eye view of America. Scott imagined the coast of America. He saw lights along the coastline of the East, with the yellow buoys of the cottages hunched along the shore. New York was a carnival of lights. The festive carnival that never slept and faced the dark Atlantic Ocean as the first sight immigrants would see when they came. He stood on the balcony of the Old World and flew back in time.

*And as the moon rose higher the inessential houses began to melt away until gradually I became aware of the old island here that flowered once for Dutch sailors' eyes—a fresh green breast of the new world.[13]*

Scott heard the surf, the soft wash of the Mediterranean outside his window. He pulled on his cigarette again and thought of Long Island, with its green lighthouse and all those people who had come to their house. America was behind them now, and he had a clear view of the playground that had opened with the beginning of the 1920s. It was more than he could have hoped for.

## CHAPTER 10

# A Northern Man's Dream of the South

### *1918*

SECOND LIEUTENANT LINCOLN WEAVER PUSHED THE STICK OF HIS plane forward and dove down through the night toward the earth. The moon was full, and he could see the white house very clearly, and Weaver knew Zelda was probably there sitting on the porch swing with another soldier. His Fokker biplane whined in protest as he dove down toward the house with the screech of the air reaching the people on the ground like a comet from space. Weaver kept his plane in the dive longer than he should have, but he wanted to give Zelda a show. At the last minute, he pulled up with a great swooping arc that sounded like a freight train swooping low over the roof. Judge Sayre burst out of the door along with Zelda's mother, staring up at the sky as the drone of the engine receded.

The biplanes screaming down from the sky had been going on for months. The soldiers had descended on Montgomery as regiments were brought up to full strength in Camp Sheridan just outside of town and this brought the aviators from Camp Taylor as well. The local newspaper said the town now smelled of khaki. Zelda sat back down behind the cavalcade of wisteria and honeysuckle casting lunar shadows. Pianos thumped up and down the streets. The Model-Ts shined dully along the road. Soldiers and girls passed by on the wooden sidewalk. Montgomery suddenly had the tempo of New York now that the world had come there to get ready to go to war.

It was a sultry night in July and Zelda had been trying to decide if she was even going to the Montgomery Country Club. She had been asked to perform the "Dance of the Hours" and, years later, described the country club as "a clubhouse sprouting inquisitively under the oaks . . . the ground around the place was as worn and used as a plot before a children's playhouse . . . it is too bad a bottle of corn liquor exploded in one of the lockers just after the war and burned the place to the ground . . . no officer could have visited it without falling in love, engaging himself to marry and to populate the countryside with little country clubs just like it."[1]

She was all of seventeen and a terrible student. There was no question she would graduate, but that was all she would do. Zelda had been spending her time with the soldiers that had swarmed down upon Montgomery like locusts, swooping up every available young girl and, most of all, swooping up Zelda Sayre as the most desirable of them all. Years later, she wrote about the change that came to Montgomery. "'War! There's going to be a war,' she thought. Excitement stretched her heart and lifted her feet so high that she floated over the steps to the waiting automobile . . . all night long Alabama thought about the war. Things would disintegrate to new excitements. . . . she convinced herself that the only thing of any significance was to take what she wanted when she could. She did her best."[2]

Zelda had been busy leading college parades as the "Belle of Montgomery," kicking in a store glass window to take a picture she wanted, drinking gin or whatever she could get her hands on, leading the entire senior class in cutting class for a day on April Fools' Day then getting expelled and then reinstated and then graduating in May, receiving the most votes for "Prettiest and Most Attractive Girl." She herself would admit, "I did not study a lot by then. I left my studies in school and as there were a lot of soldiers in town I passed my time going to dances . . ."[3]

Seventeen-year-old Zelda Sayre had been having the time of her life ever since the United States had declared war on Germany on April 6, 1917. Aviators buzzed her home to show their love, and two would eventually crash from their low dives over her home. There were dates every night with strange young soldiers with odd accents from the North. As she later wrote, "suddenly, almost the next day, everything was changed. Life had suddenly become exciting, dangerous, a crazy vitality possessed us. The war came . . . we couldn't afford to wait, for fear it would be gone forever, so we pitched in furiously dancing every night and riding up and down the moonlit roads and even swimming in the gravel pools under the white Alabama moon. . . . "[4]

And they were swarming her again on the hot dance floor in the country club. One soldier after another she danced with as each one cut in on the next. A friend, Sara Hardt, captured the view of Zelda and tried to define what made her so popular. "I saw her as she had looked at that last Christmas dance we were together, wearing a flame dress and Gold-laced slippers, her eyes starry and mocking, flirting with an immense feather fan. Her bronze-gold hair was curled in a thousand ringlets, and as she whirled about, they twinkled enchantingly like little bells. Around her flashed hundreds of jellybeans—the Southern youth of the day—in formal broadcloth and pearl-studded fronts and hundreds of other flappers in gold slippers and rainbow-colored shirts, but they somehow seemed vain and inarticulate beside her. Beauty they had, and grace, and a certain reckless abandon—yet none of them could match the glance of gay derision that flickered beneath the black edge of her eyelashes—and none of them could dance as she did, like a flame or a wind."[5]

And then a first lieutenant cut in, and the whirling dervish of the world seemed to stop. He was ridiculously handsome, with green eyes, smoothed-back blond hair, an aquiline chin, and a Brooks Brothers officer tunic and dashing yellow boots and spurs. A leading man for the leading lady. Zelda would later write, "There seemed to be some heavenly support beneath his shoulder blades that lifted his feet from the ground in ecstatic suspension as if he secretly enjoyed the ability to fly but was walking as a compromise to convention."[6]

Scott danced with Zelda in a trance and asked for her number before another officer cut in. He had to wait his turn to dance with her again, but when he did, they found in each other the very same traits they rec-ognized in themselves. *A romantic readiness such as I have never found in any other person.*[7] They both had a grand sense of life and destiny with no clear sense of purpose or how to achieve it, but the spark was bigger than the parts. In that hot Southern country club, Scott and Zelda were welded together by their demand that life should match great fiction and that great dreams were for people like them.

Scott was witty, funny, from the big city. Zelda was young, sexy, a Southern belle steeped in the mythology of the tragic South. Scott would write later, "There she was—the Southern type in all its purity . . . she had the adroitness sugar coated with sweet voluble simplicity, the suggested background of devoted fathers, brothers and admirers stretching back into the South's heroic age, the unfailing coolness acquired in the endless struggle with the heat. There were notes in her voice that ordered slaves around, then withered up Yankee captains and then soft wheedling notes that mingled in the unfamiliar loveliness."[8]

Scott fell in love with "her flaming self-respect,"[9] her beauty, but also an ideal the same way she fell in love with an ideal. He fell in love with her husky voice, her Southern accent, and the way she connected random thoughts in a stream of consciousness that would become one of her hallmarks. In *This Side of Paradise*, he turned Zelda into Rosalind Connage and described her that first night. "There was the eternally kissable mouth, small, slightly sensual, and utterly disturbing. There were gray eyes and an unimpeachable skin with two spots of vanishing color. She was slender and athletic without underdevelopment and it was a delight to watch her move about the room . . . her vivid instant personality escaped that conscious theatrical quality that Amory had found in Isabella (Ginevra)."[10]

Scott was the man destined for great things from the cosmopolitan world, and she was the heralded beauty of the South who could do no wrong and could do exactly what she wanted. After that, it was a once-in-a-lifetime love. Ginevra King had been pushed over for a young beauty whose power came from her verve, her heritage, her sense of entitlement, and her sexuality. "She saw no guilt in rapture and possessed a natural sensuality upon which she often acted, never disguising her entanglements. Scott recalled when she openly admitted that she could sleep with others and it wouldn't afflict her or make her unfaithful to him."[11]

Zelda did have a past, and in a later unpublished novel, *Caesars Things*, she hinted at intercourse that was not consensual and possibly rape behind an old school when she was fifteen with a rich older boy. "They went up to the haunted school yard so deep in shadows and creaking with felicities of murder to the splintery old swing and she was so miserable and trusting that her heart broke and for many years after she didn't want to live, but was it was better to keep going." A Southern belle would never admit to being raped or forced into intercourse. She would write about it in cryptic scenes years later, mourning, that "there wasn't any more compensatory peace of human relationships, or any more solace of the evening meal, or any more pleasure of competitive effort . . . the child could never quite remember what it was about life of which she was so heartbroken. Nor could she quite forget."[12]

True or not, Zelda's ideas of sex were radical, and Scott realized this from the start: "That any girl who gets drunk in public enjoys telling shocking stories and remarks she has kissed thousands of men and intends to kiss thousands more 'cannot be considered above reproach even if above it.'"[13] But Scott loved this type of woman who went up to the danger line and flirted and whipped up the jealous pangs. Zelda was daring and dangerous, and this made her even more desirable, and more than that, it made her his greatest heroine.

The debutante of Lake Forest, Ginevra King, her golden-girl status came from money, but Zelda's came from force of personality. The two were not even in the same universe, and from here on, Zelda Sayre was F. Scott Fitzgerald's golden girl, and all his heroines, future and past, would carry the flavor, the ignition of that young couple, swirling around in the Southern night and setting up a destiny that would reverberate far beyond their own time. But Scott had his hands full.

After they finished dancing, Scott immediately asked her for a date. "I never make late dates with fast workers,"[14] Zelda responded, but she did give him her number, which he called every day from then on. In "Babes in the Woods," Scott compared his and Zelda's personalities with fictional characters. "They had both started with good looks and excitable temperaments and the rest was the result of certain accessible popular novels and dressing room conversation culled from a slightly older set . . .

he waited for the mask to drop off, but at the same time he did not question her right to wear it. . . . "[15]

And Zelda did wear it. She was the most popular girl in Montgomery, Alabama, and she put Scott into the rotation and allowed him to call on her, where they sat on her porch swing. He walked to her home from the camp through "the hot flowery twilight . . . the four white pillars of the Calhoun house faced the street and behind them the veranda was dark as a cave with hanging weaving, climbing vines. . . . "[16] He later wrote in the short story "The Last of the Belles," "Two weeks later I sat with her on the same verandah, or rather she half lay in my arms and yet scarcely touched me—how she managed that I don't remember. I was trying unsuccessfully to kiss her and had been trying for the best part of an hour."[17]

Scott sat in the scent of honeysuckle on the swing with Zelda, her mother, Miss Minnie, in a rocker and the judge not far away reading his paper. Biplanes buzzed the house, and other suitors called even while Scott was there. On his army pay of $141 a month, he could not afford to compete with many of the locals who could take Zelda to dinner and shows. Many had cars while Scott had to take a bus from camp and then walk the rest of the way to the Sayre home. Zelda was not to be tamed easily, and once, when she saw Scott observing her at a dance, she ran into a lighted phone booth and began kissing her date. Scott was jealous and desired her even more. And she desired him.

But he quickly became aware of the darker sides of Zelda's character. "She treats men terribly. She abuses them and cuts them and breaks dates with them and yawns in their faces and they come back for more . . . she smokes sometimes, drinks alcoholic punch . . . frequently kissed . . . she is prone to make everyone around her pretty miserable when she doesn't get her way . . . "[18] The physical attraction was there, but the conversations, the rebellion against the staid life of a Sothern belle expected to marry and settle down eventually, pushed Zelda to the lightning rod that was Scott Fitzgerald. He may not have been able to offer her money at this point, but he pushed current into her dreams and made them seem real and obtainable. The hot nights where they discussed poetry, got drunk, walked in the pine groves, and the fact he may be pulled overseas into oblivion supercharged their romance. For Scott, it was the beginning of a once-in-a-lifetime love affair, and he fell in love one September night.

> *Now it was a cool night with that mysterious excitement in it which comes at the two changes of the night. The quiet lights in the houses were humming out into the darkness and there was a stir and a bustle among the stars. Out of the corner of his eye Gatsby saw that the blocks of the sidewalks really formed a ladder and mounted to a secret place above the trees—he could climb to it, if he climbed alone, and once there he could suck on the pap of life, gulp down the incomparable milk of wonder.[19]*

In the lost darkness of the Southern street, Scott lost himself. Did Zelda glimmer their destiny together at this point? The girl who would do anything saw a kindred soul in Scott. There was no youth culture, but they were fomenting a rebellion, and after that, it was the intangibility of love. He had told her of his dream to become a famous novelist, and she believed him.

> *His heart beat faster and faster as Daisy's white face came up to his own. He knew that when he kissed this girl and forever wed his unutterable vision to her perishable breath, his mind would never romp again like the mind of God. So he waited, listening for a moment to the tuning fork that had been struck upon a star. Then he kissed her. At his lips touch she blossomed for him like a flower and the incarnation was complete.[20]*

"Nothing means anything except darling self," she wrote to him later. "Don't you think I was made for you? I feel you had me ordered—I want you to wear me, like a watch charm or a buttonhole bouquet . . . sweetheart I always want to be of a help."[21] But that was in the future, and the present was so interesting. Zelda was preparing a war benefit with Sara Mayfield, and she still was seeing other men, though Scott was now her top suitor. "I'm all I'll ever be without you—and there's so much more room for growth with you . . . all my mental faculties are paralyzed with loving you—and wanting you for mine."[22]

And then, like all great loves, came the tragedy of their parting. Scott wrote in his ledger that he fell in love with Zelda on September 7, 1918. In October, Scott was sent north for the final shipping out to France. Zelda gave him a silver flask engraved "9/13/18" and the words "Forget Me Not."

It all came down to a last night Scott would immortalize in "The Last of the Belles."

"And I can still feel that last night vividly, the candlelight that flickered over the rough boards of the mess shack, over the frayed paper decorations, left from the companies' supply party, the sad mandolin down a company street that kept picking 'My Indiana Home' out of the universal nostalgia of the departing summer. . . . we toasted ourselves and the South. Then we left our napkins and empty glasses and a little of the past on the table and hand in hand went out into the moonlight itself."[23]

Scott and Zelda made love before he left.

*However glorious might be his future as Jay Gatsby, he was at present a penniless young man without a past, and at any moment the invisible cloak of his uniform might slip from his shoulders. So he made the most of his time. He took what he could get, ravenously and unscrupulously—eventually he took Daisy one still October night, took her because he had no real right to touch her hand.[24]*

The consecration of their love and the fact he might be killed pushed Scott to ask her to marry him, but Zelda held him off. He was ambitious, and she did love him, but he was unproven, and so Scott, like thousands of others, unwillingly left his girl behind to go confront the hell of war.

*On the last afternoon before he went abroad, he sat with Daisy in his arms for a long silent time. It was a cold fall day with fire in the room and her cheeks flushed. Now and then she moved and he changed his arm a little and once he kissed her dark shining hair. That afternoon had made them tranquil for a while, as if to give them a deep memory for the long parting the next day promised. They had never been closer in their month of love, nor communicated more profoundly one with another, than when she brushed silent lips against his coat's shoulder or when he touched the end of her fingers, gently, as though she were asleep.*[25]

The next day, Scott left Montgomery. "Here is my heart," he said to her before he left. Zelda carried those words with her forever. Poetry was F. Scott Fitzgerald's dream of the South, but now it was his dream of Zelda.

*"He felt married to her, that was all."*[26]

## CHAPTER 11

# Cliff Diving

## *1924*

IT'S THE TWENTIES ON THE RIVIERA. PEOPLE WEAR FULL BATHING suits that cover their bodies like comfortable, sleeveless jogging outfits. Men and women professed modesty. In a photo, Scott is sitting in the sand with Scottie and Zelda to his left. Behind is a man in a straw hat and a stripped changing tent. Scott is smiling, Scottie is smiling, Zelda's face is hidden under the brim of a large, floppy hat. There are young boys behind them, a woman in a bathing suit that looks like a dress. Scott has a self-satisfied expression. He had made it to the Riviera, and all he had to do now was write the "Great American novel" while Zelda kept herself occupied.

So she did. Zelda is now on the highest point on the point Eden Rock among the jagged cliffs and looking down. The sea breeze off the Mediterranean is magnificent. It is warm yet moist and carries the slightest tang of the ocean. Zelda hikes up to the highest point and stares at the spectroscopic blue that runs to the horizon. She is standing in her swimsuit with her short, bobbed hair recently cut by a French hairstylist in a cunning way that made people look and ask who did her hair. She is on the Riviera while her husband is working hard on his novel with that haggard, dazed look he got from too much coffee, cigarettes, and gin, when it was required. He had that look when they came back exhausted from long days in the sun with the Murphys and their children, invading the villa with sandy feet and wet suits while Scott stood up, pale-faced, wound up, exhausted, but also needing a release, which would bring on the nightlife. Zelda knew he was doing good work because he was so wound up he could barely speak until he had that first drink and then a few more to put out the fire he had been stoking all day.

Zelda had a nanny for Scottie, Mrs. Maddox, servants to keep the villa clean, servants to cook, and all she had to do was stay out of Scott's way, and to that end, she had begun to learn French and bought several novels and planned to spend her days swimming and sunning the summer away. The much-vaunted savings of coming to Europe had proved a fiction with the costs of the house, the servants that French law required to be insured, and the groceries that were more than in Great Neck. One of the novels Zelda bought was Raymond Radiguet's bestseller *Le Bal du Comte d'Orgel*. The plot of the love triangle was set in Paris after World War I. A wife devoted to her husband falls in love with a younger man while the husband allows it to happen, "only then appreciating his wife, requiring evidence of another man's desire to experience his own."[1]

Scott had bought a six-horsepower Renault for Zelda, Scottie, and Mrs. Maddox to make the two-hour drive from Valescure to the Murphy's hotel at Cap d'Antibes. Zelda, the nanny, and Scottie would leave every morning and head to Antibes to meet the Murphys. Scott set himself up in the study overlooking the Mediterranean and began writing. Zelda was picking up the language quickly. Gerald and Sara Murphy were glad to see Zelda, who promised to stay out of Scott's hair while he was writing. Zelda also had found herself out of his sex life as well. Scott believed seminal fluid was important to the creative process and, for the time being, had let Zelda know there was to be no sex until the novel was finished. Zelda was not happy about this. She wrote to her friend in Minnesota, Xandra Kalman, "Scott's started a new novel and retired into strict seclusion and celibacy. He's horribly intent on it."[2]

Usually, the day started at eleven on the Murphy beach, a spit of sand Gerald kept clear by meticulously raking away the seaweed and pebbles. The most famous photo of Gerald Murphy is not for his new avocation of painting but standing with his rake by the beach in his swimsuit. The Murphys loved swimming and sunbathing, as did Zelda, and she tanned deeply, with her hair becoming blonder with each passing day. She had lost the weight from the pregnancy, and the Murphys noticed the young men who stopped to flirt with the young twenty-four-year-old American girl. The Murphy daughter, Honoria, years later would recall that Zelda, during that summer, was "tanned and beautiful, often wearing her favorite color, salmon pink . . . a strikingly beautiful woman—blond and soft and tanned by the sun who usually dressed in pink and wore a peony in her hair or pinned to her dress."[3]

The Murphys felt Zelda's taste in clothing was all her own. They saw her as an original. Gerald found Zelda intriguing and very unique. "It was all in her eyes . . . they were strange eyes, brooding but not sad, severe, almost masculine in their directness . . . perfectly level and head on."[4] There is film that has survived from the Riviera, and in it are Scott, Zelda, and the Murphys all sitting under umbrellas with Scott in a striped shirt smoking a cigarette. It looks very bohemian, very twenties, and very much the way the world saw the Fitzgeralds. They were the glamorous young couple with the world at their feet. Undoubtedly, Scott went with Zelda to see the Murphys sometimes, where they sat on straw mats under striped umbrellas, and Gerald offered sherry and sweet biscuits to his guests and lemonade to the children playing near the water. But many times, it was only Zelda and Scottie spending the long summer days with the Murphys and the other people who were guests of the Murphys, which included Phillip and Ellen Barry, Dick and Alice Lee Meyers, and Gilbert and Amanda Seldes. Scott would write to Carl Van Vechten, "We are living here in a sort of idyllic state among everything lovely imaginable in the way of Mediterranean delights. Unlike you I have only an occasional lust for the exotic streets of the metropolis—at present I am content to work and become excruciatingly healthy under Bryon's and Shelly's and Dickens' sky."[5]

Scott still had enough money to hold off the dogs while he worked on his novel with the curtains blowing in from a Mediterranean Sea breeze. He had written to Max Perkins, "I think St. Raphael is the loveliest spot I've ever seen . . . Frejus which has aqueducts and is both Roman and Romanesque is in sight of the window . . . I'm perfectly happy. I hope to God I don't see a soul for six months. I feel absolutely self-sufficient and

I have a perfect hollow craving for loneliness, that has increased for three years in some arithmetical progress and I'm going to satisfy it at last."[6]

And now Zelda had climbed the highest peak, with the Murphys and others looking up with hands over their eyes. It was just like when she used to dive from the high board in Alabama. People just couldn't believe she was going to do it. But, of course, she was. Life had begun to settle down, and Zelda was bored. Outwardly, she had the Murphys and all their amazing friends to occupy her. There were musical events, boating trips, picnics where Gerald brought out his gramophone and the Charleston, and "Ain't We Got Fun" wafted down the hot sunbaked beach. The attire was casual, unless they were in swimsuits with the men in denim work pants and "jockey caps and women in linen trousers and with blue and white striped mariners shirts designed for the French navy. That summer Fernard Léger was a frequent guest, along with Jean Cocteau, Georges Braque, and Igor Stravinsky. Cole Porter showed up with playwright Philip Barry whose comedy *You and I* was a Broadway hit."[7] When the two-car train sounded its horn on the way to the Italian border, it was time for a siesta and lunch with everyone getting together late in the afternoon at Eden Rock, where the adults dove off the lower peaks.

The problem was the Murphys bored Zelda. The girl from Montgomery who did anything from spiking her Cokes to taking off her panties at dances and diving naked from high dives and swimming in the Plaza hotel, had fallen into the dull routine of the very rich. The Murphys were bourgeois, older, and lived a more settled life buttressed by money. Their days progressed one after another much the same with a Grecian symmetry. Gerald took up his rake with maddening regularity every morning. Sarah was the perfect hostess running her family, dispensing cordials and light fare for the beach. Everyone knew their role, and Zelda's was wife of the famous author. But she missed that famous author who offended the Murphys many times with his antics but which Zelda understood very well. Scott was pulling more and more inside himself for the novel, and for the first time, Zelda felt lonely. *"What will we do with ourselves this afternoon. . . . and the day after that and the next thirty years?"*[8] She had built her world around Scott, and now he was gone. So, she had to find thrills elsewhere.

She swam along until her arms ached. She tanned her skin a deep butternut brown. She walked the beach alone, with Mrs. Maddox watching Scottie. She began looking for thrills once again. So, climbing higher than anyone else to dive into the Mediterranean was familiar stomping ground. Zelda stared off into the distance and wondered what people were doing in New York. If there had been air travel, she would have hopped a jet and probably gone home. But she would have to find her thrills on the Riviera. One thing was for sure, she would not find it with the Murphys. No. They would never climb up to the top of the cliffs and dive off. They simply didn't have the courage, guts, or reckless abandon.

Zelda looked down at the children and the adults, then took a breath, and dove into space, arcing down toward the sparkling blue water. Even when Zelda knifed down into the cool sea and turned around, she was already wondering what she would do next. One thing was for sure. Tomorrow, she would not go to the Murphys. That she knew.

# CHAPTER 12

# The Sensible Thing

## *1918*

SCOTT RAN DOWN FIFTH AVENUE UNDER A BRILLIANT NEW YORK SKY and headed for the train station. He had just received a telegram from Zelda that made him think it might be all over. Who could have predicted the armistice would put him out of the army and into an advertising job in Manhattan, where he penned the immortal lines, "we keep you clean in Muscatine"?[1] His pay was $35 a week. Not enough to get the girl waiting for him in Montgomery to marry him after he had given her his mother's ring. Not even close. He had just received a letter from her intended for another man where she broke off another engagement. Scott was furious and said he never wanted to speak to her again. But he was desperate. Desperate like his flat in uptown Manhattan at 200 Claremont Avenue. Desperate like the rejection letters plastered all over his flat from the magazines. No one wanted his stories, and Scribner's had declined his novel completed in camp with a two-page letter.

"... the story does not seem to us to work up to a conclusion—neither the hero's career nor his character are shown to be brought to any stage which justifies an ending. This may be intentional on your part for it is certainly not untrue to life; but it leaves the reader distinctly disappointed and dissatisfied since he had expected him to arrive somewhere either in an actual sense by his response to the war perhaps, or in a psychological one by 'finding himself' as for Pendennis is brought to do.

He does go to war, but in almost the same spirit that he went to college and—school because it is simply the thing to do. It seems to us in short that the story does not culminate in anything as it must to justify the reader's interest as he follows it . . . we do not want anything we have said to make you think we failed to get your idea in the book . . . we certainly do not wish to 'conventionalize' it . . . ."[2]

Scott had lost his best shot at getting Zelda with Scribner editor Max Perkins's insightful rejection letter. So, after declaring he never wanted to speak to Zelda again for getting engaged to another man, he decided to go down to Montgomery and force her into marrying him. He sent a telegram that in the short story "The Sensible Thing" read, "letter depressed me, have you lost your nerve you are foolish and just upset to think of breaking off why not marry me immediately sure we can make it all right—"[3] Scott had already sent Zelda his mother's engagement ring, which she wore for a week and then took off. The truth was she wasn't sure anymore about the young lieutenant whom she had the intense love affair with and had given him an engraved silver flask—*All My Love Zelda*—before he boarded the train that took him away to possible death in the trenches of France.

Scott never made it to the trenches. After boarding a troopship in Long Island, he marched off when the armistice was reached. Not getting over to Europe became one of the great regrets of his life. A veteran, Sam Broomfield, who met Scott in Paris during the twenties, recalled that "the war seemed to be an obsession with him or rather the fact that he had missed out in the war and by never having active service at the front had missed the greatest experience a man could have in his generation."[4] Like the college degree he never received, the baptism of fire in war was also denied Fitzgerald, and both would spawn myths, regrets, stories, and fantasies. In "The Offshore Pirate," a young man laments missing out on the action. "It was not so bad, except that when the infantry came limping back from the trenches he wanted to be one of them. The sweat and mud they wore seemed only one of those ineffable symbols of aristocracy that were forever eluding him."[5] While waiting to get discharged in New York, Scott was caught by the Hotel Astor house detective with a naked girl, and when his regiment was ordered back to Montgomery, he was AWOL in New York and left behind. When the train arrived in Washington, Scott was at the station with two girls and a bottle. Back in Montgomery at Camp Taylor, he resumed his courtship of Zelda and asked her to marry him, but she balked at marrying an unproven writer who would not even have his $141 a month to fall back on.

She later told a date, John Dearborn, that "she didn't love Scott romantically but wanted to be his literary muse."[6] Lawton Campbell, a Princeton classmate, later recalled, "Frankly it all seemed like such a gamble . . . I told her I was sure Scott could make money from his writing and she told me about the interest some publisher had in his book and about his encouraging letters. As nearly as I can remember she said, 'If Scott sells the book, I'll marry the man, because he is sweet. Don't you think so?'"[7]

Scott had headed to New York to make good on his promise to become a successful author and prove to Zelda he was worthy of marriage. All he had was his rejected novel and a job writing ad copy he hated. "That novel begun in a training camp in the war, was my ace in the hole. I had put it aside when I got a job in New York, but I was so constantly aware of it as the shoe with cardboard in the sole, during all one desolate spring . . . so I struggled on in a business I detested . . . I walked quickly from certain places . . . from the pawn shop where one left the field glasses, from prosperous friends whom one met when wearing a suit from before the war. . . . "[8]

But all that wartime drama had vanished. Many of the soldiers were still in Montgomery, and Zelda had started dating again even as the telegrams and letters rained down from New York. "Am taking apartment immediately right under Tildes new apartment love Scott."[9] Then, "Darling Heart Ambition Enthusiasm and Confidence I declare everything glorious this world is a game and while I feel sure of you love everything is possible I am in the land of ambition and success and my only hope and faith is that my darling heart will be with me now."[10] The letters that Zelda enjoyed at first soon became a burden to reply to. "Scott you've been so sweet about writing, but I'm so damn tired of being told that you used to wonder why they keep princesses in towers. You've written that in your last six letters! It dreadfully hard to write so very much and so many of your letters sound forced—I know you love me darling and I love you more than anything in the world, but it's going to be so much longer, we just can't keep up this frantic writing."[11]

The truth was Zelda wasn't sure Scott would be successful, and marriage was the most powerful tool she had to change her life, and she couldn't throw it away on an unpublished author in a down-and-out apartment working at a low-paying advertising job. Zelda was a player, if nothing else, and she began to see other men once again.

*Through this twilight universe Daisy began to move again with the season; suddenly she was again keeping a dozen dates a day with half a dozen men and drowsing asleep at dawn with the beads and chiffon of an evening dress tangled among dying orchids on the floor beside her bed.*[12]

Scott was desperate. He had essentially quit his job when he told his boss he was leaving again for Montgomery. "He was in a mess, one of those terrific messes which are ordinary incidents in the life of the poor, which follow poverty like birds of prey. The poor go under or they go up or go wrong or even go on, somehow, in a way the poor have, but George O'Kelly (Scott) was so new to poverty that had anyone denied the uniqueness of his case he would have been astounded."[13]

Scott had lost the veneer of Princeton and the wartime glamour of a young second lieutenant. He lost all the costumes he had been wearing from the young dandy on Summit Avenue when, in reality his family lived in rented homes, to the young man among the nation's wealthy elite at Princeton where he flunked out, to the romantic image of the young officer heightened by the great tragedy of impending death, who had never even gone to war. This had all been snatched away, and he was left with a shabby suit and a rundown apartment in New York papered with literary failure. Even Scott understood he had little to offer Zelda as he wrote a friend in St. Paul, "My mind is firmly made up that I will not, shall not, can not, should not, must not marry, still she is remarkable . . ."[14]

But all Scott really had left was the golden girl down south, and now like the rest of the set pieces in his life, she was in danger of vanishing as well. He captures this time in *My Lost City*.

"As I hovered ghost-like in the Plaza Red Room of a Saturday afternoon or went to lush and liquid garden parties in the East Sixties or tippled with Princetonians in the Biltmore Bar, I was haunted always by my other life—my drab room in the Bronx, my square foot of the subway, my fixation upon the day's letter from Alabama—would it come and what would it say? My shabby suits, my poverty, and love. While my friends were launching decently into life I had muscled my inadequate bark into mid-stream. The gilded youth circling around young Constance Bennett in the Club de Vingt, the classmates in the Yale Princeton Club whooping up our first after the war reunion, the atmosphere of the millionaires' houses that I sometimes frequented, these things were empty for me . . . from them I returned to my home on Claremont Avenue—home because there might be a letter waiting outside the door. . . . I was a failure—mediocre at advertising work and unable to get started as a writer."[15]

Scott went back to Montgomery three times to persuade Zelda to marry him. April, May, and then, finally, in June. The final desperate trip in June began badly. Zelda met him at the train, surrounded by two other young men. "This is Mr. Craddock and Mr. Halt,"[16] she announced cheerfully. Scott was distraught. Scott and Zelda had sex on the last trip, with Zelda writing him after, "Sweetheart, I love you most of all the earth—and I want to be married soon Lover—Don't say I'm not enthusiastic—you ought to know."[17] But she was back on the whirlwind of dating and was impatient with Scott's inability to find success. The clock was ticking for her, too, and Zelda had to make her choice while her powers were at their peak. And her family saw Scott as wholly unsuitable. Not because he was a Catholic and a Yankee, but because he was unstable. Her father believed him to be a drunk and complained, "He's never sober."[18] Never mind that he was an Irish Catholic who had not graduated from college and had no real career except for a dream to become a bestselling author.

The truth was that the hot light of the romance was fading and this final desperate trip was to rekindle the flames before they went out for good. Scott entered Zelda's house and must have expected planes to be buzzing over the roof and soldiers to be lounging on the porch swing. The scent of honeysuckle was a painful reminder of those nights when life was intense and their love affair was burning bright. Now, "they sat together on the sofa, overcome by each other's presence . . ." Scott immediately questioned her fidelity. "'Do you expect me to never go anywhere,' Jonquil (Zelda) demanded, leaning back against the sofa pillows . . . 'and just fold my hands and sit still—forever?' Scott began to panic. 'What do you mean?' he blurted out in a panic. 'Do you mean you think I will never have enough money to marry you?'"[19]

That is exactly what she meant. The creeping panic that Zelda was slipping away was there now. "He tried to take her again in his arms, but she resisted unexpectedly, saying, 'it's hot I'm going to get the electric fan.' When the fan was adjusted they sat down again . . . 'Just when I'm ready to marry you you write me the most nervous letters as if you're going to back out and I have to come rushing down here—'

"'You don't have to come if you don't want to.'

"'But I do want to!'"[20]

Scott stared at Zelda. He didn't know that Zelda was so popular a football team at Auburn College had formed a fraternity in her name with all the members vying for her attention. He didn't know she still was getting military insignias from suitors that filled her glove box with silver and gold bars. The bloom was off the rose, and Zelda saw clearly that Scott was not the urbane visitor from the North anymore but another young man struggling to make his way after the war with a one-in-a-million shot at a literary dream with the same odds as being struck by lightning. He was the middle-class young man from the Midwest come east to find his destiny and get the golden girl . . . but it wasn't working.

Zelda broke down and cried, and "they sat there while the evening pianos thumped their last cadences into the streets outside. George (Scott) did not think or hope, lulled into the numbness by the premonition of disaster." It is all tragically obvious the next day in the Sayre home. They had each guessed the truth about the other, but of the two, she was more ready to admit the situation. Zelda spoke the silent truth in the room. "There's no use going on . . . you know you hate the insurance (advertising) business and you'll never do well at it . . . I love you with all my heart and I don't see how I can ever love anyone else but you. If you'd been ready for me two months ago I'd have married you. Now I can't because it doesn't seem to be the sensible thing."[21]

And this moniker—"The Sensible Thing"—stuck onto a short story written years later should have given Scott pause. There was a fissure here, a cold, hard decision made about his earning abilities to which some might have taken offense. But Scott believed in that love fired in the furnace of their wartime romance, and he was unwilling to let it go now. He believed in the past. "George (Scott) didn't take the situation well at all. He seized her in his arms and tried literally to kiss her into marrying him at once. When this failed, he broke into a monologue of self-pity and ceased only when he saw that he was making himself despicable in her sight."[22]

The ring is given back to Scott. Zelda had not been wearing it anyway and she regarded it much the same way she regarded the silver and gold bars from the soldiers she was still seeing. Scott was another suitor, one whom she had feelings for, but one she was unwilling to commit to unless he delivered the goods. Scott staggered through the rest of the day and through an excruciating cab ride back to the station. A final insult occurs when a young couple walks up just as he is leaving. "For an interminable five minutes they all stood there talking; then the train roared into the station and with ill-concealed agony in his face George (Scott) held out his arms toward Jonquil (Zelda). She took an uncertain step toward him, faltered, and then pressed his hand quickly as if she were taking leave of a chance friend."[23]

Scott somehow gets on the train, "dumb almost blind with pain."[24] And it here it hits him. He has lost the girl.

*The day coach—he was penniless now—was hot. He went out to the open vestibule and sat down on a folding chair and the station slid away and the backs of the unfamiliar buildings moved by. Then out into the spring fields where a yellow trolley raced them for a minute with people in it who might once have seen the pale magic of her face along the casual street.*[25]

The dream of his life created in the hot summery nights of the South has now deserted Scott along with other dreams. He was so hard up he didn't have the money for a Pullman car and had to sneak into the day coach. He is now the boy from the Midwest with nothing but an apartment in New York and the ashes of his love affair with a rejected novel sitting at home on his desk.

> *The track curved and now it was going away from the sun, which, as it sank lower, seemed to spread itself in benediction over the vanishing city where she had drawn her breath. He stretched out his hands desperately as if to snatch only a wisp of air, to save a fragment of the spot that she had made lovely for him. But it was all going by too fast now for his blurred eyes and he knew that he had lost that part of it, the freshest and the best, forever.[26]*

He rode in the train back north, "past clanging street-crossings, gathering speed through wide suburban spaces toward the sunset. Perhaps too she would see the sunset and pause for a moment, turning, remembering, before he faded with her sleep into the past. This night's dusk would cover up forever the sun and the trees and the flowers and laughter of his young world."[27]

Scott had lost Zelda and that golden part of his life. He would forever be pursuing that dream behind him already. Years later, he would reflect on the darkest time of his young life and what he lost. "It was one of those tragic loves doomed for lack of money and one day the girl closed it out on the basis of common sense."[28] The best Scott could hope for now was in the past.

> *"I wouldn't ask too much of her," I ventured. "You can't repeat the past."*
>
> *"Can't repeat the past," he cried incredulously. "Of course you can!"[29]*

# CHAPTER 13

# Passion at First Glance

## *1924*

THE *NEW YORKER* RAN AN ARTICLE IN 1926 DESCRIBING SCOTT AND Zelda on the Riviera. It is a satiric piece making light of their youth, the drinking, and Scott's rise to fame. It is a barometer of their fame as well. "All was quiet on the Riviera and then the Fitzgeralds arrived, Scott and Zelda and Scottie. The summer season opened. There had been talk about their coming. They were coming; they were not. One day they appeared on the beach. They had played tennis the day before, and were badly burned. Everybody was concerned about their burns. They must keep their shoulders covered, they must rub on olive oil."[1]

Life on the Riviera had, in fact, devolved into routine for the Fitzgeralds. Scott listens to Zelda and Scottie leave with the nanny. There is a fine breeze off the sea as he watches the curtains whip and snap. They seem to hold his characters. The sun rolls across the sea and jumps up over the sandy beach and moves on in vast ripples across the land. He and Zelda have just had a fight over what she should do. "What'll we do with ourselves?"[2] The heroine asks in Zelda's novel *Save the Waltz*. Her husband replies, "She couldn't always be a child and have things provided for her to do."[3] Zelda is complaining again about being bored. Scott can't worry about that now. His mustache has grown in. He is getting a tan. A slight headache from the night before, but no matter. Scott hears the whine of a plane out over the Mediterranean and looks up. It is a biplane, and for a moment, he thinks of the war he never went to. It is one of the regrets of his life. He watches the plane coming in low for a moment, then looks down and begins to write.

Zelda also hears the whine of the plane and opens her eyes on the beach. She had been for her morning swim and was letting the sun bronze her skin to the dark golden color of tawny pine. The airy beach and the soft swish of the water breaking on the beach with a lost child's voice came across, then the sputtering sound of the airplane motor that reminded her of the aviators who flew low over her home in Montgomery. She opened her eyes in time to see the bright yellow biplane make a turn and fly straight toward the beach. Zelda sat up and watched the plane almost skimming the water suddenly lift up in a long arcing swoop and caught sight of the pilot's slicked-back dark hair as he raised his hand. She waved back and watched the plane turn back out to sea and thought of the young aviator she had met the day before.

She laid back down. Zelda didn't feel like driving to the Murphys. Not every day. Once Scott shoed them out of the villa and the nanny had her daughter, Zelda was left to her own devices. The days lately were halcyon on the Riviera with a mild temperature of eighty degrees and a northerly mistral blowing in from the Alps. There was no rain to speak of, just blue sea and blinding yellow sand with the faint whoosh of the surf. She had bought several French novels, but her eyes bothered her and French was difficult. Scott had that strange detachment she noticed whenever he was in the middle of a story or a novel. He went through the motions and gave the correct responses, but that was up until he drank, then he came back in like a radio turned to a loud station. But mostly, he was remote, distant, celibate.

So Zelda tanned herself and swam, and then after a few hours, she went to the café by the beach, the Café de la Flotte. It wasn't noon yet, but she had recently become very, very bored. Zelda swam far out to sea many times, working off her psychic and physical steam. She later wrote Edmund Wilson, " . . . everything would be perfect if there was somebody here who would be sure to spread the tale of our idyllic existence around New York . . . it's fine to be away from the continual necessity of revolt of New York."[4]

She was alone until Scott wanted to go out at night and while the Murphys were nice and the people were interesting, she couldn't just sit and watch Scottie play with the Murphy daughter, Honoria, all day. She couldn't be that mom all the time or F. Scott Fitzgerald's wife. So she went to the beachside café and ordered a Pastis, "an anise flavored cordial served neat with a jug of water." She mixed it herself and sat at the bar, feeling the lull of the alcohol. It was hard to say when she started to talk with the French aviators from the nearby base. There were four who had entered the café. "Bobbe Croier, a veteran of the Verdun; Robert Montagne, older than the rest, who had fought in the war of the Riff and was fluent in Arabic; Jacques Bellando, recently awarded his flight wings at the seaplane training school in Berre west of Marseille; and the handsomest of the group, a twenty-five-year-old lieutenant named Edouard Jozan."[5]

Jozan is tall and dark, athletic, and knows little English. He is the son of a French army officer and has the military bearing, dark features, the commanding eyes that Zelda recognized in the aviators who had crowded around her in Montgomery. In photos, he looks into the camera with casual, cool eyes. He is used to being a leader. Zelda basks in the attention from the officers, and the Southern belle takes another lap. It is all very innocent and there is talk of meeting her husband. Zelda, later in her novel *Save Me the Waltz*, would describe Jozan. "The flying officer who looked like a Greek God was aloof . . . he seemed not too content with the official purpose which had brought him there and was not casually available."[6]

Zelda would portray that first meeting differently in works of her fiction. In her novel *Caesars Things*, she has the first encounter on San Raphael's beach near the Café de al Flotte. In this more dangerous version, she and Scott meet the young aviator together on a path leading to the pavilion. Scott encourages her to talk to the Frenchman. "'I don't feel I ought to . . .' The husband, Scott, pushes her. 'Oh go on, he's just a young Frenchman looking for a good time.' She responds, 'What's that got do with it? I don't know French.' He responds, 'Never mind, he does.'"[7]

The aviator declines the invitation for a drink, promising some other time they would all drink together. Then another version in *Save Me the Waltz*, the café's owner invites her and Scott in for a drink, promising food and dancing later. "My establishment would be honored if you accept an American cocktail after your bath."[8] But it is here Zelda reveals her immediate attraction and experienced *un coup de foudre* (a flash of lighting, or *passion at first glance*). "As her eyes met those of the officer, Alabama experienced the emotion of a burglar unexpectedly presented with the combination of a difficult safe by the master of the house . . . she felt as if she had been caught red handed in some outrageous act."[9] However they met, it was enough for Zelda to immortalize the moment in two novels years later.

Somewhere Zelda returns to the beach, where it has gotten hotter, and she goes for a long swim to cool down and looks back at the beach and can see the aviators watching her from the café. Eduardo Jozan is intrigued. He has met her in the café or on the beach. It doesn't matter. His English is terrible, and he cannot really follow what she was saying, but she is vivacious, pretty, witty, American; there is something in her voice he can't place.

Up above, sitting at his writing table in the villa, after a swallow of gin, Scott defines it for him. *"It was the kind of voice that the ear follows up and down, as if each speech is an arrangement of notes that will never be played again."*[10]

# CHAPTER 14

# Repeating the Past

## *1918*

SCOTT FITZGERALD SAT ON THE TOP OF THE TRAIN CAR IN THE HOT sunshine nailing into the boards lining the roof. He had just bought new overalls, and he was feeling good. After two long months, he had completed the rewrite of his novel and had given it to his friend "Tuddy" to deliver to New York. It had only been three months since he left New York, but it felt like an eternity. After coming back from Montgomery, Scott went on a three-week bender and emerged amazingly hungover. He then walked the hot sidewalks of New York in his shabby suit, realizing he was just one of the multitudes.

> *I felt a haunting loneliness sometimes, and I felt it in others—poor young clerks who loitered in front of windows waiting until it was time for a solitary restaurant dinner—young clerks in the dusk, wasting the most poignant moments of night and life.[1]*

In the short story "May Day," Gordon Skerritt is a penniless artist who can't get going in New York. He visits an old friend from college, Dean Phillips, in his hotel room. The scene mirrors Fitzgerald's penurious state. "Gordon rose and picking up one of the many shirts, gave it a minute examination. It was of very heavy silk, yellow, with a pale blue stripe—and there were nearly a dozen of them. He stared involuntarily at his own shirt cuffs—they were ragged and linty at the edges and soiled to a faint gray. Dropping the silk shirt, he held his coat sleeves down and worked the frayed shirt cuffs up till they were out of sight. Then he went to the mirror and looked at himself with listless, unhappy interest. His tie, of former glory, was faded and thumb creased—it served no longer to hide the jagged button holes of his collar. He thought, quite without amusement, that only three years before he had received a scattering vote in the senior elections at college for being the best dressed man in his class."[2]

Later, he would write, "I wandered through the town of 127th Street, resenting its vibrant life or else I bought cheap theatre tickets at Gray's drugstore and tried to lose myself for a few hours in my old passion for Broadway. I was a failure—mediocre at advertising work and unable to get started as a writer. Hating the city, I got roaring, weeping drunk on my last penny . . ."[3]

On July 4, Scott left New York, and on the train ride back west, he decided to take another crack as his novel. "The idea of writing *This Side of Paradise*," he remarked later, "occurred to me on the first day of last July. It was a sort of substitute form of dissipation."[4] Scott went back to St. Paul, where his parents let him have his old room back on the third floor. "I retired not on my profits, but despair, and a broken engagement and crept home to St. Paul to finish a novel."[5] Scott put a schedule on his curtain, and with lots of Coca-Colas and cigarettes, he buckled down for two months of hard work in the hot attic space of 599 Summit Avenue and ignored imploring letters from his old friend Bunny Wilson to write him a story and a position offered by a local insurance company.

Scott was going for broke to win back Zelda. He was going back to repeat the past like a master tinker and fix the problem and then proceed from there. "This is an attempt at a big novel," he wrote Max Perkins of Scribner's toward the end of August. "And I really believe I have hit it . . . "[6] It was after he finished *This Side of Paradise* that Scott took the job nailing boards into the Union Pacific cars and left his fate up to a group of men in Manhattan sitting around a table with his manuscript on the dark walnut. The young editor, Max Perkins, sat at the conference room at Scribner's Publishing Company, smoking a Camel nonfilter. Mr. Scribner sat with the greasy manuscript in front of him that looked like it had been lost in a taxi. It had. Fitzgerald's friend Tuddy had been entrusted to get it to Scribner's and then left it in a cab, and fortunately, the cab driver was not a literate man but an honest one and retuned the manuscript.

So here it sat with the young editor down at one end of the table and Mr. Scribner and his son at the other end. Max Perkins was the editor brought on board to spice things up and get Scribner's into the twentieth century with a crop of talented young writers that could open up new markets. But this rough manuscript . . . this hodgepodge of conversations, prose, poetry, riffs from plays, vignettes, sex, drinking, strange language, dangling storylines, storylines that went nowhere, faked literary references, all held together with kite string . . . this was too far. The entire Scribner office looked down on the book. A sister of a sales associate had been given the book to read, and her trusted opinion had rendered many bestsellers. "So when it was known that he had taken *This Side of Paradise* home for the week-end, his colleagues were agog on Monday morning. 'And what did your sister say?' they asked in chorus. 'She picked it up with the tongs,' he replied, 'because she wouldn't touch it with her hands after reading it and put it into the fire.'"[7]

And the author was a nobody. Just another returning soldier taking his shot with a novel that a first-year English professor would roll his eyes at and probably throw in the trash.

"Charles Scribner sat at the head of the table glowering. His brother Arthur sat by his side. Brownell was there too, a formidable figure for he was not just the editor in chief but one of the most eminent literary critics in America . . . he looked eager to argue against any of the half dozen other men sitting around the table who might want to accept it. Old CS held forth. 'I'm proud of my imprint. I cannot publish fiction that is without literary value.' Then Brownell spoke for him when he pronounced the book frivolous. The discussion seemed over—until old CS with his forbidding eyes, peered down the conference table and said, 'Max, you're very silent.' Perkins stood and began to pace the room. 'My feeling . . . is that a publisher's first allegiance is to talent. And if we aren't going to publish a talent like this, is a very serious thing . . . if we were going to turn down the likes of Fitzgerald, I will lose all interest in publishing books.' There was a silence and then Mr. Scribner said he wanted more time to think it over."[8]

Scott spent his time going down to the corner drugstore, borrowing money from his friend Tubby for cigarettes and cokes since his parents had let him know they wouldn't support him. And then he got the job at Union Pacific. "At 6:30 the following morning carrying his lunch, and a new suit of overalls that had cost four dollars he strode self-consciously into the Great Northern car shops," he wrote late in the short story "Forging Ahead." "It was like entering a new school, except that no one showed any interest in him or asked if he was going out for the team. . . . He found that nailing nails into a board was more technical than nailing tacks into a wall. . . . 'Hey, you! Get up!' He looked down. A foreman stood there, unpleasantly red in the face. 'Yes you in the new suit. Get up!'"[9]

Scott rose from sitting, which he had found much easier than standing when nailing boards. It didn't matter; after his new coveralls were stolen, he was laid off. "Basil (Scott) received four dollars and lost his coveralls. Learning that nails were driven from a kneeling position had cost him only cab fare."[10] And then. Then everything changed . . . "The postman rang and that day I quit work and ran along the streets stopping automobiles to tell acquaintances about it—my novel *This Side of Paradise* was accepted for publication. That week the postman rang and rang and I paid off my terrible small debts, bought a suit, and woke up every morning with a world of ineffable toploftiness and promise."[11]

Max Perkins had put his job on the line for an unknown writer who had flunked out of Princeton, been a bad solider, had a drinking problem, lost his girl, and had ended up back in his parents' home like a wayward millennial, but it had worked. Mr. Scribner had relented to the young new editor, Max Perkins, who would remain Fitzgerald's lifelong editor, companion, banker, and friend.

"Dear Mr. Fitzgerald, I am very glad, personally, to be able to write to you that we are all for publishing your book, *This Side of Paradise*. Viewing it as the same book that was here before, which in a sense it is, though translated into somewhat different terms and extended further, I think that you have improved it enormously. As the first manuscript did, it abounds in energy and life and it seems to me in much better proportion. I was afraid that when we declined the first manuscript you might be done with us conservatives . . . "[12]

Fitzgerald lost no time in rectifying the past. He signed with the Harold Ober agency in New York and immediately began selling stories to the magazines *The Smart Set* and *Scribner's Magazine* for $215.00 and $300.00. "Of course I was delighted to get your letter," he wrote back to Perkins. "Would it [be] utterly impossible for you to publish the book by Christmas or say by February? I have so many things dependent on its success—including of course a girl—not that I expect to make a fortune, but it will have a psychological effect on me and all my surroundings and open up new fields. . . . "[13]

Scott was now ready to go back down to Alabama and get the golden girl. After lunching at the Princeton Club, he ran into Lawton Campbell on the stairs with a color-illustrated jacket cover of *This Side of Paradise*. Scott showed him the cover and told him, "You'll probably recognize some of your friends . . . you might even recognize yourself." Then Lawton told him he had seen Zelda in Montgomery. "He thanked me and then looked at the jacket cover. He knitted his brow a minute as if to indicate the months of hard labor on the book would be rewarded in more ways than one. Scott smiled and said, 'I phoned her long-distance last night. She's still on the fence and I may have to go to Montgomery to get her but I believe this will do the trick.'"[14]

Zelda had written him after he told her of his success. "I've been wanting to see you . . . but I couldn't ask you." She then told him she was recovering from an affair with Auburn's starting quarterback and asked if he would bring her a court of gin. "So funny Scott, I don't feel a bit shaky and do dontish like I used to when you came—I really want to see you, that's all, Zelda."[15]

It had been five months since he had seen Zelda. He wrote to his friend Fowler before he left, " . . . not even the family knows I'm going to Montgomery so keep it dark . . . God knows tho Lud, I may be a wreck by the time I see you. I'm going to try and settle it one way or the other."[16] The train ride back to Montgomery in the fall was bittersweet with nostalgia. He and Zelda had not corresponded for months since the breakup.

He reached Montgomery and checked into a hotel. "He was breathing hard—he noticed this but he told himself that it was excitement, not emotion. He was here; she was not married—that was enough." Scott then went to Zelda's house in the cooling twilight and saw that it had changed. "There was nothing changed, only everything was changed. It was smaller and it seemed shabbier than before—there was no cloud of magic hovering over its roof and issuing from the windows of the upper floor."[17]

Already his dream of conquering Zelda once and for all was smashing up against the reality of time passed. He sat in the dusky parlor, and "then the door opened and Jonquil (Zelda) came into the room—and it was as though everything in it suddenly blurred before his eyes. He had not remembered how beautiful she was and he felt his face grow pale and his voice diminish to a poor sigh in his throat. And now the young couple went for a walk but not before Scott asked her the question.

'You don't love me anymore do you?'

'No.'"[18]

They go for a walk to the Confederate cemetery and then when they returned, they found themselves back in the parlor where it had all fallen apart last summer. "Then dinner was over and he and Jonquil were alone in the room that had seen the beginning of their love affair and the end. It seemed to him long ago and inexpressibly sad. On that sofa he had felt agony and grief such as he would never know again. He would never be so weak or so tired poor and miserable. Yet he knew that boy of fifteen months before had had something, a trust, a warmth that was gone forever . . . The sensible thing, they had done the sensible thing. He had traded his first youth for strength and carved success out of despair. But with his youth, life had carried away the freshness of his love."[19]

And then Scott asks her to sit in his lap like they used to while he relates what had happened in the last few months. In the story "The Sensible Thing," he becomes the hero of an engineering expedition in Peru, but in real life, he seals himself into his parent's top floor and uses every bit of talent he possesses to forge his first novel out of pain and despair. And here is where the coals of their romance flame up and Scott can't help himself. They kiss, and their fate is sealed.

*There must have been moments even that afternoon when Daisy tumbled short of his dreams—not through her own fault but because of the colossal vitality of his illusion. It had gone beyond her, beyond everything. He had thrown himself into it with a creative passion, adding to it all the time, decking it out with every bright feather that drifted his way. No amount of fire or freshness can challenge what a man can store up in his ghostly heart.*[20]

Zelda and Scott get back together and have sex on this trip using early-twentieth-century birth control, which many times was nothing at all. Sometime before Zelda consented to be Mrs. F. Scott Fitzgerald, Scott had taken a ride through Central Park in a hansom with Rosaline Fuller. They had met at a Plaza Hotel party and the young English actress had no sexual inhibitions. When Scott suggested they leave, they took a nighttime ride through Central Park under a blanket in a carriage. He later wrote that the "clip clop of the horses hooves made a background to our discovery of each other's bodies." Rosaline would follow this up in her diary by writing, "we made love everywhere, in theatre boxes, country fields, under the sun, moon, and stars . . . no end to our delight and discovery of one another."[21] At a time when contraception was not widely available, this was risky business.

After Zelda consented to marry Scott, they had their own scare. Scott sent her some pills to terminate the pregnancy and Zelda wrote back, "I wanted to for your sake, because I know what a mess I'm making and how inconvenient it's all going to be—but I simply can't and won't take those awful pills—so I've thrown them away. I'd rather take carbolic acid. You see, as long as I feel that I had the right, I don't mind much what happens—and besides, I'd rather have a whole family than sacrifice my self-respect. They just seem to place everything on the wrong basis—and I'd feel like a damn whore if I took even one."[22] It turned out she wasn't pregnant.

The marriage was set for April 3, and Zelda's parents declined to come to New York, sending their daughter off on the train to be wed in Manhattan's St. Patrick's Cathedral. A crowd of Zelda's friends saw her off at the station, and she boarded a train for New York. In her later novel,

Zelda describes the parting: "The judge put her on the train. 'Goodbye daughter.' He seemed very handsome and abstract to Alabama. She was afraid to cry, her father was so proud. 'Goodbye daddy.' 'Goodbye baby.' The train pulled Alabama out of the shadow drenched land of her youth."[23]

The Southern belle was going to marry a man with no real pedigree in a ceremony that was one step up from a Las Vegas wedding. They were married in the cavernous St. Patrick's Cathedral just off Fifth Avenue. There were no flowers and Scott didn't even wait for Zelda's sisters, Marjorie and Rosaline and their husbands to arrive. It is amazing that the Belle of Montgomery was sneaking off and getting married in a "suit of midnight blue with a matching hat trimmed in leather buckles and ribbons . . . holding the orchid corsage Scott had sent earlier with some white Swainsonia to freshen it up."[24] It is amazing these two young twentysomethings had decided to marry in New York; it was a place neither of them was familiar with and there was no parental support from either side. There was no luncheon, and when Zelda's sisters arrived, they were furious with Scott for starting the ceremony earlier.

Rosalind recalled later that "Scott did not communicate with us until the day before the wedding when he phoned to her say that it would take place at St. Patrick's the next morning . . . "[25] There was no photographer, no music, no reception. Just the cavernous echoing hall of the majestic church. There was Ludlow Fowler, his best man, and a few friends. They might as well have been married by the justice of the peace, but Zelda had decided to throw the dice with Scott Fitzgerald in New York City.

Zelda's mother had written Scott before the wedding, warning of taking on her daughter. "It will take more than the pope to make Zelda good for you . . . you will have to call on God Almighty direct . . . she is not amiable and she is given to yelping when she does not get her own way."[26] Scott would tell his daughter years later that he later regretted the hasty marriage. "I decided to marry your mother after all, even though I knew she was spoiled and meant no good to me. I was sorry immediately I had married her."[27]

But Scott was dedicated to his dream of rectifying the past.

*He looked around him wildly, as if the past were lurking here in the shadow of his house, just out of reach of his hand. "I'm going to fix everything just the way it was before," he said. He talked a lot about the past, and I gather that he wanted to recover something, some idea of himself perhaps, that had gone into loving Daisy. His life had been confused and disordered since then, but if he could return to a certain starting place and go over it all slowly he could find what that thing was. . . . [28]*

The priest admonished Zelda to be a good Episcopalian and Scott to be a good Catholic. Scott and Zelda emerged from the church into spring sunshine and walked the ten blocks up Fifth Avenue, which was still wet with morning dew. They walked in the silence of New York on a Sunday morning with Model-Ts sputtering blue smoke down the avenue and reached Scribner's publishing house. They stopped and peeked into a Scribner window with the reflection of a young man in a suit and hat and a young woman from the South with a white orchid on her shoulder. They peered in and saw a large poster advertising F. Scott Fitzgerald as "The Youngest Writer for whom Scribner's ever Published a Novel."

It was 1920, and they were poised to rule the world.

# CHAPTER 15

# A Playmate

## *1924*

SAND WAS IN HIS SHOES FROM THE BEACH THE DAY BEFORE. THE DAMP scent of the Mediterranean came in through the patio doors. Sometimes Scott took a walk before he wrote, but mostly, he just sat down with his coffee, Chesterfields, and gin. Nobody worked out. Even Hemingway had never jogged or biked in his life. Working out belonged to future generations. No, Scott faced his blank pages and his pencils without the adrenalin lift of exercise. His lift was nicotine, caffeine, and gin. And not in that order. But his paper was damp today, his pencils smudging. And he had a headache from the night before.

So he started drinking, staring moodily off the verandah at the sea. He had a couple fingers of gin out on the balcony in the strong Mediterranean sunshine. Zelda and Scottie had cleared out, of course, but now he wanted some company. The book was coming in really short, maybe 50,000 words, and in 1924, people did not like short books. There was no television, and films were just beginning to make serious inroads as a form of entertainment. People wanted to settle in for a nice long book. Short books were suspect. They wanted something big and thick. Part of it was the new form he had adopted. Scott could say more in one sentence than a lot of writers could in ten. The second thing was the plot was simple, and there was no veering from that. A love story, really, or maybe a love triangle . . . but it was all beginning to back up on him, and by evening, he needed to get away.

The problem was there wasn't much of an audience anymore. He missed that. He missed the adulation and the audience that put up with his antics. The Murphys were rich and almost formal in their dinners, and he had gotten drunk, and he "began throwing Sara's gold flecked Venetian wineglasses over the garden wall. He had smashed three of them this way before Gerald stopped him. As the party was breaking up Gerald went up to him and told him that he would not be welcome in their house for three weeks."[1]

Scott was repentant, but the ban stayed in place. The truth was he needed people to pay attention to him. Didn't they know he was writing the most brilliant novel of his time? Didn't they care? They didn't seem to, and they were stuffy and rich, and his nest egg was down to two grand, and he resented the Murphys, with their twin fortunes and their other rich friends. So he threw glasses over the wall. He threw figs at other guests. He got drunk and asked personal questions about how much sex the couples were having. He couldn't help himself. He couldn't stand not being the center of attention. Especially when drunk. He accused the Murphys of liking Zelda over him. Once, when they were leaving a casino, he fell down drunk, and Gerald refused to pick him up. "This is not Princeton and I'm not your roommate, get up yourself,"[2] Gerald told him. Reflecting years later on Scott's behavior, Gerald said, "He really had the most appalling sense of humor, sophomoric and . . . well trashy."[3]

But the interrogation of friends and the Murphys that Fitzgerald unleashed at dinner parties like well-aimed grenades for effect reached a breaking point that summer with Sarah, and she chastised him in a letter. "You can't expect anyone to like or stand a continual feeling of analysis and sub analysis and criticism—on the whole unfriendly—such as we have felt for a while. It is definitely in the air—and quite unpleasant—it certainly detracts from any gathering . . . we cannot at our age and stage in life be bothered with sophomoric situations like last night."[4] They just didn't know what to do with Scott when he was drunk, where he became surly, abusive, and, sometimes, violent. While he was banished, he took revenge by hurling a garbage can up over the stone wall onto the patio while the Murphys were dining with friends.

Scott needed a fresh audience. After gin, cigarettes, and coffee and wrestling with a book that was coming to him in fits, he needed the balm of adulation. Enter the French aviators. Usually, around seven, he and Zelda drove into San Raphael, "where moonlight cast shadows over palm trees by the harbor and the band played waltzes in the pavilions."[5] Scott was delighted with the officers in their white ducks who were impressed with the famous author and his wife while they sat at the bistro tables with the breeze blowing in. Scott would often pay, flashing money around, buying his gin, Zelda a stinger or brandy and crème de menthe.

Deeply tanned from flying, Jozan observed the high-flying author flashing money, getting drunker by the moment, while the young aviator watched and kept his eyes on Scott's beautiful wife. Jozan and the other officers insisted they pay, but Scott would not hear of it. He was the rich American, and he waved his arms about in the "cave [bar] decorated in a North African motif with scimitars on the walls, brass trays on drumheads, and tiny mother of pearl tables. It smelled of brine and incense."[6] In Zelda's novel *Save Me the Waltz*, David (Scott) "warns that if he catches her making eyes at the Frenchman he'll wring his neck."[7] But Jozan speaks little English, and he watches Fitzgerald in the warm darkness, swinging his arms wildly, going on diatribes. Jozan would later describe the Fitzgeralds as "brimming over with life. Rich and free, they bought into our little provincial circle brilliance, imagination, and familiarity with a Parisian and international world which we had no access."[8] That was for the public. Privately he saw Scott as "a proud, domineering, man, sometimes tender, sometimes cruel, who appeared more concerned with commercial than artistic success, despite talent and imagination."[9]

But on Zelda, Jozan had no ambivalence. He saw her as a "shining beauty, a woman who overflowed with activity, radiant with desire to take from life every chance her charm, youth and intelligence provided so abundantly. . . . "[10] He put Zelda against Scott and saw her as more elemental. Someone who liked "the relaxed life on beaches . . . trips by car, informal dinners."[11] The music has become louder, and the aviators are clustered around the Fitzgeralds while Scott weaves back and forth.

He was never able to hold his liquor, and now he was getting wild, falling down. The officers watched as the conversation became heated.

"Ford," Scott proclaimed, "runs modern society and not the politicians who are only screens or hostages."[12] Jozan did not believe in materialism and struggled to make Scott see his point of view. He believed in the old-world values of honor and sacrifice that he had seen in the war, another point that irritated Scott, who had not gotten to the war. Jozan believed these values trumped commercial profit. Jozan later summed up the conversation: "In short, we were young romantics arguing with a man better versed in the practicalities of life."[13]

Scott continued drinking, burning through his cigarettes, getting smashed outside the café. The night ended somewhere, and Scott and Zelda drove back to their villa, where another fight broke out. She was bored, and Scott was boorish. Sometimes glasses were thrown, bottles broken. Doors slammed. Scott would later write John Bishop from the Riviera: "Zelda and I sometimes indulge in terrible four-day rows that always start with a drinking party but were still enormously in love and the only truly happily married people I know."[14]

Zelda now had a playmate in Jozan. They met in the afternoons and often swam together and "were seen lying on the wide canvas beach mats in the sun, sunburned and laughing together while they invented new cocktails."[15] It was no different than her friendship with Ring Lardner or Ludlow Fowler or any of Scott's friends who enjoyed being with the vivacious young beauty who flirted openly and could drink more than her husband. Zelda had lots of male friends. "No one paid much attention to them and they seemed content to be in each other's company without joining the other bathers."[16] In a way, Scott was relieved. His biggest problem in writing was finding something for Zelda to do so he could focus on his novel. Jozan was tall, dark, and handsome and reminded her of the aviators who buzzed her home in Montgomery. In fact, Eduardo began to do stunts over their villa.

The Southern belle took it all in stride.

# CHAPTER 16

# The American Dream

## *1920*

DOWN THE HOT SUNBAKED STREETS OF MANHATTAN THEY CAME, walking, running, stumbling. It didn't matter how they came; the youth culture arrived. Twenty years into the new century, an urban culture bled out from New York into the rest of the country just waking up from the great rural experiment of a farm-based, small-town democracy. Gin. Cigarettes. Sex. Women who wanted sex. Women who raised their dresses. Women who swam, swore, smoke, and drank. Men who did the same. The youth culture materialized in the blond-haired, green-eyed young man and his wife with the burnt honey hair and the husky Southern accent.

The blue smoke of new cars rose between the buildings as they rode on top of taxis and fell down drunk in the Plaza Hotel. Probably never before had two people been so perfectly matched for the time they were living in. Scott and Zelda Fitzgerald pulled the cork on the champagne that was the twenties, and they were right there at the beginning with a bestselling novel that summed up the youth of their generation, and New York claimed them as their own. It was straight-up fantasy. A country on the brink of a spree that would turn into a ten-year party, with Zelda and Scott on the top of the wave, if not a taxi, and riding it all the way to the crash of 1929. The couple peering at *This Side of Paradise* on that Sunday morning in the Scribner window had no idea that it was their golden ticket to everything they could desire. Even measured against today, the Fitzgerald fame burned white-hot at a time when mass culture was just getting started and authors were still celebrities.

Sheer decadence. They stayed at the Plaza Hotel; the gilt-edged elegant hotel just off Central Park was one of the most expensive in Manhattan. They were in the Plaza fountain, with water spangling into the sunshine air. *This Side of Paradise* had just passed 50,000 copies, a surprise runaway bestseller, and Scott was selling one story after another to the magazines, and the movies and the money were gushing in, and why not jump into the fountain in their knickers and splash around and swim and then get on a taxi and have Zelda ride on the hood with Scott on top and why not take off your clothes in the middle of a musical like Scott did? And why not drink all the time and smoke because there was no roadmap for any of this? The country was running at full-tilt, and these two twentysomethings had stumbled into the middle of the storm as a new American Dream was forming in front of them. Get the golden girl and become wealthy and live in exotic places, and that dream coalescing through the nineteenth century was now reaching its zenith in the twentieth century. And, of course, to be absurdly young was required, as an article in the *New Yorker* noted: "That the Fitzgeralds are the best looking couple in modern literary society doesn't do them justice, knowing what we do about beauty and brains. That they might be the handsomest pair at any collegiate house party, inspiring alumni to warnings about the pitfalls ahead of the young, is more to the point, although Scott really looks more as the undergraduate would like to look, than the way he generally does."[1]

So Scott and Zelda cashed in on the new American Dream. It is amazing how much the dream gave up. The media could not get enough of F. Scott Fitzgerald. He was absurdly handsome and looked sharp in his Brooks Brothers suit, complete with a cane. Then the reviews came in on *This Side of Paradise*. Harry Hansen of the *Chicago Tribune* wrote Scribner's, "My how that boy can write!"[2] *The Chicago Review* lauded the novel in a review by Burton Rascoe: "*This Side of Paradise* gives him, I think, a fair claim to membership in that small squad of contemporary

American fictionists who are producing literature . . . it bears the impress, it seems to me, of genius."[3]

Then the royalties for the novel. Then more money for articles. Eleven stories brought $4,625, and then movies bought three stories for $7,425. Scott put hundred-dollar bills in his top pocket and strutted around the Plaza Hotel. He was twenty-four. Zelda was twenty. They had no idea what they were doing, but they were now famous. They gave interviews and drank. They arrived late at parties and drank. It was bewildering, but the media saw *This Side of Paradise* as emblematic of the jazz age and the flapper and the newly liberated woman, and Scott was its trumpeter, and Zelda was its heroine. The dream of fame and fortune descended like a cloak, and Scott later wrote, "I who knew less of New York than any reporter of six months standing and less of its society than any hall room boy in a Ritz stag line was pushed into the position of spokesman for the time but of the typical product of that same moment. I, or rather it was we, now did not know exactly what New York expected of us and found it rather confusing."[4]

One party led to another and one hotel to another. They bounced from the Biltmore to the Plaza to the Waldorf. Many times, they were asked to leave for being too noisy or leaving the water on in the tub and flooding the hotel room. It didn't matter that the money was flowing and the gin was flowing and the Fitzgeralds were flowing from one party of movers and shakers to another. In his second novel, *The Beautiful and the Damned*, Scott would portray himself and Zelda as Gloria and Anthony. "The magnificent attitude of not giving a damn altered overnight; from being a mere tenet of Gloria's it became the entire solace and justification for what they chose to do and what consequence it brought. Not to be sorry, not to lose one cry of regret, to live according to a clear code of honor toward each other and to seek the moment's happiness as fervently and persistently as possible."[5]

Poured across Manhattan, they were the hit of the town, and everyone wanted to meet them. Staggeringly attractive, Zelda and Scott were a couple out of a movie sunset. "Fitzgerald was so tall and straight and attractive," remembered H. L. Mencken, "that he might have been called beautiful . . . he cast himself in the role of the playboy, yet the playboy he incessantly mocks. He is vain, a little malicious, of quick intelligence and wit, and has an Irish gift for turning language into something iridescent and surprising." Zelda was "a woman of astonishing prettiness . . . Zelda's honey gold hair seemed to give her a burnished glow."[6]

They were perfect for the new celebrity culture. As Scott later wrote, "The first speakeasies had arrived, the toodle was passe, the Montmartre was the smart place to dance . . . we felt like small children in a great bright unexplored barn. Summoned out to Griffith's studio on Long Island, we trembled in the presence of the familiar faces of Birth of a Nation . . . when I first met Dorothy Gish I had the feeling that were both standing on the North Pole and it was snowing."[7]

America had awakened to an urban culture fueled by money and illegal booze. They made the speakeasy circuit in Manhattan, which ran from the seedy to extravagant hotel rooms. "Some speakeasies were deluxe, with silk festooned interiors and doormen, but most were crowded, noisy smoke filled basement or backroom dives, cheaply decorated with magazine pictures shellacked onto the walls, where they served lethally astringent cocktails."[8] Zelda and Scott found people shoving membership cards in their palms. On the back of the speakeasy cards were pornographic photos or cocktail recipes. When Scott died, three cards were found in his papers: "Louis and Armand, at 46 East Fifty Third Street, Ye White Horse Tavern at 114 West Forty Fifth Street, and Club Des Artistes at Broadway and Sixty fourth."[9] A lot of people made their own gin, including the Fitzgeralds. Scott also left behind a recipe that called for "80 drops juniper berry oil, 40 drops coriander oil, 3 drops aniseed oil, take 40 percent alcohol, 60 percent distilled $H2O$, put five drops of mixture, 23 oz of alcohol and water, add 1 oz of sweetening to each 23 ozs of above, liquid rock candy syrup is the best sweetening."[10]

Scott and Zelda went to Princeton to the Cottage Club, where he introduced Zelda as his mistress, got drunk, made a scene, with the president of the club asking him to leave. No matter; they returned to Manhattan and began the rounds once again. New York gave herself to the young couple and it became their home. The city finally lived up to Scott's and Zelda's dream of urban paradise. Zelda later wrote, "Twilights were wonderful after the war. They hung above New York like indigo wash, forming themselves from the asphalt dust and sooty shadows . . . the far away lights from the buildings high in the sky burned hazily through the blue, like golden objects lost in deep grass . . ."[11]

The New World of New York is where they rode the wave and learned that, for now, hedonism was good, drunkenness was good, sex was good, smoking was good, not sleeping was good. The new decade was being launched off the deck of old agrarian America and everyone was waiting to see how far it could sail. They ate lunch with George Nathan in the Japanese Gardens in the Ritz with *Ziegfeld Follies* star Kay Laurel and at the Montmartre Club. They were tossed out of a Broadway show for laughing, giggling at all the wrong spots, and then falling drunkenly off their chairs. The press loved all of it, and their antics continually appeared in "Society" and "About Town" columns. Zelda and Scott were fundamentally middle-class people who now found themselves with the cream of society. Zelda was a provincial Southerner who had some notoriety in the very small pond of Montgomery but now was expected to carry on with urbane people who wanted to know her.

Scott later wrote an essay, "Early Success," where he described those early days: "With its publication [*This Side of Paradise*] I had reached a stage of manic depressive insanity. Rage and bliss alternated hour by hour. A lot of people thought it was a fake and perhaps it was, and a lot of others thought it was a lie which it was not. In a daze I gave out an interview—I told what a great writer I was and how I'd achieved the heights. Heywood Broun who was on my trail, simply quoted it with the comment that I seemed to be a very self-satisfied young man, and for some days I was notably poor company. I invited him to lunch and in a very kindly way told him that it was too bad he had let his life slide away without accomplishing anything. He had just turned thirty and about then I wrote a line that certain people will not let me forget, 'She was a faded but still lovely woman of twenty-seven.' In a daze I told the Scribner Company that I didn't expect my novel to sell more than twenty thousand copies and when the laughter died away I was told that a sale of five thousand was excellent for a first novel. I think it was a week after publication that it passed the twenty thousand mark, but I took myself so seriously that I didn't even think it was funny."[12]

To handle it all, Zelda, like Scott, got smashed and acted out. Author Rebecca West met the Fitzgeralds, and her impression of Zelda differed from a lot of people. "My relations with Mrs. Fitzgerald were few and fragmentary. I don't know if you'll find anybody to confirm my impression that she was very plain. I had been told that she was very beautiful, but when I went to a party and saw her I had quite a shock. She was standing with her back to me, and her hair was quite lovely, it glistened like a child's. I am sure this was natural. Then she turned around and startled me, I would almost go so far as to say her face had a certain craggy homeliness. There was a curious unevenness about it, such as one sees in Gericault's pictures of the insane."[13]

West might have been smarting from a party where she was to be the guest of honor, but nobody bothered to pick her up. This is one of the Fitzgerald's legendary drunk episodes; too smashed to bring the guest of honor, Scott spent the entire time criticizing her writing at dinner. West would later say Zelda got drunk at a party and "flapped her arms and looked very uncouth as she talked about her ballet ambitions . . . the odd thing to me always was that Scott Fitzgerald who might have been expected from his writings to like someone sleek like Mrs. Vernon Castle, should have liked someone who was so inelegant."[14] There was no love lost between Mrs. West and the Fitzgeralds.

Zelda's daughter, Scottie, years later would say of her mother's transition to a Manhattan socialite, that "in the South, life was cozy and so full of love that it formed a cocoon. To step out into the world of New York . . . constantly exposed to parties where mother was supposed to be witty and glamorous companion to a famous, difficult and demanding man was something she was ill-equipped to cope with."[15] But no matter. All was forgiven. Scott and Zelda, at this point, could do no wrong. They saw Charlie Chaplin in a yellow coat, thought they saw Gloria Swanson and bandleader Paul Whiteman. People telephoned each other. "We're having some people over," everybody said to everyone else, "and we all want you to join us . . . all over New York people telephoned. They telephoned from one to another to people on other parties that they couldn't get there."[16]

Their life was frantic, frenetic, out of control. They were early rock-stars blazing the way that many rock stars would follow, where drugs, money, sex, booze, youth were served in abundance. But they were the first. And they spent money like water. Scott, who had watched his father fail in the shadow of the McQuillan fortune, now declared his victory over money by spending like a drunken sailor. He gave out lavish tips, wasted money on hotel rooms he and Zelda never occupied but for a few nights, and then wrote another story. "All big men have spent money freely. I hate avarice or even caution,"[17] he wrote his mother after she questioned his lifestyle.

Lawton Campbell was invited to lunch and went up to the Fitzgerald's room at the Biltmore. "When I entered, the room was in bedlam. Breakfast dishes were all about, the bed unmade, books and papers scattered here and there, trays filled with cigarette butts, liquor glasses from the night before. Everything was untidy and helter skelter. Scott was dressing and Zelda was luxuriating in the bathtub. With the door partly open, she carried on a steady flow of conversation. 'Scott . . . tell Lawton about . . . tell Lawton what I said . . . Now tell Lawton what I did. . . . '"[18]

Zelda recounted the previous night's wild escapades from the bathroom while Scott laughed. She told of going into the Waldorf Hotel and dancing on the tables and taking the chefs headgear and then being escorted out by the hotel detectives. Then Zelda appeared, buttoning up her dress while poor Lawton realized his lunch hour was over. Another friend, the former editor of the *Daily Princeton*, Alex McKaig, visited the Fitzgeralds nine days after their wedding and kept a diary of his encounters. "Called on Scott Fitz and his bride . . . latter temperamental small town Southern belle. Chews gum shows knees. I do not think marriage can succeed. Both drinking heavily. Think they will be divorced in three years. Scott writes something big then die in a garrot at thirty two."[19]

Edmund Wilson and John Bishop visited the Fitzgeralds in room 2019, where Zelda gave them orange blossoms made with bootleg gin and then "spread herself elegantly on the sofa."[20] Wilson later said she was "very pretty and languid,"[21] but then later said she had "an unpredictability combined with 'Southern exoticism.'"[22] Zelda's own memory of their honeymoon in the Biltmore was one of booze and people complaining.

"People in the corridors complained, there was a tart smell of gin over everything, for years the smell of her trousseau haunted her . . . corsages died in the ice water tray and cigarettes disintegrated in the spittoon."[23]

The cult of youth had arrived with the Sothern girl and the St. Paul author. A column reported on a speech Scott gave, "We watched him wave his cigarette at an audience one night not long ago and capture them by the nervous young ramblings, until he had the room (mostly 'flappers') swaying with delight. Then the autograph hunters! This admiration embarrassed him much—but after he had escaped into the outer darkness he acknowledged, with a grin, that he rather liked it."[24]

The truth was that even as Scott and Zelda rode this rollercoaster, they knew little of each other. They had courted through a long-distance relationship punctuated by long separations. They were "Babes in The Woods," a Fitzgerald story, and, later, a chapter in *This Side of Paradise* in all aspects. "Isabelle and Kenneth were distinctly not innocent, nor were they particularly hardened. Moreover, amateur standing had very little value in the game they were beginning to play. They were simply very sophisticated, very calculating and finished, young actors, each playing a part that they had played for years. They had both started with good looks and excitable temperaments and the rest was the result of certain accessible popular novels, and dressing-room conversation culled from a slightly older set."[25]

But they were different. Scott was prone to fits of the jitters that he used alcohol to combat, which Zelda did not understand. He had trouble sleeping and needed the room totally dark while Zelda could fall asleep anywhere. Zelda had no real domestic skills and let the laundry pile up while Scott complained about the lack of fresh laundry. Zelda was picky about her food while Scott ate anything. They didn't even know how to drive. Leon Ruth was called upon to give advice when they went car hunting. "Neither of them could drive much," she later recalled. "Scott used to borrow my car in Montgomery when he was courting Zelda, so I knew fairly well the limits of his ability. As I remember it we went down to the battery and it was a choice between a new sedan and a secondhand Marmon sports coupe. Of course they couldn't resist the Marmon. Well we bought it and I drove them to 125th Street. I showed Scott how to shift on the way and both of them knew something about steering. Then they put me out and we struck off."[26]

No driver's license. No driver's education. The traffic lights in Manhattan were not much help either. On some, the green light meant stop. On other stoplights, the green light meant go. On top of all the traffic lights was a policeman whose job was to switch out the lights from red to yellow to green. People routinely died in head-on collisions with no clear laws on what side of the road cars should drive on. The country, like the Fitzgeralds, was just getting used to the modern age and had yet to catch up with itself. The city was not conducive to writing, and they took the Marmon and discovered a cottage in Westport, Connecticut, so Scott could begin another novel. But the parties continued unabated. Alexander McCaig came out for one of the parties and later wrote in his diary, "Fitz and Zelda flighting like mad—say themselves marriage can't succeed."[27]

During one of the parties, Zelda pulled a fire alarm, and it made the papers, which wrote that charges might be brought against the Fitzgeralds. Scott went to court and said he would pay the expenses of the fire department coming out to their home. The parties continued with drunken excess and some amount of danger. George Jean Nathan, the editor of *The Smart Set*, was very attracted to Zelda and began to flirt with her. He began to send Zelda letters addressed only to her. "Dear Blonde, why call me a polygamist when my passion for you is at once so obvious and so single. Particularly when I am lit. Is it possible that Southern girls are losing their old perspicacity? I am very sorry to hear that your husband is neglectful of his duties to you in the way of chewing gum. That is the way husbands get after five months of marriage."[28]

Nathan even offered to publish Zelda's diaries, but Scott refused, citing them as literary property he used for his own work. Zelda flirted openly, and suddenly Nathan was not invited to the parties anymore. Scott had gleaned it had gone beyond flirtation, that Nathan was falling in love with Zelda. He managed to head off that crisis, but he watched Zelda more closely now, a man who had recently discovered that something was going on in his own house. Many guests received apologetic notes from Zelda after drunken nights. "I am running wild in sack cloth and ashes because Scott and I acted like two such drunks the other night—Aside from the fact that you were horribly bored, I am sorry because we saw nothing of you. It's been years since we three spent a satisfactory night together—so won't you please come back Saturday or Sunday or whenever you will so we can astound you with our brilliant conversation."[29]

The music played on. The parties played on. The gin poured on. The parties blended together.

> *The lights grow brighter as the earth lurches away from the sun, and now the orchestra is playing yellow cocktail music and opera of voices pitches a key higher . . . suddenly one of the gypsies, in trembling opal, seizes a cocktail out of the air, dumps it down for courage and moving her hands like Frixco, dances out alone on the canvas platform. The party has begun.[30]*

The Fitzgeralds continued to dance to the music, wildly drunk, wildly satiated, stamping their mark on the decade like braille. They just needed to keep being young.

# CHAPTER 17

# Jozan

## *1924*

SCOTT AND ZELDA WERE HAVING BREAKFAST ON THEIR PATIO WITH the brilliant blue sea below. They had been out late the night before with the young French pilots at the casino, where Zelda got drunk enough to get up and dance on the tables. Scott got drunk enough to almost get beat up by the bouncer, but somehow, they managed to get him out of the casino. But now, the night was a blur, and they were having croissants and coffee, bleary-eyed, thick-headed. It would not be a good writing day, this Scott knew.

Jozan had driven them back to their villa the night before and helped Scott up the stairs. Jozan could drink heavily and not show it while Scott was drunk after just two drinks. It was just one of many of the extreme differences between the men Zelda noted. While Scott got louder, Jozan became more in control, quiet, quick-thinking. Where Scott became boastful, Jozan asserted his natural leadership through his body language of quick, short, deft movements. These qualities made him such a good test pilot. The man did not get rattled. Scott would later create a character, Tommy Barban, based on Jozan, who is a mercenary and very dangerous. One of Scott's entries in his notebooks from this time reads, "I wouldn't go to war unless it was in Morocco or the Khyber Pass."[1]

It is probably straight from Jozan's mouth. But this is in the future. Right now, Scott is smoking a Chesterfield and nursing his hangover.

Zelda is sipping her coffee. She first hears the whine of the biplane and looks up, and the double-decker World War I plane is now in front of them, and Scott sees it too. The plane roars off the villa walls as it barrel-rolls and then loops twice. Scott is staring open-mouthed while the plane defies gravity with the long whine of the engine straining to reach the heavens then suddenly going backward in an amazing roll with wings twirling. "It was so low they could see the gold of Jacques hair . . ." Zelda later wrote in *Save Me the Waltz*. "As the plane straightened itself, they saw Jacques wave with one hand and drop a small package in the garden." The dispatch box held a note with his regards, *"Toutes me amitiesw du haut de mon avion."*[2] And then the plane flew back into the sun, leaving Scott shakily smoking a cigarette and staring after the man who could defy gravity and drop a package just a few feet from their breakfast table.

Jozan flew back to his base, knowing exactly what he was doing. The stunts were a risk and so was dropping the note. But he was used to taking risks. It had started when he was fifteen when he and some boys had descended into a crypt beneath a church. The crypt smelled like death. Cold and clammy. They were under the church after lifting the heavy trap door. The boys fell down onto the dirt floor, their eyes adjusting to the darkness. A skeleton grinned against the wall, then turned into a statue. A skull was found on the far wall, and the boys put a candle in it, the eyes luridly glowing in the death chamber. "It was startling to see its red eyes and the shinning mouth grimacing in the darkness,"[3] Eduardo wrote later. The boys scratched their names into the walls, then scurried up and pulled the trap door back in place. The fifteen-year-old was caught. At the military training academy, punishment could be severe. "The authorities are making a colossal affair of this little escapade and they treated us like criminals,"[4] he wrote in his journal. Sentenced to sleep in the Pleu for a week, he had to carry his mattress down there every night for a week. Eduardo didn't mind. He liked taking risks and understood risks had consequences.

The young man from the military family applied to the Naval Academy at Brest. When he was accepted, he and two friends celebrated in Paris and were arrested. One of his friends was Jean Hourcade, the son of a high-level prosecutor. When they were bailed out, they returned to Hourcade's residence at 195 rue de La University. Eduardo's handsome figure and confidence gave him an entrée into the family that introduced him to the Parisian elite. Many times on leave from the Naval Academy, they would go the Grande Markets in Paris, where the women fell like flies. "What do you expect," Eduardo said to Jean, "we are so handsome."[5]

When World War I ended, Eduardo was assigned to test seaplanes. Flying was extremely dangerous, and every time he flew, he was taking his life in his hands. "With unreliable instruments and few navigational aids, flying required courage and daring—just a man and machine. Buffeted by wind in open cockpits, aviators guided their planes by intuition and feel with engine failures and crashes common. 'Flying by the seat of their pants,' accurately described the situation. With seats the contact point, pilots could sense engine vibrations through their jodhpurs and variations in gravity indicated whether they were climbing up or down. A pilot was pressed into his seat when climbing and felt heavier, but when diving felt lighter."[6]

Eduardo was used to improvising and had the cool, calm detachment required for a cloth-and-wire plane, where engine failure could mean death. Flying at eight thousand feet with only a white scarf, goggles, and a leather helmet, pilots were the jousting heroes of old, and in the twenties a test pilot was as glamorous as a movie star. Jozan was certainly flying by the seat of his pants as he met the intriguing American woman every day to swim and enjoy a light lunch of wine and cheese. In Zelda's novel, *Save Me the Waltz*, Alabama asks Jacque, "'Aren't you afraid when you do stunts?' He replies with a shrug, 'I am afraid whenever I go in my areoplane. That is why I like it.'"[7]

Jozan and the other aviators became regulars at the Fitzgeralds' dinners and parties. Scott and Zelda were socially starved and Scott needed release at night from writing. He later wrote, "It is twilight as I write this . . . in half an hour Rene and Bobee, officers of aviation, are coming to dinner in their white ducks. Afterwards in the garden, their white uniforms will grow dimmer as more liquid dark comes down until they like the heavy roses and the nightingales in the pines, will seem to take an essential and invisible part of the beauty of this proud gay land."[8]

Zelda had always flirted with Scott's friends, and flirting with the young aviator in front of Scott was just more of the same. The dinners were exotic under the moon. "The ritual Provencal dish as Zelda noted on her recipe card must be serviced under special conditions according to the custom of Marseilles with at least seven or eight convivial people. The Frenchman came to supper most weekends, curious meals Zelda recalled, served on large porcelain plates with tricolored ribbons and culminating with strangely fluorescent drinks. . . . Victrola music drifted into the garden as French mingled with English amid clinking toasts of Cristal Brut."[9]

Scott held court with the Frenchmen, smoking, drinking, going into strange diatribes. Eduardo and the Frenchmen listened attentively, but they tolerated Scott. Sometimes, famous friends attended the dinners and impressed the young Frenchmen. "Donald Ogden John Dos Passos, or Archibald MacLeish and his wife Ada."[10] Eduardo listened to Scott bloviate but kept his eyes on Zelda in the darkness. Zelda responded to the very qualities Scott lacked. "There was air of assurance about him, a quality of natural leadership that Zelda respected and responded to. Leadership, athletic prowess, a smart military air were precisely those qualities Scott Fitzgerald lacked. It was as if Jozan and Fitzgerald were opposite sides of a coin, each admiring the others' abilities, gifts and talents, but the difference in the equipment they brought to bear on life was clear."[11]

When Zelda described Jozan in *Save Me the Waltz*, it was in the romantic terms of a warrior. "Jacque moved his sparse body with the tempestuous spontaneity of a leader."[12] While Scott wrested with his novel high in the villa, Jozan and Zelda liked to swim in the strong currents and lay in the sun. The idyllic setting where the Frenchman stretched out next to her was evident in the passages later from Zelda's novels. "He aimed to conquer . . . It didn't seem to make any difference what she wanted to do or intended either . . . life suddenly offered possibilities to a reckless extravagance which she didn't like."[13] The very foreignness of Jozan was exotic to Zelda. "Eduardo's lack of language might have accelerated the attraction. How much more romantic than to be on the beach with a young Frenchman who only knew bits of English, resorting to French to convey his feelings. '*Je te boi des Yeux* (I drink you with my eyes). *Je t'em-brasse partout* (I kiss you all over). *Nous sommes faits pour entendre* (We are meant to get along).'" Zelda later referred to his language. "His English was more adequate about love than anything else."[14]

The basis of Scott's and Zelda's fights was Zelda's constant need to be entertained, but when people saw Zelda and the aviator on the beach and in the bistros, they began to assume an affair. And when he became a frequent guest at the Fitzgeralds, Scott saw the attraction, but this had happened before. "Jealousy titillated him and he admitted being excited by another man's interest in Zelda. Early in their relationship he discovered the best way to hold on to one another was to torture each other through jealousy."[15] Scott would later write that Zelda was always looking for a stronger male. "I am half feminine, that is, my mind is. In the last analysis, she is a stronger person than I am. I have creative fire but am a weak individual. She knows this and really looks up to me as a woman."[16]

But Jozan was a warrior of the skies who saw his quarry from above and pursued it. In "Image of the Heart," a story Scott wrote later, the couple is in their car when a plane comes out of nowhere. "The plane had come out of its dive, straightened out and was headed straight for them. Tom caught at Trudy's hand trying to pull her from the car, but he had misjudged the time and the plane was already upon them and away."[17] This is much more ominous than the stunts in front of the villa with the note dropped into the garden. In this story, the pilot is now hunting the couple, getting behind them in the sun, which is standard procedure before going in for the kill.

Eduardo, for his part, was smitten with the American woman so different from the French girls. "Her vitality was a breath of fresh air, yet mystery enveloped her and she appeared elusive and sensual, more intangible than pretty with an undercurrent of necessity. Her eyes were full of secrets and body so assertively adequate that someone once remarked she often looked as if she had nothing on underneath. . . . "[18] And Zelda, who was preoccupied with cleanliness and took baths frequently, especially after sex, had come to associate Jozan with all that is good in her life. "There was a clean scent about him she adored, something to do with his starched white uniform . . . that fresh smell lingered, and she couldn't eliminate it from her mind. Nor did she want to; she felt intoxicated by it."[19]

And while this all unfolds, Scott struggles on with his novel, amazed to realize that something was going on at the very dinners that he swings his glass of gin around and proclaims, *"Nowadays people begin by sneering at family life and family institutions and next they'll throw everything overboard and have intermarriage between black and white!"*[20]

# CHAPTER 18

# A Perfect Fool

## *1921*

ZELDA WAS LEAVING SCOTT. PUFFING GIN AND CIGARETTES, SHE WAS running down the railroad tracks to New York with her slippers catching on the rocks and the railroad ties, hearing a train behind her. She was going to the city after another horrible fight, and Scott was coming after her. It was only after she boarded the train she realized he was on the train but had no money for a ticket. Zelda refused to give him any money even when the conductor threatened to put Scott off. The conductor stared at Scott and threatened to put him off the train. When Zelda reached New York, she took a cab to Alex McKaig's apartment, who was keeping a journal of his encounters with the Fitzgeralds.

"In the evening Zelda—drunk—having decided to leave Fitz and having nearly been killed walking down RR track, blew in. Fitz came in shortly after. He had caught the same train with no money or ticket. They threatened to put him off but finally let him stay on—Zelda refusing to give him any money. They continued their fight while here. . . . Fitz should let Zelda go and not run after her. Like all husbands he is afraid of what she may do in a moment of caprice. None of the men however she knows would take her for a mistress. Trouble is Fitz absorbed in Zelda's personality. . . . she has supplied him with all his copy for women."[1]

Scott needed to finish his second novel, *The Beautiful and the Damned*, and they rented a cottage in Westport, Connecticut, fifty miles west of New York, close to Long Island Sound. "It was dark when the real estate agent of Marietta showed them the gray house. They came upon it just west of the village where it rested against a sky that was a warm blue cloak buttoned with tiny stars. The gray house had been there when women who kept cats were probably witches. . . . "[2] New York commuters swarmed the beaches, and at Campo beach, "wooden bath houses lining the boardwalk could be rented by the hour. . . . "[3] But the Fitzgeralds had their own small beach and a dock, where a picture was snapped of Zelda in a black bathing suit. The house immediately became overwhelmed with dirty laundry and dishes as they looked for a servant. "We have a house with a room for you," Zelda wrote Ludlow Fowler. "And a ruined automobile because I drove it over a fireplug and de-intesinted it." Zelda, at this point, also believed she was pregnant. "Only by the time you do come I'll probably have grown so fat like this [drawing of a stick woman] that you won't be able to recognize me. . . . "[4]

It turned out she was not pregnant.

The gin-soaked weekends begin anew with friends from New York staying over many times all weekend. McKaig was one of them and noted, "Visit Fitz at Westport . . . terrible party. Fitz and Zelda fighting like mad."[5] The house became the model for Gloria and Anthony's honeymoon cottage in *The Beautiful and the Damned*, and later, Scott would use it one more time. *"I had just left a country of wide lawns and friendly trees so when a young man at the office suggested that we take a house together in a commuting town, it sounded like a great idea. He found the house, a weather beaten cardboard bungalow at eighty a month. . . . "*[6]

Zelda had grown bored and told Sara Mayfield she found the town depressing and began to pester Scott to go to parties in New York. A trip South was then proposed to go see Zelda's parents so Zelda could have peaches and biscuits. They had the 1918 Marmon and it was logical they would take a trip. Besides, Zelda was homesick, so they went down to Montgomery to see her parents. Scott wrote an article, "The Cruise of the Rolling Junk," that celebrated their breakdowns, blowouts, lost wheels, speeding fines, inflated garage bills, their inability to read maps. The 1,000-mile trip from Connecticut to Alabama took a week (actually, it was from New York to Alabama, but the article had parameters that

Scott wanted to exploit). It would take two years to sell the story after the *Post* and others turned it down. The travel segment finally appeared in *Motor Magazine* in 1924.

"The Cruise of the Rolling Junk" gives a glance afforded few into the personal lives and prejudices of Fitzgerald. The prose developed to a fine point in *Gatsby* is evident, but also, for the first time, the patina of New York is torn away, and we realize America is still a rural country that fifty-seven years before had experienced a Civil War. "Slow short hills climbed in green tranquility toward a childish sky. And already there were antebellum landscapes—featuring crazy cabins inhabited by blue black gentlemen and their ladies in red checked calico. The South now—its breath warm upon us . . . the sun was at home here, touching with affection the shattered ruins of once lovely things. Still, after fifty years we could see the chimneys and wall corners that marked the site of old mansions."[7]

In Virginia, they are denied a hotel room because of their white-matching knickerbocker suits (women were not supposed to wear knickers, and by Greensboro, North Carolina, Zelda was wearing a skirt over hers to placate Southern mores). Their trip becomes eerie, passing through the battlefields in Virginia at night. "At sunset we plunged into the Wilderness—the Wilderness where slain boys from Illinois and Tennessee and the cities of the Gulf still slept in marshes and the wooded swamps—but over the bloody ground there was only the drone of the cicadas now and the sway of the lush vines."[8] A "highwayman" then attempts to stop them with a pistol.

"—a man stepped suddenly into the road about twenty yards in front of us. The glare of the depressed headlight fell on him for a moment and we saw that his face, brown or white, we could not determine which, was covered with a black mask, and that in his right hand was the glint of a revolver."[9] The Fitzgeralds hunched down to avoid being shot while Zelda, who was driving, stomped on the gas and "with a gasping cry the masked man took a quick sidestep and avoided the bull-like leap of the car by inches."[10]

This might have been pure hyperbole, but traveling down through the Deep South on country roads at a time when most roads were not policed did open up travelers to robbery and the crimes of opportunity. Scott laments that he did not buy a revolver in Washington. The roads in 1922 were awful, and their 1918 Marmon 34, which was a swanky car capable of speeds up to sixty miles an hour, had passed its prime and would become stuck many times during the 1,200-mile journey. To drive 1,200 miles anywhere in 1922 was to tempt fate, but to go down South where the roads devolved into the muddy red clay slides that cars became helplessly stuck in was considered foolish. Scott keeps a running commentary during the travelogue and tries to get some gas at a gas station from some African Americans. "I drew up alongside, where we were immediately joined by two aged negroes and a quartet of little black boys from whom I demanded gasoline."[11]

Another young man who helps the Fitzgeralds get their car going again in Alabama stares at Zelda and shakes his head at her knickerbockers. "It's a pity a nice girl like you should be left to wear those clothes."[12] Scott and Zelda are confronted with rural America bashing up against their own rarified world of New York once again. "It was fifty years of provincialism speaking," Scott writes. "It was the negative morality of the poor white and yet it filled me with helpless and inarticulate rage."[13] They nurse their car up to seventy miles an hour and a policeman pulls them over and takes $5.00 from the Fitzgeralds. "If you don't want to come to the courthouse you can give me the five dollars and I'll see it gets to the judge."[14] It is a shakedown, but Scott has little choice. "So I handed over a precious bill where at the guardian of the roads thanked me, tipped his hat and drove hastily away."[15]

When they hit Montgomery, Zelda burst into tears as she realized Montgomery had changed for her; "Suddenly Zelda was crying, crying because things were the same and yet not the same. It was for her faithlessness she wept and the faithlessness of time."[16] Zelda's parents happened to be away, and Scott and Zelda drove to the Country Club, then stayed with Zelda's friend, Katharine Elsberry. Katharine would later write that she heard Zelda call out before breakfast, "Scott what did you do with the toothbrush?"[17] Katharine thought this was strange as Zelda was a clean freak and constantly bathing. Scott would build this into his heroine Gloria Gilbert in *The Beautiful and the Damned*. "I loathe women . . . they never seem clean to me, never, never, never,"[18] Gloria cries out. When Anthony Patch asks why she wants to marry him, she replies, "Well because you're so clean. Your sort of blowy clean, like I am. there's two sorts . . . ones . . . clean like polished pans. You and I are clean like streams and winds. I can tell whenever I see a person whether he is clean and if so, which clean he is."[19]

The trip lasted less than two weeks with disapproving eyes toward Scott from Zelda's parents. The 1918 Marmon was sold off, and they took a train back North. Scott reflects on the youthful trip in the final lines. "My affection goes with you Rolling Junk—with you and with all the faded trappings that have brightened my youth and glittered with hope or promise on the roads I have travelled—roads that stretch on still, less white, less glamorous, under the stars and the thunder and the recurrent inevitable sun."[20]

Gluttons for punishment, Zelda's parents visited in August, where they found Scott and Zelda again not up to their standards. Zelda wrote Ludlow Fowler, "Scott's hot in the midst of a new novel and Westport is unendurably dull but you and I might amuse ourselves—and both of us want to see you dreadfully . . . it's been a wild summer . . . at present I'm hardly able to sit down owing to an injury sustained in the course of one of Nathan's parties in NY. I cut my tail on a broken bottle and can't possibly sit on the three stitches that are in it now . . . I was boiled . . . The place was a tub somewhere."[21]

Zelda often took baths when she arrived at parties while Scott napped on a nearby couch. This time, there was a broken bottle in the tub. She followed this by telling Ludlow she was glad to see her parents, who arrived to find two drunk friends of Scott asleep in the hammock. Zelda sent Scott and his friends off to a hotel, but they were back by 3:00 a.m., drinking gin and tomato juice with Scott at the kitchen table. When Zelda came downstairs, she found the kitchen a wreck and tried to take the gin bottle from Scott. He knocked her hand away and her face hit the swinging door. Zelda ended up with a nosebleed and swollen eyes. Judge Sayre glared at Scott accusingly in the morning. In a repeat, the trip was cut short, and the Sayres left the Wakeman cottage a week early.

Scott bared down on *The Beautiful and the Damned* while Zelda fired up the New York social whirl once again. It was then the fight broke out that had Zelda running down the railroad tracks to New York. "I look down the tracks and see you coming—and out of every haze and mist your darling rumpled trousers are hurrying to me—without you, dearest dearest I couldn't see or hear or feel or think or live," she wrote him later, professing her love after she tried to leave him. "I love you so and I'm never in all our lives going to let us be apart another night . . . come quick, come quick to me . . . I could never do without you if you hated me and were covered with sores like a leper—if you still ran away with another woman and starved and beat me—I still would want you I know—"[22]

The parties continued, and McKaig kept a running chronicle of the Fitzgeralds' life. "John (Bishop) spent weekend at Fitz—new novel sounds awful—no seriousness of approach. Zelda interrupts him all the time—diverts in both senses."[23] The cottage in Westport was finally given up in the fall for a small apartment on West Fifty-Ninth Street close to the Plaza Hotel. Scott wrote in his ledger, "Work at the beginning but dangerous at the end. A slow year, dominated by Zelda and on the whole happy."[24] Zelda needed to be occupied so Scott could work on *The Beautiful and the Damned*, and McKaig became her escort. They dropped into Lawton Campbell's apartment with the announcement they were there so "Scott could write." Campbell later recalled that "she would stretch out on the long sofa in my living room with her eyes to the ceiling and recount some fabulous experience of the night before or dream up some exploit she thought would be a cute idea. . . . If her remarks were occasionally non sequitur one didn't notice it at the time. She passed very quickly from one topic to another and you didn't question her."[25]

Zelda was on the loose, many times without Scott to entertain her. McKaig became her companion, observer, chronicler of the Fitzgerald whirlwind. "Went to Fitzgerald's. Usual problem there. What shall Zelda do? I think she might do a little housework—apartment looks like a pig sty. If she's there Fitz can't work—she bothers him—if she's not there he can't work—worried what she might do . . . Fitz on the wagon eight days, talks as if it were a century. Zelda increasingly restless—says frankly she simply wants to be amused and is only good for useless pleasure giving pursuits, great problem, what is she to do? Fitz has his writing of course—God knows where the two of them will end up . . . went up to Fitzgerald's to spend evening. They just recovered from an awful party . . . much taken with idea of having a baby."[26]

McKaig one evening shaves Zelda's neck to make her bobbed hair more defined. He is slowly falling in love with her and notes her "wonderful hair—eyes and mouth."[27] Scott needs Zelda occupied, and McKaig spends more and more time with her taking her to a cocktail party at John Cole's and then to a tea at the Biltmore. In the taxi, Zelda turns to McKaig and asks him to kiss her. He wrote later, "In taxi, Zelda asked me to kiss her, but I couldn't. I couldn't forget Scott, he's so damn pitiful."[28] This seems to be the only thing holding Zelda back, who had also asked John Bishop to give her a bath once. Soon after McKaig had taken the taxi ride, he received a message from Scott. "The most awful thing had happened, would he go to their apartment immediately, it would be a test of their friendship."[29]

McKaig went to the apartment immediately and found Scott on the phone. "When I got there . . . he said hello casually and went on talking . . . I asked him in Christ's name what the matter was . . . it seemed they had a quarrel. Zelda went into the bathroom, turned on the water to hide noise of footsteps and walked out the door. Instead of trying to find her himself he . . . telephoned all his friends."[30] Obviously Scott suspected Zelda might have been with McKaig and demanded he rush over to prove she wasn't. Jealousy was Scott's constant companion, and there were incidents that sometimes turned violent. One quarrel turned dangerous when Zelda barricaded herself in the bathroom and Scott broke down the door. "In Zelda's version he 'hurt her eye.' In Scott's ledger he notes the bathroom incident and the 'black eye.'"[31]

Zelda believes that sex means less than love, and she even gives Scott permission to have an affair, seeing a girl he was staring at after she said, "If you want to take her out go ahead. . . . I don't mind. I know it isn't love."[32] McKaig, Zelda, and Scott go to see a Broadway show, *Enter Madame*, but get kicked out when Zelda falls off her seat drunk. Zelda ingratiated, flirted, and often treaded dangerous ground with Scott's friends. In a second novel, *Caesar's Things*, Zelda paints a picture of men who "knew what kind of cold cream she used, who confessed their preferences in women to her and who slumbered over the grill stairs and left their hats all over town. . . . " She continues on and describes her role in those first years of marriage. "He owned her, bundled her up and set her in taxis beside him . . . showed her off to an inclusive set of college friends. . . ."[33]

Christmas 1921 was lonely in their small New York apartment. Scott commented, "finding no nucleus to which we could cling, we became a small nucleus ourselves and gradually fitted our disruptive personalities in the contemporary scene of New York."[34] Then, on Valentine's Day, Zelda realized she was pregnant and headed down to visit her parents in Montgomery alone. She took part in the annual Les Mysteriousness Ball with a Hawaiian theme. Lawton Campbell happened to go to the ball and later recorded what happened. "During this number, the audience began to notice that one masker was doing her dance more daring than the others. All eyes were concentrated on her. Finally the dancer in question turned her back to the audience, lifted her grass skirt over her head for a quick view of her pantied posterior and gave it an extra wiggle for good measure. A murmur went over the auditorium in a wave of excitement and everybody was whispering, 'That's Zelda!'"[35]

She clearly wanted her homecoming to be memorable, and it was. Scott finished *The Beautiful and Damned* in April, and they decided to go to Europe with Zelda two months pregnant. But before they left, an incident occurred in the Jungle Club in New York. Once again, Lawton Campbell was the witness to the Fitzgerald debacle. "I was sitting one evening at a table with three friends, when I spied Scott at the door of the bar. He was obviously under the influence and rather uncertain on his feet. I noticed he was having words with the bouncer."[36] The bouncer had decided Fitzgerald was too drunk to go back into the bar, and Lawton interceded and got Scott outside and away from the door. "In a few minutes Zelda appeared at the door of the bar, looking around for Scott." Lawton took her to his table, explaining her husband had an altercation with the bouncer, and he "tried to divert her with a dance. No thank you, she was going back to the bar and Scott was coming with her."[37]

Zelda went outside and found Scott. "No so and so bouncer can prevent Scott from going anywhere he pleases."[38] They went to the door, where the bouncer stopped Scott again. Zelda turned to Scott and demanded he do something. Scott "took a feeble punch at his opponent which missed its mark. A few other phantom attempts and finally the bouncer lost his patience and gave Scott a shove that sent him halfway across the room, crashing into a table."[39] Zelda was furious, but Lawton got Scott to his feet and outside to a taxi when Zelda burst out onto the sidewalk without her coat and shouted, "Scott, you not going to let that so and so get away with that."[40] She then pulled him out of the taxi and led him back into the Jungle Club, where he was beaten badly by the bouncer. Zelda was fearless; Scott was not.

Both McKaig and Lawton Campbell believed Zelda was his muse. "I have always thought Zelda did more for Scott than Scott did for Zelda."[41] Zelda, for her part, grew bored and resorted to making Scott jealous. She flirted with Townsend Martin and proclaimed Townsend and John Bishop had missed out on wedding kisses and then kissed both men in front of Scott. He played along, "Oh yes, they really have kisses coming to them because they weren't at the wedding and everybody at a wedding always gets a kiss."[42] But after that, she asked Townsend to give her a bath and tried to climb into John Bishop's bed, Scott became angry, and later, Zelda would admit that summer she became "romantically attached."

Carl Van Vechten, a fortysomething novelist, noticed right away Scott's inability to hold his alcohol. "He could take two or three drinks at most and be completely drunk. . . . "[43] He later summed up the Fitzgeralds in his novel *Parties,* turning them into David and Rilda Westlake, who "loved each other desperately, passionately. They cling to each other like barnacles cling to rocks but they want to hurt each other all the time." In the novel, Rilda complains to David about "our damned faithfulness . . . our clean 'fidelity, doesn't get us very far. We follow each other around in circles, loving and hating and wounding. We're both so sadistic. . . . '"[44]

In her unpublished novel, *Caesar's Things*, Zelda saw her situation clearly. "Jacob [Scott] went on doing whatever it was that Jacob did.

. . . He was more important than Janno; she always felt as if she should be helpful about his tinkerings; they were intricate enough to need an assistant. She didn't really do anything but wait on his will. While Jacob painted she went to the hairdresser and bought things. . . . "[45] The parties continued that summer in New York with one gin-soaked party blurring into another and another and another in Zelda's and Scott's small apartment high above the skyline of Manhattan.

> *Yet high over the city our line of yellow windows must have contributed their share of human secrecy to the casual watcher in the darkening streets and I saw him too, looking up and wondering. I was within and without, simultaneously enchanted and repelled by the inexhaustible variety of life.*[46]

It was still only 1921.

Scott and Zelda Fitzgerald in 1923. Wikimedia Commons

Scott and Zelda in Westport, Connecticut, in 1920. Some believe that Westport and not Long Island was the inspiration for the setting of *The Great Gatsby*. Wikimedia Commons

The Fitzgeralds' passport book for their escape to Europe. Wikimedia Commons

Scott, Scottie, and Zelda in Paris in 1925. Photofest

Gerald and Sara Murphy. Yale University Libraries

Scribner editor Maxwell Perkins in 1943. Perkins's criticism of *The Great Gatsby* did much to improve the final manuscript. Library of Congress

The original jacket for *The Great Gatsby*. Wikimedia Commons

The lobby card for the first film adaptation of *The Great Gatsby* in 1925. Wikimedia Commons

# CHAPTER 19

# Smooth as Two Cats

## *1924*

SCOTT STARED OFF THE PATIO AT THE COBALT-BLUE MEDITERRANEAN. He was a blunted, empty bucket. The novel and the unexpected magazine stories had exhausted him. He had been writing hard for a month, and he was at the point where the wall existed. Scott had been there before, and he didn't want to blow it by forcing a resolution on the book. The setup was there; the real question was, where was it going? On a short story, he knew before he started where it began, ended up, and then resolved itself. It was like a three-jump sprint. And he had all his runners in place and the starting gun was loaded. He just had to give the runners the signal, but he wasn't sure of the denouement or the resolution. He wasn't sure where the journey was taking him. It was the journey, after all, and not the destination.

But it wasn't all work. There are pictures of the Fitzgeralds where Zelda is sitting in a field of flowers with Scottie in her lap. Scott is holding his daughter aloft in the surf in a one-piece bathing suit that looks like a black tank top and shorts with a belt. Zelda is sitting on a rock with Scottie, who is fast becoming a little girl, chubby, her legs crossed, blond hair shining. Then they are on the balcony of their villa; Scott is in knickers with Zelda on his right and Scottie on the balcony veranda with Scott holding her, sporting a small French mustache. They have a gramophone. "Ain't Misbehaving" floats in the languor of summer in the South of France. This is in midsummer in the Riviera, and during the writing of *The Great Gatsby*, there is a family vacation in there also. But like all families, money becomes tight, and Scott has to swing off from *Gatsby* to write two short stories for *The Saturday Evening Post*; one is "How to Live on $36,000 a Year," set in Great Neck, and the other is "How to Live on Practically Nothing," set in the Riviera.

"Now when a family goes abroad to economize, they don't go to Wembley exhibition or the Olympic games—in fact they don't go to London and Paris at all but hasten to the Riviera, which is the Southern coast of France and which is reputed to be the cheapest as well as the most beautiful locality in the world. Moreover we were going to the Riviera out of season which is something like going to Palm Beach for July. When the Riviera season finishes in late spring, all the wealthy British and Americans move up to Deauville and Trouville . . . immediately prices fall . . . for two reformed spendthrifts the Riviera in summer had exactly the right sound. So we put our house in the hands of six real estate agents and steamed off to France amid the deafening applause of a crowd of friends on the docks."[1]

The reality was Scott and Zelda had quickly gone through their nest egg of $7,000, and in his essay, Fitzgerald was taking on one of the reasons they had come to the Riviera: to reduce expenses. The irony of writing the Great American Novel about the American Dream was that it was being done under the crush of financial pressure. "How to Live on $36,000 a Year" ends up with the couple acclimating themselves to the Riviera. "Perhaps you have already recognized in these two cultured Europeans the same barbaric Americans who had left America just five months before . . . the secret is they had entered fully into the life of the Old World. Instead of patronizing 'tourist' hotels they had made excursions to quaint little out of the way restaurants with the real French atmosphere . . . yes our summer had been a complete success. And we had lived on practically nothing—that is, on practically nothing except our original seven thousand dollars. It was all gone!"[2]

But now, the novel was stalled. Scott smoked his cigarette, leaning off the balcony and staring down at the beach. There were some kids running along the thin spit of sand, some nannies in chairs, some striped umbrellas, and two people sitting close together watching the surf. It was lunchtime. The isolation of the Riviera had given him a time much like when he was writing on the top floor of his parent's home in St. Paul. But he was out of money and would have to start begging Max Perkins for an advance on the novel. He owed Scribner $6,000 already and hoped the novel would clear the books for him. One thing was for sure, the Riviera had not turned out to be the place to live on nothing. The French law requiring Fitzgerald to insure all his servants was particularly irksome.

"Exactly where the money went we don't know—we never do. There were the servants for example: I was very fond of Marthe and Jeanne (and afterwards of their sisters Eugenie and Serpolette, who came in to help) but on my own initiative it would never have occurred to me to insure them all. Yet that was the law. If Jeanne suffocated in her mosquito netting, if Marthe tripped over a bone and broke her thumb, I was responsible. I wouldn't have minded so much except that the 'little on the side' that Marthe made in doing our marketing amounted, as I figure about forty five percent."[3]

Then there was Zelda. Thank God she had found a playmate to spend time with; otherwise, Scott would get nothing done. Scott pulled on his cigarette, his eyes drifting down to the two people sitting close together on the beach and watching the sea. He stared at the two heads that came together several times and pulled the cigarette from his mouth. The short, bobbed, blond-haired woman and the slicked-back, dark-haired man put their heads together again. Scott leaned forward, feeling a tickling down in the center of his stomach. He lit another cigarette and continued staring at them. Jozan was now lounging back on a towel while Zelda was sitting up with her arms braced in the sand. To the world, they looked like a couple; to Scott, he felt like he had come upon the scene of an accident.

The French aviator had come over for dinner the night before with the other officers. Scott had felt outnumbered, but he played the successful author while the young men fell in love with Zelda. Of course they did. He considered it flattering in a way, and again, he was glad for the distraction. Zelda needed to be entertained, and the darkly handsome Frenchman seemed up to the task. Zelda had been leaving early and returning late, and many times, she had been drinking and didn't want to go back out when Scott needed to blow off steam. She was having the time of her life, it seemed to him, and hadn't given much thought to what she was doing all day. Zelda was being Zelda. But here she was on the beach with Jozan. . . .

Scott stubbed his cigarette and put on his swimsuit. He didn't like the beach. He became restless many times when Zelda was tanning or swimming and often returned alone to the villa. Many times, he went down at lunch and swam with Zelda and Scottie, but Scottie was off with the nanny, who was efficient and made Zelda feel more inadequate as a mother.

Scott left the villa and walked down the road to the beach and across the shifting sands. It was hot, but he had kept his shoes and socks on. He didn't like people to see his feet. Ever since childhood, he had been this way. He had several jammed toes on his right foot, bunched at the joint and fairly deformed. Zelda had once taken a picture of his feet when she found out about his feet phobia, and he had torn the picture to pieces. Now he was walking, breathing heavily from cigarettes and the two fingers of gin. The sun was blazing and giving him a headache, and he realized he had also forgotten his sunglasses. The two people remained in front of him. Zelda immortalized the moment later in *Save Me the Waltz*.

"David [Scott] walked to the beach to join Alabama for a quick plunge before lunch. He found her and Jacques sitting on the sand like a couple of—well a couple of something, he said to himself distastefully. They were as wet and smooth as two cats who had been licking themselves. David was hot from the walk. The sun in the perspiration of his neck stung like a nettled collar.

"'Will you go in with me again?'

"He felt he had to say something.

"'Oh David [Scott]—it's awfully chilly this morning. There's going to be wind.'

"Alabama employed an expletive tone as if she were brooking a child's unwelcome interruption.

"David swam self-consciously alone, looking back at the two figures glittering in the sun side by side. 'They are the most presumptuous people, I have ever seen,' he said to himself angrily.

"The water was already cold from the wind. The slanting rays of the sun cut the Mediterranean to many silver slits and served it up on the deserted beach. As David left them to dress, he saw Jacque lean over and whisper to Alabama through the first gust of the mistral. He could not hear what they were saying.

"'You'll come,' Jacque whispered.

"'Yes, I don't know, yes,' she said."[4]

Scott stood in the water and stared. He felt a prickly heat crawling up his back. He had been in his world a long time, but seeing the two of them side by side, it was obvious. They sat like school children caught suddenly going out of bounds. Jozan's body lounged long and tan and muscular next to Zelda, who was continually turning toward him. Scott stared and felt the heat of the Riviera sun as a searing comet on his shoulders and neck.

*"Who wants to go to town," demanded Daisy insistently. Gatsby's eyes floated toward her. "Ah," she cried. "You look so cool." Their eyes met and they stared together at each other, alone in space. With an effort she glanced down at the table. "You always look so cool." She had told him that she loved him and Tom Buchannan saw. He was astounded. His mouth opened a little and he looked at her then at Gatsby, and then back at her as if he had never seen her before.*[5]

Sarah and Gerald Murphy, years later, said they had observed Zelda and the young officer "on the beach together and dancing at the casino, they said it was impossible not to notice what was happening. I don't know how far it really went," Gerald Murphy recalled. "I suspect it wasn't much, but it did upset Scott a good deal. I wonder whether it wasn't partly his own fault."[6]

Scott continued staring as if in a trance, then swam out of the water and put back on his shoes and socks hurriedly and left Zelda and Jozan, who had decided to go for a walk. He watched them stroll down the beach side by side, then walked off and headed back to the villa. He had to get back to his writing table while the fire was still burning.

# CHAPTER 20

# A Beautiful Little Fool

## *1921*

ZELDA WALKED OUT OF THE CLUBHOUSE OF THE MONTGOMERY swimming pool in her tank suit and squinted against the glaring sunshine. The heat had been oppressive, even for Montgomery, Alabama, with the cars too hot to touch and everyone sitting on the front porches in the evenings while homes dissipated the heat. Scott couldn't stand the heat and no longer saw the South as the idyllic land of his courtship. The South was now just a hot, quiet town with Zelda's parents, who looked at him with suspicion if not outright loathing. Zelda was pregnant, and Scott and Zelda had decided to leave New York and have the baby in Montgomery. "It seemed inappropriate to bring a baby into all that glamor and loneliness."[1]

This was after their three-month trip to Europe that was less than stellar. They had even considered having the baby in Europe, but Scott found little to his liking. "Goddamn the continent of Europe. It is of merely antiquarian interest. Rome is only a few years behind the Tyree and Babylon."[2]

Too young. Too bored. Too restless. They went back to New York and then left for Montgomery. The Fitzgeralds had been discussing the baby for a while, and their personal scribe, McKaig, had noted on October 21 that the baby was the center of their thinking. "Went up to Fitzgerald's to spend evening. They just recovered from an awful party. Much taken with the idea of having a baby. Have just planned a good baby and a bad baby—former has Scott's eyes, Zelda's nose, Scott's legs, Zelda's mouth, etc. Latter has Zelda's legs, Scott hair, etc. Scott hard up for money in spite of the fact he made 20,000 in the past twelve months."[3]

But now they were in Montgomery, and Zelda had gained a lot of weight, and it looked as if she might be having twins. The women at the country club pool who asked her to leave were polite, and the men who asked her to leave did not meet her eyes. In the South, women in the delicate condition of pregnancy were not expected to appear in public and certainly were not expected to appear at a swimming pool in a bathing suit. Zelda tried several pools, but the Southern mores stuck. "Had she remained on the pool's sidelines, there might only have been whispers, but when she dove into the artesian waters, she got ordered out. Combined with her father's edict of no alcohol being allowed in the house they headed for St. Paul."[4]

Their daughter, Scottie, years later would reflect on the change of venue for her birth: "I was supposed to be born in Montgomery, Alabama, but there was a terrible heat wave in September of 1921 . . . and my father, I'm sure it was my father because he seems to have made the decisions at all times, decided to wait for the event in St. Paul, Minnesota."[5] They took a house in Dellwood on White Bear Lake outside of St. Paul. In his ledger, Scott wrote, "No work. Slow deteriorating depression with outbreak around the corner."[6]

In September, he noted Zelda's weight had made it difficult for her to move. Zelda wrote, "In the fall we got to the Commodore in St. Paul and while leaves blew up the streets we waited for our child to be born."[7] Zelda had met Scott's parents, and she found them provincial and boring. Edward, being from the South, got a little more latitude, but Northern women, like the North itself, Zelda found alien. In the short story "The Ice Palace," Sally Harper comes north to visit her fiancé Harry for the first time. "Home was a rambling frame house set on a white lap of snow, and there she met a big gray haired man of whom she approved and a lady who was like an egg and who kissed her, these were Harry's [Scott's] parents." Zelda was miserable in the cold and wrote later, "There were the

Indian forests and the moon on the sleeping porch and I was heavy and afraid of storms."[8]

Zelda later told Sara Mayfield that Scott's parents had "neither Southern charm nor New York sophistication, that Mollie Fitzgerald was badly dressed and painfully eccentric while Scott's father, with his cane, flowing cravats and Vandyke beard, struck her as an ineffectual cardboard figure from a bygone age."[9] It was no wonder that Scott, who always felt some shame when introducing his mother and was sensitive to his father's failure in life, put off introducing them to his young bride. His father liked to ride in Scott's Buick downtown to get cigars, but other than that, the couple avoided his parents. "I don't do much but read," Zelda wrote to Max Perkins after he sent her a book. "We are quite popular out here and are enjoying our importance and temperance . . . but I'm homesick for Fifth Avenue."[10]

They quickly found a young married set, and Zelda began to enjoy herself again, smoking on the backs of trolley cars, talking loud at movies and commenting on the actors, and dancing with young men, whispering, "My hips are going wild, you don't mind do you?"[11] It wasn't the South, but even in the North, pregnant women were not expected to go out and drink and smoke and enjoy themselves. Her weight gain increased, and Scott, used to having the Belle of the Ball by his side, began to comment on her weight. He wrote in his ledger, "Zelda's weight . . ."[12]

Zelda captured her impression of the community around White Bear Lake in the unpublished story "The Girl Who the Prince Liked." "When summer came, all the people who liked summertime moved out to the huge clear lake not far from town, and lived there in long, flat cottages surrounded with dank shrubbery and pine trees and so covered by screened verandas that they made you think of small pieces of cheese under large meat safes. All the people came who like to play golf or sail on the lake . . . all the young people came whose parents had given them white bungalows . . . and a great many handsome sun-dried women of forty or fifty with big families and smart crisp linen costumes that stuck to the seats of their roadster when they went to meet their husbands escaping from town in the five o'clock heat."[13]

Even with her antics, Zelda felt invisible in St. Paul. Scott, on the other hand, was the local celebrity, interviewed by Thomas Boyd, the literary editor of the *St. Paul Daily News*, with the headline, "SCOTT FITZGERALD HERE ON VACATION RESTS BY OUTLINING NEW NOVELS." Scott addressed the St. Paul's Women's City Club, where he spoke about his work and flappers. Scott also completed a short story, "Winter Dreams," based on Dexter Riley, who goes East to find success but is anchored by his winter dreams formed in St. Paul. The very weather Zelda felt so soul-deadening energized Scott's prose. "In April the winter ceased abruptly. The snow ran down into Black Bear Lake scarcely tarrying for the early golfers to brave the season with red and black balls. . . . Dexter knew there was something dismal about this Northern spring just as he knew there was something gorgeous about the fall. Fall made him clench his hands and repeat idiotic sentences to himself and make brisk abrupt gestures of command to imaginary audiences and armies."[14]

The Fitzgeralds were asked to leave their home around White Bear Lake after some plumbing problems, and they moved into the Commodore, a hotel close to Summit Avenue. Scott then took a downtown office, where he worked on the proofs for *The Beautiful and the Damned*. Zelda once again was left on her own as the due date approached. On October 26, 1921, Zelda went to the Miller Hospital and endured a hard labor. Her friend, Xandra Kalman, later said "that Scott kept popping in and out of the delivery room jotting things down in the little notebook he always carried. When I asked him what he hurriedly scrawled during Zelda's labor, he replied 'help' and 'Jesus Christ!' When I asked him why he wrote it down, he said 'I might use it some time.'"[15]

The doctors had enough of the author with the notebook and told him to wait outside. Scott then threatened to kill himself if Zelda died from childbirth complications. Frances Scott Key Fitzgerald (Scottie) was delivered safely. When Scott realized Zelda was going to pull through, he went back to his role as scribe and wrote down Zelda's first comments post-delivery: "Oh God goofo, I'm drunk. Mark Twain. Isn't she smart—she has the hiccups. I hope it's beautiful and a fool—a beautiful little fool"[16]

*"Listen Nick; let me tell you what I said when she was born. Would
you like to hear?"*

*"Very much."*

*"It'll show you how I've gotten to feel about—things. Well she
was less than an hour old and Tom was God knows where. I woke
up out of the ether with an utterly abandoned feeling and asked the
nurse right away it was a boy or a girl. She told me it was a girl and
so I turned my head away and wept. All right," I said. "I'm glad it's a
girl. And I hope she'll be a fool—that's the best thing a girl can be in
this world, a beautiful little fool."*[17]

Zelda later wrote Landon Ludlow that "she is awfully cute and I am
very devoted to her."[18] Scott lost no time in announcing her arrival with
telegrams. "LILLIAN GISH IS IN MOURNING CONSTANCE
TALMAGE IS A BACK NUMBER AND A SECOND MARY
PICKFORD HAS ARRIVED."[19] Winter descended on St. Paul as
Zelda tried to recover, but losing the baby weight was difficult for her.
"Scottie was born and we went to all the Christmas parties and a man
asked Sandy 'Who is your fat friend?'"[20] For a former Southern belle
like Zelda Sayre, this was unthinkable, but she grimly tried to endure
the winter that swallowed up life as she knew it. Scott sums up Zelda's
reaction in his short story "The Ice Palace."

"A sudden thaw had nearly cleared the streets before but now they
were traversed again with a powdery wraith of loose snow that traveled
in wavy lines before the feet of the wind and filled the lower air with a
fine particle mist. There was no sky—only a dark ominous tent that drape
in the tops of the streets and was in reality a vast approaching army of
snowflakes . . . it was a dismal town after all she thought . . . dismal."[21]

In the story, the Southern girl has come north only to turn around
and go back south as she realizes her impending marriage and the climate
are one and the same: a barren, icy hell she cannot endure. "Sometimes
at night it had seemed to her as though no one lived here—they had all
gone long ago—leaving lighted houses to be covered in time by tombing
heaps of sleet. Oh if there should be snow on her grave! To be beneath

great piles of it all winter long, where even her headstone would be a light shadow against light shadows."[22]

But for Scott, the party continued, and he would invite friends over to their small apartment, and Zelda would tell the same people, "You won't come up will you. The baby wakes up and the place is too small. We don't want you." Then Scott would follow this up by saying, "Zelda's got this silly notion that we can't have anyone in the place . . . you'll come up won't you and help me cure her of this idea."[23] They moved in November of 1921 to a Victorian house on 626 Goodrich Avenue. The parties continued again. When her friend Xandra stopped by, she "recalled how she and Oscar found that the baby, whom Zelda was breastfeeding, had hiccups. The angry nanny loudly blamed it on Zelda's excessive gin consumption the previous night."[24] Zelda hated the weather, St. Paul, she detested Scott's parents, and disliked the way she was left behind while Scott played the local celebrity. She wrote to Ludlow Fowler, "I certainly miss you and Townsend and Alec . . . in fact I am very lonesome."[25]

In the climax of "The Ice Palace," the character Sally Harper becomes trapped in a palace of ice constructed in St. Paul. "Then on an instant the lights went out and she was in complete darkness. She gave a small, frightened cry and sank down into a cold little heap on the ice. She felt her left knee do something as she fell but she scarcely noticed it as some deep terror far greater than any fear of being lost settled upon her. She was alone in this presence that came out of the North, the dreary loneliness that rose from ice-bound whalers in the Arctic seas, from smokeless, trackless wastes where were strewn the whitened bones of adventure. It was the icy breath of death; it was rolling down low across the land to clutch her."[26]

Zelda is rescued from the brutal winter cold in the spring with the publication of *The Beautiful and the Damned*. She and Scott leave for New York for a two-week trip to attend the publication party on March 22, 1922. They had no real home, but New York was about as close as they could get.

# CHAPTER 21

# Jumping off the Cliff

## *1924*

ZELDA AND JOZAN WERE DANCING IN A CORNER OF THE CAFÉ. THE other officers and Scott were outside at a bistro table. The moonlight drenched the tables, and Zelda could see their profiles lit against the night. She put her hand around the back of Jozan's neck. In *Caesars Things*, Zelda describes how far things had gone with the young French Aviator. " . . . They kissed again, a long time before his friends . . . Janno [Zelda] loved him so that she never questioned his good faith. Another night after dancing with him, she kissed Jacque [Jozan] on the neck . . . the kiss lasted a long time . . . she did not mean to do this. The young officer treated her preciously and she knew that no matter what it would be tragedy and death; ruin is a relative matter. Janno recognizes she should have never kissed him. . . . "[1]

But the night continues, and they head back to their villa, where "the party soared on the babble of French phrases senseless to Alabama." Zelda later recorded in her novel *Save Me the Waltz*, "'Do let me offer you a taste of the Doges dress,' she said slipping into the currant jelly or a nice spoonful of Rembrandt. They sat in the breeze on the balcony and talked of America and Indo China and France and listened to the screech and moan of night birds out in the darkness. The jubilant moon was tarnished with much summer use in the salt air and the shadows black and communicative. A cat clambered over the balcony. It was hot."[2]

As dawn approaches, the other aviators leave, and Zelda, Scott, and Jozan are left alone. Zelda later writes, "The ice melted on the pantry floor, they cooked eggs in the blackened iron pans of the kitchen." Then another adventure looms, and they decide to drive to nearby Agay. Jozan drives, with Zelda in the passenger seat and Scott in the back. "Alabama and David and Jacque drove in the copper dawn to Agay against the face of the cool golden morning into the patterns of the creamy sun on the pines and the white odors of the closing flowers of the night."[3]

> *"Shall we go in my car?" suggested Gatsby. He felt the hot green leather of the seat. "I ought to have left it in the shade."*
>
> *"Is it a standard shift," demanded Tom.*
>
> *"Yes."*
>
> *"Well you take my coupe and let me drive your car to town."*
>
> *The suggestion was distasteful to Gatsby. "I don't think there's much gas," he objected.*
>
> *"Plenty of gas," said Tom boisterously. He looked at the gauge. "And if it runs out I can stop at a drugstore. You can buy anything at a drugstore nowadays."[4]*

"'Those are the caves of the Neanderthal man,' David [Scott] said, pointing to the purple hollows in the hills. 'No,' said Jacque [Jozan]. 'It was at Grenoble, that they found the remains.'" Correcting the author in the back seat, Jozan drives his car aggressively, with Scott's wife in the passenger seat. "He drove it like an areophane, with much speed and grinding and protesting tensions scattering echoes of the dawn like swarms of migrating birds. 'If this car were my own I'd drive it into the ocean,' he said. They sped down the dim obliteration of Provence to the beach, following the languorously stretching road . . . 'It was going to cost five hundred francs at least to get the car repaired,' thought David."[5]

There was another party at the Murphys in the Villa American, with Scott getting drunk and asking offensive questions, throwing olives at the backs of the Murphy's titled guests. Gerald clearly saw the problem between Zelda and Scott that summer. "Zelda swam and baked in the sun; she tried very hard to keep out of Scott's hair during the day while he wrote: she read a little, but her eyes bothered her and she preferred being active to the immobility of reading. She was left alone with little to do. After all Scott had his writing. Zelda had Scott and she didn't have very much of him while he was working. . . . "[6]

So when Scott acted up at the Murphy's dinner, Zelda had enough and suggested they go to the cliffs at Eden Roc at the tip of the Cap Antibes where she had swum before. The Murphys and others tried to talk Scott and Zelda out of going there. It was dark, and the rocks below the thirty-five-foot cliff were dangerous. Scott waved it all away, and they drove to Eden Roc in the warm night. Zelda was the swimmer, and she knew Scott would go along, but she also knew he was terrified.

They reached the cliffs and Zelda stripped off her evening frock and began to climb the rocks. Scott followed her. As they climbed, he became more nervous. Zelda was more athletic, more nimble. The dawn was now over the Mediterranean, and the Murpheys and others were far below. Scott looked for footholds, grabbing onto the jagged rocks. He still had his shoes on while Zelda was barefoot, moving stealthily like an Indian. She was always a few steps ahead of him and, of course, a much better swimmer and had all her life been diving off high points while he watched. She had already reached the top as Scott shakily moved higher with the gin thumping in his temples, the cigarettes tightening his chest from smoking all night. The air was thick and it was still very warm. He was sweating profusely, and as he climbed, something flashed by him. Zelda had already dived off the top down to the water below. Scott looked out and saw the white splash, and then she turned and waved.

He continued, moving slowly toward the top. By the time Scott reached the plateau, he was soaked, and his head was pounding. The people below were a small, glowing bunch of faces looking up. The water was far below and he saw white splashes where the surf hit the rocks. If he hit one of those rocks, he was dead. He cursed Zelda for getting him into the situation. She was always pushing him. Always pushing him into uncomfortable, dangerous situations and leaving him to extricate himself. He could have let her dive and just watched, but he never did that. He had to go where she led him. In an essay written for *Metropolitan Magazine* in 1922, "Eulogy on the Flapper," Zelda defines the very character that was tormenting Scott now.

"She flirted because it was fun to flirt and wore a one piece bathing suit because she had a good figure, she covered her face with powder and paint because she didn't need it and she refused to be bored chiefly because she wasn't boring. She was conscious that the things she did were the things she had always wanted to do. Mothers disapproved of their sons taking the Flapper to dances, to teas, to swim and most of all to heart. She had mostly masculine friends, but youth does not need friends, it needs only crowds and the more masculine crowds the more crowded for the flapper."[7]

Scott stared down with a faint sea breeze fluffing his hair, his eyes watering. He was not a good swimmer. He was not a good diver. He was a follower, really. Scott swore, wished strangely for his notebook, then realized that was ridiculous as it would be soaked or lost if he killed himself. Scott looked down again and saw Zelda wave to him. He realized then he still had his shoes on and took them off, putting them with the socks neatly on some rocks. His hairless white feet looked awful in the darkness. He stared down again at the water, his heart thumping in his chest. In an interview shortly after the publication of *This Side of Paradise*, Scott examined his own creation: "Thus it is, that we find the young woman of 1920 flirting, kissing, viewing life lightly, saying damn without a blush, playing along the danger line in an immature way—a sort of mental baby vamp."[8]

So now he was out on the edge of a cliff because of the very character he had created. Well, what did he expect? Scott looked down again and saw the dawn was getting stronger over the water. He thought of his book. He was getting closer. He just had to work out the ending. It was almost there. Resolution. You never knew until it happened in the climax of the novel, but he was getting close. You just had to jump off the cliff and trust it would all work out. You had to follow the character wherever she went. Scott swore again, shut his eyes, then dove off into the scattering darkness, into the abyss, following Zelda once again.

CHAPTER 22

# The Beautiful and the Damned

## *1922*

THE TOILET WATER WAS BLOODRED. THAT WAS IT. NO MORE BABY. THE Plaza hotel bathroom was brilliant white tile and the porcelain of the toilet made the baby water all the more horrible to Zelda. The pennyroyal or angelica that caused abortive bleeding had done the trick. The nasty pills Zelda wouldn't take before they were married, she took this time. There was no way she was going through another pregnancy when she still hadn't lost the weight she gained from the first pregnancy. In *The Beautiful and the Damned*, Anthony, upon learning that Gloria is pregnant, says, "talk to some woman and find out what's best to be done. Most of them can fix it in some way."[1] Zelda stood up and flushed the toilet.

Scott noted later in his ledger, "Zelda and her abortionist . . . pills and Dr. Lackin . . . lamenting that his son went down the toilet of the XXX hotel after Dr. X pills."[2] Scott would later comment on the "chill mindedness of his wife." They were back in New York with money in the bank from Scribner's and staying at the Plaza Hotel, the place of their honeymoon. Zelda had been waiting to get out of the frozen northland and the publication party for *The Beautiful and the Damned* was just the ticket. She wrote Ludlow, "This damned place is eighteen below zero."[3] So they left and began drinking and hitting the speakeasies and a party at George Jean Nathans then had lunch with Edmund Wilson, John Peale Bishop, and Donald Ogden Stewart. Wilson's impression of the

Fitzgeralds was not flattering. "Scott looked weary and Zelda decidedly matronly."[4] Zelda was worried she had lost her figure for good.

*The Beautiful and the Damned* was published and went on to sell fifty thousand copies. It was a success for Fitzgerald, but the $15,000 he received from royalties and $7,000 from serialization was not enough to get him out of bondage to the magazines. He was in debt to Scribner's for $5,600, and after he cleared that debt, his expenses ate into the rest. Zelda was asked by Burton Roscoe of the *New York Tribune* to write a humorous review of the novel based on the two main characters, Gloria and Anthony Patch, who are leading alcoholic lives in New York while waiting for an inheritance from his family. The couple is distinctly the Fitzgeralds and mirrors their life. Scott would admit to Max Perkins in a letter: "The girl is excellent . . . somewhat like Zelda . . . but the man . . . is a sort of debauched edition of me."[5]

*The Beautiful and the Damned* is Scott and Zelda. The plot revolves around young marrieds in New York, Anthony and Gloria Patch, who are waiting for Anthony to inherit his grandfather's fortune. It is a novel of slow disintegration, with both characters drinking themselves into oblivion while carrying on affairs. In 1930, Fitzgerald would reflect on the novel in a letter to Zelda: "I wish *The Beautiful and the Damned* had been a maturely written book because it was all true. We ruined ourselves—I have never honestly thought we ruined each other."[6]

The two characters betray Fitzgerald, later telling his daughter that Gloria and her mother were very different people and is confirmed again in a letter about *This Side of Paradise* from 1920: "I married her (the flesh and blood Rosalind-Zelda) eventually and now writing a . . . more 'honest' book about her."[7] Scott and Zelda come through in the descriptions of the characters. Gloria discovers Anthony is "an utter coward toward any one of a million phantasms created by his imagination. . . . " Anthony discovers Gloria is "a girl of tremendous tension and of the most high handed selfishness . . . almost utterly without physical fear." In an eerie section of the book, Gloria has an affair with an aviator who crashed later "when his plane fell 1,500 feet . . . gasoline engine smashed through his heart."[8]

Zelda's review of the novel is illuminating. "It seems to me that on one page, I recognized a portion of an old diary of mine, which mysteriously disappeared shortly after my marriage and also scraps of letters which, though considerably edited sound to me vaguely familiar. In fact Mr. Fitzgerald, I believe that is how he spells his name, seems to believe that plagiarism begins at home." But the lightheartedness of the review vanishes as Zelda zeroes in on the book's weakness. "The other things I didn't like in the book, I mean the unimportant things—were the literary references and the attempt to convey a profound air of erudition. It reminds me in its more soggy moments of the essays I used to get up in school at the last minute by looking up strange names in the Encyclopedia Britannica."[9]

Zelda's criticism is just, but John Peale Bishop nails what Zelda dances around. "*The Beautiful and The Damned* concerns the disintegration of a young man who, at the age of twenty-six has put away all illusions but one; this last illusion is a Fitzgerald flapper of the now famous type— hair honey colored and bobbed, mouth rose colored and profane."[10] Scott did use Zelda's diary, the same one he refused to turn over to George Jean Nathan for publication. Zelda's review was lighthearted and flip, but at one point, she defends the loosely cloaked charter of Gloria. "I think the heroine is most amusing . . ." Lawton Campbell later told Sara Mayfield, "*The Beautiful and the Damned* was pure Zelda."[11]

In a foreshadowing section of the novel, Anthony has an affair that could stand in for Gloria, whose infidelity has also contributed to the demise of their marriage. "Anthony's affair with Dorothy Raycroft was an inevitable result of his increasing carelessness about himself. He did not go to her desiring to possess the desirable, nor did he fall before a personality more vital, more compelling than his own, as he had done four years before. He merely slid into the matter through his inability to make definite judgements."[12]

*McCall's* magazine asked Zelda to write an article titled "Where Do Flappers Go?" *The Metropolitan Magazine* published another piece, "Eulogy on the Flapper." Zelda sums up the character she had lived and created: " . . . the flapper awoke from her lethargy of sub-deb-ism bobbed her hair, put on her choicest pair of earrings and a great deal of audacity and rouge and went into the battle . . . now audacity and earrings and one-piece bathing suits have become fashionable and the first flappers are so secure in their positions. . . . "[13]

Zelda's writings were delivered with F. Scott Fitzgerald in the byline. The assumption was that without this moniker, people would not be as interested in reading the article. Scott then was interviewed by *The New York World*, where he gave his view of a woman's role in a marriage. "I think that just being in love, really in love, doing it well, you know, is work enough for a woman. If she keeps her house the way it should be kept and makes herself look pretty when her husband comes home in the evening and loves him and helps him with his works and encourages him, oh I think that's the sort of work that will save her."[14]

This fantasy woman had no resemblance to the woman he had married, but it did not seem to bother him. It was almost as if he had a make-believe wife in mind that Zelda could not possibly be, and if that was the case, then what was Zelda to him? She certainly didn't deserve a career. There was to be a movie version of *The Beautiful and the Dammed*, and the Fitzgeralds were offered screen tests to play themselves. Zelda had been taking some acting lessons and wanted to try out for the movie, but Scott shut her down. She had just played a Southern flapper in the Junior League Frolic when they returned to St. Paul on April 17, but Scott, for reasons of his own, closed the door to his wife. He wanted Zelda the character all for himself, and a movie would have exploited her character, used up his material, and opened the world to Zelda that now came through her famous husband. When the movie came out, Scott denigrated it, and Zelda was so furious, she never spoke of it again.

In the serial version of *The Beautiful and the Damned*, Scott tries to bring meaning to the chaos, the drinking, the infidelity, the debauchery of Gloria's and Anthony's lives and, more importantly, his and Zelda's. "That exquisite heavenly irony which has tabulated the demise of many generations of sparrows seems to us to be content with the moral judgements of man upon fellow men. If there is a subtler and yet more nebulous ethic somewhere in the mind, one might believe that beneath the sordid dress and near the bruised heart of this transaction there was a motive which was not weak but only futile and sad. . . . "[15]

Zelda, whom the novel was based on, protested against this over-blown, inflated, purple prose and convinced Scott to cut it for the novel and go with a modern ending of dramatic dialogue. On December 23, 1921, Scott had wired Max Perkins, "Zelda thinks book should end with Anthony's last speech on ship she thinks new ending is a piece of morality. Let me know your advice."[16] Perkins agreed with Scott's muse, and the ending was cut for the final lines of Anthony whispering to himself, "I showed them. It was a hard fight but I didn't give up and I came through."[17]

In the summer, they took another place on White Bear Lake, where the parties began again, and they were soon asked to leave. Zelda played golf that summer with her friend, Mrs. Kalman, who later recalled that "she was very athletic and wanted to be out doing something. Zelda was rather a good golfer, or at any rate, far better than Scott. She was not all interested in going out with the girls and when Scott wanted to remain at home, Zelda stayed with him . . . she and Scott were always thinking up perfectly killing things to do . . . she was a natural person who didn't give a damn about clothes . . . but there weren't many people she liked."[18]

They decided to leave Minnesota, and the Fitzgeralds left Scottie with his parents while they went back to New York for the publication of *Tales of the Jazz Age*. At The Plaza, they met Ring Lardner and John Dos Passos. Dos Passos later recalled the day: "Scott called and asked me if I would care to join him for lunch; Sherwood Anderson would be there and it might be fun if I came along. I did. That was when I first met Zelda. She was very beautiful, she possessed a sort of grace—a hand-some girl, good looking hair—everything about her was very original and amusing. But there was also this strange little streak."[19]

They collected John Dos Passos and went house hunting on Long Island and ended up in Great Neck, a town of about 1,200 people with a view of Manhattan skyscrapers fifteen miles in the distance. Bootleggers, new money, showbiz people, and industrialists peopled the small community in 1922. They looked at several mansions and mocked the salesman's pretension in calling the mansions "gentlemen's estates." After enlisting the help of famed journalist Ring Lardner, who was drunk, and Zelda remarked that "Ring is drinking himself to an embalmed state so he'll be ready for the grim reaper. I don't think he'll have long to wait if he keeps on."[20]

They found a house on Gateway Drive situated across the inlet from Sands Point.

*I lived at West Egg, the less fashionable of the two, though this is a most superficial tag to express the bizarre and not a little sinister contrast between them. My house was at the very tip of the egg, only fifty yards from the Sound, and squeezed between two huge places that rented for twelve or fifteen thousand a season.*[21]

A lease was signed for $300 a month, a governess hired for $90 a month, and a live-in couple for $160 to cook and clean. Zelda went back to St. Paul for Scottie's first birthday while Scott stayed behind. When they came East, he picked them up in a used Rolls-Royce, and the party began again out on Great Neck, Long Island.

# CHAPTER 23

# You Never Loved Him

## *1924*

SCOTT IS WRITING, OVERLOOKING THE MEDITERRANEAN. THE PENCILS are lined up. Papers are on the floor. Notes are on the floor. He breathes in the smoke that hurts his chest. Tuberculous. He had it in college, or at least he believed he had it. He always thought of himself as tubercular. At night, he turns restlessly in bed from too much coffee. The sunshine outside on the verandah was a distraction. The halcyon day was a distraction. How could the sky and the sea be that color of cobalt blue? It was paradise, and paradise was pushing in on his world. He needed to know. He needed to know what she would do. He held his pencil. He rubbed his eyes. Zelda had left early. Scottie and the nanny had gone to the Murphys. The stories had drained him. His money was drained; it was the middle of July, but he was at the point of no return . . . he had to push through to the end now, but he needed to know what she would do. . . .

Zelda sat on the beach, listening to the gentle surf. Scott didn't even like to sit on the beach with her. His wet suit bothered him. His bunched toes shamed him. Zelda looked up behind her and saw the window to his study. He encouraged her to flirt with the officers. "Go on, they look like interesting officers . . . go meet them."[1] No sex for a month now. She might as well be alone. He was up there now writing and using her. He always used her. One way or another. Zelda felt the shadow over her now. It was Jozan. "The flying officer who looked a Greek god."[2]

He plopped down next to her, and they sat watching the morning sun sparkling on the Mediterranean. They could do that. Just not talk. It didn't matter if his English was bad. They communicated with glances, murmurs, moods, gestures, hugs, kisses. They had been doing this awhile and they had become a couple. Everyone knew it but Scott, and Zelda suspected he even knew it, and that in a way made her even more determined. Jozan was looking at her now and the French words for love were tumbling out of his mouth. The summer was going fast. Eventually, Scott would finish his book and they would leave. They both knew this. Jozan was pouring sand from one hand into the other. The morning peace of the beach was there. The gentle surf was a symphonic backdrop. The gulls. They had kissed in front of his friend the night before. Zelda had kissed his neck, and now he was leaning in and facing her, his broad, dark chest leaning toward her. And he asked the question just like that. They both knew what it meant. It was time. She could not hang on like this forever. Here was love. Pure and simple.

"If things didn't work out, there would always be the memory . . . she preferred to consider that she was merely feeling her way and that any moment she could withdraw . . . he told her to come to his apartment. She said she would; she was horrified. She could not possibly do so."

"'Yes,' she said."[3]

He had asked her to go to his apartment in Fréjus before, and she had demurred, but now, she did not. She glanced up toward the villa where Scott sometimes watched them, but there was no one on the patio. Scottie was with the nanny and Zelda was with Jozan. They wordlessly stood like two people in a play and drove toward his apartment in Fréjus. It "was the oldest Roman city in Gaul, now comprising Belgium, France and Holland, Fréjus was established during the Julius Caesar era and still contained remnants of a first century amphitheater."[4] They drove back in time.

"Birdsong filled the air along with the clang of a blacksmiths hammer and tolling of distant church bells. Long roads wound implacably up and over into the pine fragrant depths," Zelda later recalled. "Gardens dropped into the sea. The baritone of tired medieval bells proclaimed disinterestedly a holiday from time to time. Lavender bloomed silently over the rocks. It was hard to see the vibrancy of the sun."[5] They drove with Jozan taking the turns in the early morning sunshine and reached the village. Then they walked and Zelda felt like they were walking even further back in time. "They wandered through alleys as narrow as trenches, dipping under vaulted passageways, where windows and doors popped open in unexpected places."[6]

And then into Jozan's apartment, where the morning sun shone through the open windows. Zelda felt him against her as the sand from the beach sprinkled the cool, clean sheets. He was dark and strong in the half-light. So different from Scott. He was a warrior and his dark eyes and sandy wet hair fell against the pillow. They had no clothes now. Her suit. And his. Gone. This is what they had danced around all summer and this is what Zelda had seen a thousand times. There was none of Scott's clumsiness in bed, his awful reservations, his strange prudishness. There was just love with the curtains moving slowly and the light trellising into the room. The white plaster of the walls and the windowsill and the indiscernible clean scent of him. He was of the sea and the air and this European village. He was something out of the ages and he fed her soul. He did not use her. She did not shine for him to make himself greater. He just loved her. He loved her for who she was. Jozan saw her then as "a shining beauty, a creature overflowed with activity, radiant with desire to take from life every chance her charm, youth and intelligence provided so abundantly."[7] She kissed him; she kissed his neck. This had been growing and growing, and she had been plotting for a month the ways to meet him without Scott knowing.

She nuzzled his chest. "There was a clean scent about him she adored, something to do with his starched white uniform. Maybe she thought, they added bouquet to the misting water while ironing. That fresh smell lingered and she couldn't eliminate it from her mind, nor did she want to. She felt intoxicated by it."[8] She had been going into town without Scott lately to find Jozan. "With heightened expectations she made excuses to drive into San Raphael and look for him by the harbor."[9] Sometimes, she went with Miss Maddock, more often alone. "It was an improbable affair, full of passion,"[10] she later wrote in *Caesar's Things*. "Sometimes they went to the tin pan picture show and sometimes they wandered around the plane trees."[11] She was tired of seeking him out. They were together now in the bed, and "he drew her body against him till she felt the blades of his bones carving her own. He was bronze and smelled of the sand and the sun and she felt him naked underneath the starched linen. She didn't think of David. She hoped he hadn't seen but she didn't care. She felt as if she would like to be kissing Jacques Chervez Feuille on top of the Arc de Triumphe."[12]

Zelda's life vanished then. This was her new life. This man whom she was making love to in the old village in France in this old apartment in this bed with his uniform draped over a chair. This was her new life. The life of the fights, the money problems, the drinking, Scott's demands, her loneliness . . . that, that was all behind her now. This life was the new one. She came and she never knew it could be like this. With Scott, her pleasure was infrequent. He was Victorian in his approach to sex, and of course, they hadn't had any sex all summer. The Catholic hangover was always in their bed unless they were plastered. Now here was pure pleasure. Here was a man who made love to her and didn't use her the way Scott used her, her entire life. She simply felt young again . . . free. Fidelity was something she was never sure of. It had no real meaning to her.

In *The Beautiful and the Damned*, Gloria explains her view of sex to Anthony in bed. "'Haven't you ever kissed anyone like you kissed me?' 'No' she answered simply. 'As I've told you men have tried . . . oh lots of things. Any pretty girl has that experience . . . you see,' she resumed. 'It doesn't matter to me how many women you've stayed with in the past, so long as it was merely a physical satisfaction, but I don't believe I could endure the idea of your ever having lived with another woman for a protracted period. . . . '"[13]

Jozan's cigarette was filling the air now as Zelda nuzzled against him. Their voices were murmurous. They both were exhausted, satiated. How rare to have an equal sexual relationship. It was nothing short of amazing. He murmured in French and then, "What will you say to your husband?"[14] Zelda paused, staring at the curtains waving in the windows. The light moved around the room and reflected in the mirror over the small walnut bureaus. Church bells rang in the distance. Zelda moved her finger across his chest.

"I'll have to tell him."[15]

She heard the soft crackle of his cigarette, the smoke rolling out over the bed. He spoke slowly, haltingly. "It would be unwise. We must hang onto our benefits."[16]

Zelda continued staring at the curtains waving in the morning breeze. If only they could stay this way forever. In *Caesar's Things*, Janno (Jozan) quotes the bible to her. "He who looketh on a woman to lust after hath committed adultery with her in his heart already . . . adultery was adultery and it would have been impossible for her to love two men at once, to give herself to simultaneous intimacies."[17] She had veered and, for the first time, taken her attention away from Scott, and it was liberating. Zelda had never really believed in marriage, and the very words Scott used in *The Beautiful and the Damned* for Gloria were hers. "What grub-worms women are to crawl on their bellies through colorless marriages! Marriage was created not to be a background but to need one. Mine is going to be outstanding. It can't—shant be the setting—it's going to be the performance, the live, lovely, glamorous performance, and the world shall be the scenery. I refuse to dedicate my life to posterity. Surely one owes as much to the current generation as to one's unwanted children. What a fate—to grow rotund and unseemly, lose my self-love, to think in terms of milk, oatmeal, nurse diapers . . . Dear dream children, how much beautiful you are, dazzling little creatures who flutter on golden wings. Such children, however, poor dear babies, have little in common with the wedded state."[18]

In this way, it was always a matter of time for Zelda. The world was away and she felt that young girl with the world at her fingertips. "If he was unable to marry she thought, they could make other arrangements."[19] Zelda didn't want to think about all that. She didn't want to think that at this very moment, Scott was sitting at his table, seeing the scene. It was impossible they should be in the same universe. Her world was all that mattered now. This was not his life; it was hers. But Scott had found his rhythm again . . . and the pencil was moving quickly.

*"Daisy that's all over now," he said earnestly.*

*"It doesn't matter anymore. Just tell him the truth—that you never loved him—and it's all wiped out forever."*

*She looked at him blindly. "Why—how could I love him—possibly?"*

*"You never loved him."*

*She hesitated. Her eyes fell on Jordan and me with a sort of appeal, as though she realized at last what she was doing —and as though she had never, all along intended doing anything at all. But it was done now. It was too late.[20]*

# CHAPTER 24

# Absolution

## *1922*

GIN-SMASHED AGAIN. THE CARAVAN PARKED IN THE FRONT. PEOPLE never left. Scott slept on the lawn. Zelda slept on the lawn. Guests slept in the hammock, on the floor, in the basement. Everyone remained passed out until noon. Scott and Zelda posted a list of rules for guests at the Great Neck House. "1. Visitors may park their cars and children in the garage. 2. Visitors are requested not to break down doors in search of liquor even when authorized to do so by their host and hostess 3. Weekend guests are respectfully notified that the invitations to stay over Monday issued by the host and hostess during the small hours of Sunday morning must not be taken seriously."[1]

They were back in Great Neck and Scott took a shot at his novel between the parties and the wild weekends in New York. But it didn't go well. "A series of parties—the Boyd's, Mary Blair, Chas and Kaly, Charlie Towne. Drunk . . . no ground under our feet,"[2] were his ledger entries. Rage now entered the picture. Anita Loos had come over for dinner and Scott got smashed and then went into a rage and "locked Zelda and Anita in the dining room and threw a wine cooler, a lighted candelabra, a water carafe and a leg of lamb at them screaming, 'Now I'm going to kill you two!' Anita shaking and incredulous and Zelda highly distressed but still loyal to Scott were forced to flee to Ring Landers."[3]

But Scott could not control his drinking or his writing now. His concept for the new novel went off the rails, and he wrote Max Perkins he was going to "come at it from a new angle."[4] "Absolution" was published in June of 1924, a product of his attempt to come to grips with what the new book would be about. He later wrote Perkins, "I'm glad you like 'Absolution.' As you know it was to have been the prologue of the novel but it interfered with the neatness of the plan."[5]

In "Absolution," a boy, Rudolph Miller, lies in confession and goes to the house of a priest to be forgiven. His father is a local freight agent who is violent and oppressive, and Rudolph goes to see a priest who sits inside his house tormented by the physical, sensual world outside his house. "Sometimes, near four o'clock, there was a rustle of Swede girls along the path by his window, and in their shrill laughter he found a terrible dissonance . . . At twilight the laughter and the voices were quieter, but several times he had walked past Romberg's Drug Store when it was dusk and the yellow lights shone inside and the nickel taps of the soda fountain were gleaming . . . "[6]

Rudolph comes for absolution for his sin of lying in confession, and the priest gives it to him, but Rudolph repeats to himself, "Blatchford Sarnemington, Blatchford Sarnemington . . . when he became Blatchford Sarnemington a great suave nobility flowed from him."[7] Rudolph (Scott) finds his life intolerable and creates another persona.

> *His parents were shiftless and unsuccessful farm people—his imagination had never really accepted them as his parents at all. The truth was that Jay Gatsby of West Egg, Long Island, sprang from his platonic conception of himself. He was a son of God—a phrase which, if it means anything, means just that—and he must be about His Fathers business, the service of a vast, vulgar and meretricious beauty.*[8]

The priest starts to have a breakdown, fascinated with the boy and his own desires, and tells Rudolph, "Go and see an amusement park . . . it's a thing like a fair, only much more glittering. Go to one at night and stand a little way off from it in a dark place, under dark trees. You'll see a big wheel made of lights turning in the air and a long slide shooting boats down into the water. A band playing somewhere and a smell of peanuts and everything will twinkle. . . . " The priest then frowned. "But don't get up to close . . . because if you do, you'll only feel the heat and the sweat and the life."[9]

Rudolph then realizes "that there is something ineffably gorgeous that had nothing to do with God. . . . "[10] Rudolph realizes then that it is his own dreams that give life color and comes into his own. "At that moment when he had affirmed immaculate honor a silver pennon had flapped out into the breeze somewhere and there had been the crunch of leather and the shine of silver spurs and a troop or horsemen waiting for dawn on a low green hill."[11]

Scott had his theme, if not his novel, and now he went to work on gathering the new material.

*The most grotesque and fantastic conceits haunted him in his bed at night. A universe of ineffable gaudiness spun itself out in his brain while the clock ticked on the wash stand and the moon soaked with wet light his tangled clothes upon the floor. Each night he added to the pattern of his fancies until drowsiness closed down upon some vivid scene with an obvious embrace. For a while these reveries provided an outlet for his imagination; they were a satisfactory hint of the unreality of reality, a promise that the rock of the world was founded securely on a fairy's wing.*[12]

Ring Larder wrote an article, "In Regard to Genius," a satirical takedown on Fitzgerald. "Another prominent writer of the younger set is Mr. F. Scott Fitzgerald. Mr. Fitzgerald sprung into fame with his novel *This Side of Paradise* which he turned out when only three years old and wrote the entire book with one hand. Mr. Fitzgerald never shaves while at work on his novels and looks very funny along towards the last five or six chapters. His hobby is leashing high bred dogs and when not engaged on a book or a story can be seen most any day on the streets of Great Neck leashing high bred dogs of which there is a great number. He cannot bear to see any of them united."[13]

Meanwhile, at Great Neck, Scott got drunk and climbed under the table. Scott got drunk and lit twenty-dollar bills on fire and used them to light his cigarettes. Zelda got drunk and drove their Rolls-Royce off the pier into the bay, but the water was so shallow the car didn't sink but was stuck in the mud up to the hubcaps. Scott now greeted his guests by saying, "I'm an alcoholic." Zelda's friend, Eleanor Browder, came up to visit, and they went to meet Scott in New York at the Plaza and found him being escorted out of the Palm Court for drunkenness. They drove back to Great Neck for dinner and Scott got drunk again and "ripped off the tablecloth sending food in every direction. Seemingly unruffled, Zelda rose calmly and suggested they have coffee in another room."[14] The tornado that was their life took a toll on their relationship to their child. One party guest remembered that when Scottie was brought in, Zelda told her to "kiss mother, dear, that the child vehemently shook her head, at which point, Zelda quipped that Scottie only loathed her but hated Scott."[15]

When Scott tried to get going on his new novel, Zelda was left on her own to fend for herself with visitors from Montgomery, which brought her friend, Livre Hart's mother, out to Great Neck. Mrs. Hart then invited Scott and Zelda for tea at the Astor Hotel in New York, but "they arrived separately too drunk to locate each other in the hotel lobby."[16] Mrs. Hart then forbade her daughter to visit the Fitzgeralds.

Weekends in New York, then. A dinner party at Ernest Boyd's apartment on East Nineteenth Street where Scott and Zelda arrive late. They fall asleep over their soup from being up all night at a party and someone picks up Zelda and puts her in a bedroom, where "she lay curled and asleep like a silky kitten."[17] Scott wakes up and orders two cases of champagne and a fleet of taxis to take everyone to a nightclub. Boyd might have dismissed Fitzgerald as riding the fame train to its logical end, but he later said, "Fitzgerald was one of the few serious people capable of so much frivolity."[18] Drunk driving was standard as Scott, who had no license, drove he and Zelda back to Great Neck at night along with other people inside and outside on the running boards. When Scott could no longer drive, he turned the wheel over to someone else who had no experience driving and went to sleep with the rest of the drunkards in the back seat. Amazingly, they always made it back.

The Great Neck parties continued, and Rosalind, Zelda's sister, came to visit in July. Scott had been gone for three days on a bender with Ring Lardner and then fell asleep on the lawn. Zelda didn't care for Ring initially. "He's a typical newspaperman whom I don't find very amusing . . ." she told her sister. "He is six feet tall and goes on periodical sprees lasting from one to six weeks. He is on one now, which is probably the reason he will call on us."[19] They went to a party at one of the Long Island mansions and Scott refused to leave even though they had stayed through the night. They finally left without him and took a cab home. Zelda leaned over to her sister and whispered, "I never did want to marry Scott."[20]

"Still drunk,"[21] Scott's leger tells it all. The new novel collapses, leaving only the characters Jordan, Vance, Ada, and Carraway, and the story is told in the third person. Two pages survive. The rest is discarded for the cyclone that is Great Neck, stuffed with show businesspeople and the parties at Clarence Mackay's mansion, a French chateau "*that was a colossal affair by any standard—it was a factual imitation of some Hotel de Ville in Normandy, with a tower on one side, spanking new under a thin beard of ivy, and a marble swimming pool and more than forty acres of lawn and garden.*"[22]

Besides the sportswriter Ring Lardner, Scott got to know the wealthy Tommy Hitchcock, who was, at the time, one of the best polo players in America and a war hero. Physically, he was imposing and "*had a body capable of enormous leverage.*"[23] He had recently come over from England after spending a year at Oxford, "*an opportunity they gave to some of the officers after the armistice.*"[24] Scott would go watch his matches at the Meadow Brook Polo Club, where the "horses were worth thousands and the riders worth millions."

In the morning, bleary-eyed and hungover, Scott and Zelda would smoke and drink coffee out on the porch, reading about the Fuller McGee case that was in the headlines detailing how their Long Island neighbor had swindled investors out of millions with his stock firm that declared bankruptcy listing six million dollars in debt. Everyone wanted to be in on the market, and Fuller was indicted "on a twelve count charge that included operating a bucket shop for illegally gambling with customers fund."[25] Four trials later, Fuller would only serve a year in jail for making himself wealthy with other people's money. They would turn the page and there might be a story on gambler Arnold Rothstein accused of fixing the 1918 World Series. "*He's the man who fixed the 1918 World Series Old Sport.*"[26] Rothstein would later be murdered outside the old Manhattan Park Central Hotel.

*It was four o'clock in the morning then and if we had raised the blinds we would have seen daylight . . . Then he went out on the sidewalk and they shot him three times in his full belly and drove away.*[27]

Then Scott and Zelda would wait for the night, where they might see some of their other neighbors. Maybe the bootlegger Max Von Gerlach, who always addressed Scott as "Old Sport."

*"That's a great expression of yours isn't it?" said Tom sharply.*
*"What is?"*
*"All this Old Sport business. Where'd you pick that up?"*[28]

Or Robert Kerr, who would tell the story again about how, as a young man, he saved a man's yacht from breaking up against the rocks. "*It was James Gatz who had been loafing along the beach that afternoon in a torn green jersey and a pair of canvas pants but it was already Jay Gatsby who borrowed a rowboat pulled out to the Tuolomee and informed Cody that a wind might catch him and break him up in half an hour. . . .*"[29] Or their more famous neighbors, "Groucho Marx, Basil Rathbone, producers Sam Harris and Arthur Hopkins . . ." Or they would drive the twenty miles into Manhattan along the Northern Boulevard and go across the Corona Dumps, where a lone gas station sat near the railroad drawbridge. They could see the landfill of ashes, horse manure, and garbage if they went by train or car where a lone billboard loomed over the desolation.

*This is a valley of ashes, a fantastic farm where ashes grow like wheat into ridges and hills and grotesque gardens where ashes take forms of houses and chimneys and rising smoke and finally with a transcendent*

*effort of men who move dimly and already crumbling through the*
*powdery air . . . but above the gray land and the spasms of bleak dust*
*which drift endlessly over it, you perceive, after a moment, the eyes of*
*Doctor T. J. Eckleburg.*[30]

Many times, Scott returned from New York after a two- or three-day binge, unable to remember where he had been. By 1923, he was battling insomnia, with notes in his ledger that his old "dream of baseball player, football player, and general to put me to sleep"[31] was no longer working, and he noted in February "still drunk." This was followed a month later with "tearing drunk."[32] The couple he described in *The Beautiful and the Damned* had become themselves. "The magnificent attitude of not giving a damn altered over night; from being a mere tenet of Gloria's it became the entire solace and justification of what they chose to do and what consequence it brought. Not to be sorry, not to lose one cry of regret, to live according to a clear code of honor toward each other and to seek the moment's happiness as fervently and persistently as possible."[33]

After sleeping in until noon, Scott and Zelda were ready for another party. Many times, the Fitzgeralds would drive into New York for the weekend and cross the Queensboro Bridge in the hard sunlight of morning.

*Over the great bridge with the sunlight through the girders making*
*a constant flicker upon the moving cars, with the city rising up across*
*the river in white heaps and sugar lumps all built with a wish out*
*of non-olfactory money. The city seen from the Queensboro Bridge is*
*always the city seen for the first time, its first wild promise of all the*
*mystery and beauty in the world.*[34]

Sometimes they would go to a Princeton football game with the Bucks, Gene and Helen, who warned their friends that if they wanted to invite the Fitzgeralds over, their furniture would "be ruined by spilled drinks and cigarette butts."[35] All these people and more crossed Scott's and Zelda's lives during the two years they lived in Great Neck.

*Once I wrote down on the empty spaces of a timetable the names of those who came to Gatsby's house that summer . . . July 5th 1922. From East Egg came the Chester Beckers and the Leeches and a man named Bunsen, Whom I knew at Yale, and Doctor Webster Civet, who was drowned last summer in Maine. And the Hornbeams and the Willie Voltaires and a whole clan named Blackbuck . . . a man named Klipspringer was there so often and so long that he became known as the "boarder" . . . all these people came to Gatsby's house in the summer.[36]*

Even though Scott was making twenty times what the average American made, he was severely in debt and not getting anywhere again on his novel. Zelda later wrote of this time, "They were proud of themselves and the baby, consciously affecting a vague bouffant casualness about the fifty thousand dollars they spent on two years worth of polish of life's baroque façade. In reality, there is no materialist like the artist, asking back from life the double and the wastage and the cost on what he puts out in emotional usury."[37] Zelda, while a Southern belle, had not come from money. The judge's salary was a middle-class existence and probably a tight one at that. Suddenly, the girl from the provincial South could buy whatever she wanted in New York City.

*"My dear," she cried. "I'm going to give you this dress as soon as I'm though with it. I've got to get another one tomorrow. I'm going to make a list of all the things I've got to get. A massage and a wave, and a collar for the dog, and one of those cute little ash-trays where you touch a spring and a wreath with a black silk bow for mother's grave. . . . "[38]*

Scott's play "The Vegetable" had become his ticket out. The title was based on a satirical essay by Mencken. "Here is a country in which it is an axiom that a businessman shall be a member of the Chamber of Commerce, an admirer of Charles M. Schwab, a reader of the *Saturday Evening Post*, a golfer, in brief, a vegetable."[39] Scott had written musicals and plays at Princeton, but he could never master the straight dramatic form, and the play failed miserably.

And now he is back over the garage with the oil stove, and it has been a long slog of writing the stories to pay the bills. It was the oldest story in the world for the writer. Doing the work that allowed for the writing. He had to write the damn magazine stories, but now he had enough ahead. It was time to leave. Already they had used up what New York had to offer. In *My Lost City*, Scott laments that the best is already behind them. "But we were no longer important. The flapper, upon whose activities the popularity of my books was based, had become passe by 1923—anyhow in the East. I decided to crash Broadway with a play, but Broadway sent its scouts to Atlantic City and quashed the idea in advance, so I felt that, for the moment, the city and I had little to offer each other. I would take the Long Island atmosphere that I had breathed and materialize it beneath unfamiliar skies."[40]

So it was time to go and economize in Europe. He had to do it. And after writing, Scott would go back down to the beach by the bay at night and stare at the green light beaming from the Long Island lighthouse that beamed from his own dreams begun as a boy in the Midwest.

*He stretched out his arms toward the dark water in a curious way and far as I was from him, I could have sworn he was trembling. Involuntarily I glanced seaward and distinguished nothing except a single green light, minute and far away, that might have been at the end of the dock.*[41]

Scott could see the great mansions across the bay, and he knew he was, in fact, writing, writing, writing . . . and now he was in the hot breezy villa on the Riviera a year later, and he had used just about everything he had. He had used his entire life, culminating in the Great Neck years, but now he had to cross the Rubicon. He drank more gin. Smoked three cigarettes. Sweated more pearls. Nothing was working. He needed to know what had happened. He needed to know where it was all going. He did not have Zelda's diary like the one he used in *The Beautiful and the Damned.* He had no heroine to whom he could ascribe every value like *This Side of Paradise.*

In a review of *The Beautiful and the Damned*, John Peale Bishop hits on Scott's deficiency in writing. "The most interesting thing about Mr. Fitzgerald's book is Mr. Fitzgerald. He has already created about himself a legend . . . the true stories about Fitzgerald are always published under his own name. He has the rare faculty of being able to experience romantic and ingenuous emotions and a half hour later regard them with satiric detachment. He has an amazing grasp of the superficialities of the men and women about him, but he has not yet a profound understanding of their motives, either intellectual or passionate."[42]

For Scott to understand the deep well of human motivation, he needed his muse. He knew what the green light portended, but . . . "*what foul dust floated in the wake of his dreams. . . .*"[43] He needed Zelda to tell him what happened next.

CHAPTER 25

# The Foul Dust

## *1924*

SCOTT AND ZELDA STOOD IN THE SULTRY AIR. SHE HAD COME TO HIM
at last. Much like every story, every novel, even his play. She had filled
in the gaps and told him what he needed to know. And now Zelda was
staring at him with her cheeks flushed, perspiration shining on her forehead. She knew the answer, and now she was going to tell him. Besides,
it was too hot to write. The noon heat was close to one hundred degrees.
Scott kept sweating on his manuscript pages. Worse, the heat made him
tired, unable to think.

> *"Hot!" said the conductor to familiar faces. "Some weather! . . .
> Hot . . . Hot! . . . Hot! . . . Hot! Is it hot enough for you? Is it hot? Is
> it . . . ?" My commutation ticket came back to me with a dark stain
> from his hand. That anyone should care in this heat who flushed lips
> he kissed, whose head made damp the pajama pocket over his heart!*[1]

The gin had turned against him as well, and the old trick of getting
just enough lift from a mouthful was not working. It was just making
him tired. No wonder everyone left the Riviera for the summer. He had
written Max Perkins a few days before, "I'm not going to mention my
novel to you again until it is on your desk. All goes well."[2] But all wasn't
going well. Not well at all. And now, this heat made progress almost

impossible. They would have to get out soon and find somewhere cooler. But Scott had to finish first, and he was headed for the big showdown, but he couldn't see how it finished up. He had the main characters at a ballgame, but that wasn't really working . . . no . . . he needed more, and all he wanted to do was take a nap. Scott pulled back his hair, and that's when he heard the door to the villa open.

Zelda had come straight from the apartment with Jozan to find Scott with the crazed look he always had after writing. He seemed relieved that she had interrupted him, and now they were facing each other, with the warm sea breeze twisting up the long curtains. She was breathing heavily, almost hyperventilating, but this was how it must be done. She loved Jozan "because he was attractive but also because she is afraid of love and must confront and overcome her fear."[3] Driving over from the apartment, she had reasons that "it was expedient, unexpected and miserable that she should be in love. . . ."[4] Zelda had experimented before with George Jean Nathan and even asking Scott's friends to kiss her, bathe her, telling Scott that if he wanted to take a girl, it was alright. Maybe it was as simple as that "after five years of marriage and the experience of motherhood, Zelda feared she had passed the peak of her beauty and had to prove that she was still attractive to men."[5] Maybe it was simply lust, but she knew one thing: she wanted a divorce. "By turns upset and embarrassed by Scott's drinking and pushed into a world of writers, artists and actors as something of a marital appendage, she sought to recover her once strong sense of identity."[6]

Scott stared at her, stunned into silence. His novel had stalled. He was running out of money. He had suspected Zelda might have been toying dangerously close to an affair, but he could not let himself think about it. But now, here it was. It was there in her flushed expression, her declaration that she was in love with Jozan and that she wanted a divorce. All the psychic steam exploded just then. He didn't remember later what he said, just that Zelda accused him of ruining her life and that somebody loved her for who she was and she didn't want to be married to him anymore. Daggers in his heart. Thank God the Nanny and Scottie were not there. They were standing in the villa in the noon heat now. Zelda was watching him, and he could see the pile of the manuscript that had gone no further for the last week. It had just stalled, but now he was writing again. He wanted a confrontation.

*"I suppose the latest thing is to sit back and let Mr. Nobody from Nowhere make love to your wife. Well it that's the idea you can count me out. . . . "*[7]

Scott then "demanded Zelda and Eduardo declare their love before him."[8]

*"You're crazy!" he exploded. "I can't speak about what happened five years ago, because I didn't know Daisy then and I'll be damned if I see how you got within a mile of her unless you brought the groceries to the back door. But all the rest that's a Goddamned lie. Daisy loved me when she married me and she loves me now."*
*"No," said Gatsby shaking his head.*
*"I want to know what Mr. Gatsby has to tell me."*
*"Your wife doesn't love you," said Gatsby. "She's never loved you. She loves me."*
*"You must be crazy," exclaimed Tom automatically.*
*Gatsby sprang to his feet, vivid with excitement.*
*"She never loved you, do you hear?" he cried. "She only married you because I was poor and she was tired of waiting for me. It was a terrible mistake, but in her heart she never loved anyone except me!"*[9]

Zelda refused a showdown, saying Jozan would never consent to that. In fact, Zelda had asked Jozan to fight for her and that she was going to confront Scott and tell him. "I cannot fight," he said gently. "I am much stronger than he."[10] Zelda repeated that she wanted a divorce, and Scott laughed and said he would never give her a divorce. Zelda said she never loved him and that they should have never married.

*"I never loved him," she said with perceptible reluctance.*
*"Not at Kapiolani?" demanded Tom suddenly.*
*"No."*

*"Not that day I carried you down from the Punch Bowl to keep your shoes dry?" There was a husky tenderness in his tone. "Daisy?"[11]*

Zelda shook her head, keeping the image of Jozan in the clean, white sheets smoking a cigarette. She had even ventured to say to him "when we are married," but Jozan had quickly knocked that down. "That's absurd. She loved him so that she never questioned his good faith. If he was unable to marry she thought they could make other arrangements."[12] Scott was shaking his head now, walking back and forth. This was visceral. A gut punch. He knew Zelda flirted. He knew he had to keep his eye on her. But he never thought she would step over the line. But she had. He felt a panic descending on him. He was at the precipice. His marriage was breaking apart, the book he had put his whole career on was not progressing . . . he could not let her go. Scott picked up the glass of gin and threw it down, then marched across the room. He began pacing back and forth, writing again.

*"Daisy loved me when she married me and she loves me now."*
*"No," said Gatsby shaking his head.*
*"She does though. The trouble is that sometimes she gets foolish ideas in her head and doesn't know what she's doing." He nodded sagely.*
*"And what's more, I love Daisy too. Once in a while I go off on a spree and make a fool of myself, but I always come back, and in my heart I love her all the time."*
*"You're revolting."[13]*

Scott stopped and walked up to Zelda and told her he was going "to make a formal complaint to Eduardo's commanding officer and demand that he be transferred."[14]

*"Who are you anyhow?" broke out Tom. "You're one of that bunch that hangs around with Meyer Wolfsheim—that much I happen to know. I've made a little investigation into your affairs and I'll carry it further tomorrow."[15]*

Scott walked around the room and would later brag that he tried to engage Jozan in a fight. "I could have annihilated him in two minutes . . . the kid didn't know his left hand from his right."[16] But he didn't; the best, the only thing he could do was to keep Zelda from seeing Jozan. At least until he finished his book. Scott had referred many times in his letters to Zelda that he understood why they kept princesses locked in towers. He said it so many times she'd requested he quit making the reference in his letters. But now he knew why you locked princesses in towers . . . so they wouldn't go out and have affairs and leave.

Scott stared at the bedroom. "Interior doors in French villas secured from the inside and out, so all Scott most likely did was shut Zelda in a bedroom and pocket the key."[17] He put his drink down and grabbed his wife by the wrist. She fought back, but he dragged her into the bedroom and pushed her down. Zelda spit at him. Scott grabbed her by the arms. He then took three steps out and pulled the door, locking it from the outside. Zelda slammed the door with her fists.

*"I've got my wife locked up in there," explained Wilson calmly. "She's going to stay there till the day after tomorrow and then we're going to move away."[18]*

Scott could hear her crying and then screaming. He poured himself another glass of gin and sat down at his writing table again.

*Mrs. Wilson's voice loud and scolding, downstairs in the garage. "Beat me!" he heard her cry. "Throw me down and beat me, you dirty little coward!"[19]*

This was Zelda's prison. "From July 13 until August when guests arrived, Zelda was confined to Villa Marie. As she writes in *Caesar's Things*, life's possibilities suddenly vanished. It was inexpedient, unexpected and miserable that she should be in love. Janno told her husband that she loved the French officer and her husband locked her in the villa."[20] Scott later wrote in his notebook a feeling of remorse for "proxy in passion, strange encouragement—he was sorry, knowing how she would pay."[21] But it was too late now. Scott went back to the door, still holding the skeleton key. She was crying, of course.

> *The voice begged again to go. "Please Tom! I can't stand this anymore."*
> *Her frightened eyes told that whatever intentions, whatever courage she had, were definitely gone.*
> *"You two start on home Daisy," said Tom. "In Mr. Gatsby's car."*
> *She looked at Tom, alarmed now, but he insisted with magnanimous scorn. "Go on. He won't annoy you. I think he realizes that his presumptuous little flirtation is over."[22]*

Scott then walked over to his writing table and sat down. He picked up his pencil and listened to his wife crying in the locked room. He heard the door handle turn, and then the door slam against the jam. She was throwing her body against it. She was screaming now, her screams going out over the villa patio. It was so damn hot, and Scott wiped his face. Even when she told him she wanted a divorce, he was there, but he was also watching from above. He didn't have all the answers, but he had enough. For now. Scott took one more swallow, listened to his wife crying and slamming the locked door, then began to write once again.

> *Gatsby walked over and stood before her. "Daisy, that's all over now,"*
> *he said earnestly. "It doesn't matter anymore. Just tell him the truth—*
> *that you never loved him and it's all wiped out forever."*
> *She looked at him blindly. "Why—how could I love him—possibly?"[23]*

## CHAPTER 26

# The Confusion of a Simple Mind

## *1924*

BANG! BANG! BANG!

Scott worked on *The Great Gatsby* with his wife locked in his bedroom, drinking gin, smoking Chesterfields, occasionally glancing at the bedroom door that seemed at times it might come off the hinges. *"'Your wife doesn't love you,' said Gatsby. 'She has never loved you. She loves me.'"*[1] The writing was going along very well now. *"I can't tell him in his own house . . . I can't do that, Old Sport."*[2] Scott continued writing with Zelda banging on the door, shouting, and then crying. The pages flew along. *"I did love him once but I loved you even more don't you see?' Gatsby's eyes opened and closed. 'You loved me too?' he repeated."*[3]

"Big Crisis July 13," Scott writes in his ledger. Then several days later, "Good work on novel,"[4] he notes in his ledger again. Years later, Scott would write, "her affair with Eduardo Jozan . . . shook something out of us." Several months later, Scott admitted, "That September 1924, I knew something had happened that could never be repaired. . . . "[5]

-Scott looked up from his desk. She was quiet now. Jozan must be wondering what happened, Scott mused. He looked back down and continued writing, *"So we drove on toward death through the cooling twilight."*[6]

There were explosions outside Zelda's bedroom window. "It was Bastille Day, July 14, the founding of the Republic and in San Raphael a brass band played in the pavilion and there was dancing in the streets."[7] Zelda squinted at the sunshine, feeling like she had been through a war.

The fireworks made it sound like a war had erupted. She gazed out the half-open window at the sun shimmering on the cobalt-blue sea. Her eyes were swollen from crying, and her fist hurt from pounding the door. Her breakfast had been brought in by Scott after he told Scottie mommy was sick and could not be disturbed. She had stayed awake most of the night, listening for Jozan. She had told him she was going to tell Scott, and he must have wondered what happened.

She expected Jozan to fight for her and listened for his footsteps on the drive. He loved her as she loved him, and now he must fight for that love. Zelda stared out the window. "How could she remain with her husband when she loved another? If she loves him there wasn't any answer . . . Adultery is adultery and it would have been impossible for her to love two men at once, to give herself to simultaneous intimacies."[8] She continued to listen for his footsteps on the gravel drive. Zelda paced in the room. He would come. Of course he would and free her from this locked-in prison while Scott sat outside like a troll, writing. But one day passed to another and there was no Jozan. Zelda could not understand how he could have abandoned her and not fought for her. She began to wonder if she had misinterpreted the affair altogether.

Zelda, for all her worldliness, still had a Southern belle's view of the world. "She was accustomed to American men and used to wielding power over them."[9] She didn't speak French very well, and Jozan had only rudimentary English. Later, in her novel *Caesar's Things*, she wrote, "She so hardly spoke the language and was never quite sure what she was saying."[10] Sex had probably the biggest part to play in the affair. Scott had never been the ardent lover and still had Irish Catholic hang-ups if not prudishness about intercourse. He and Zelda never had a satisfactory sex life. "He was not very interested in sex," a friend, Oscar Kalman, recalled. "Not a very lively male animal. Scott liked the idea of sex for its romance and daring but was not strongly sexed and inclined to feel the actual act of sex was messy."[11] Add to that drinking, enforced celibacy, "a tendency toward premature ejaculation and what could only be described as a modestly sized penis."[12]

Zelda had confused sex with love. "She believed that he [Jozan] loved her, but that he avoided any confrontation shows how casually he viewed the romance and how seriously his career. To create a scandal was one thing, but to assume responsibility for someone else's spouse was something else entirely. He [Jozan] wanted a mistress not a wife, best let her go, which he did."[13] But now her husband had "locked her up in the villa."[14] In *Caesar's Things*, Jacob (Scott) tells her "not to leave the premises and Janno (Zelda) wearily replies, 'a locked door is not difficult to comprehend.'"[15]

Zelda would never see Jozan again. He was transferred to Hyères, where the Fitzgeralds had visited earlier in the summer and their relationship ended. He was a young man beginning his career and did not want a wife. Unfortunately, Zelda was a fling on the beach for him where a very interesting American woman had come into his life, but he was content she should get out of it as well. The Riviera was dead for Zelda now. She later wrote, "San Raphael was dead . . . the lush promenade under the trees, so rich and full of life and summer seemed swept of all its content. There was nothing but a cheap café and the leaves in the gutter and dog prowling about."[16]

Later, an aviator's wife gave Zelda a letter from Jozan along with a picture. "Unable to read it she tore it in a hundred little pieces. . . . Thought it broke her heart, she tore the picture . . . what was the use of keeping it . . . there wasn't a way to hold onto the summer . . . whatever it was that wanted from Jacque [Jozan] he took it with him . . . you took what you wanted from life, if you could get it and you did without the rest."[17]

Outside the bedroom, Scott's pencil continued to dance.

*I came into the room half an hour before the bridal dinner and found her lying on her bed as lovely as the June night in her flowered dress . . . and drunk as a monkey. She had a bottle of Sauterne in one hand and a letter in the other. "Graduate me," she muttered. "Never had a drink before, but oh how I do enjoy it.". . . . I rushed out and found her mother's maid and we locked the door and got her into a cold bath. She wouldn't let go of the letter. She took into the bathtub*

*with her and squeezed it up into a wet ball and only let me leave it
in the soap dish when she saw that it was coming to pieces like snow.*[18]

Scott and Zelda struggled through the next few weeks. When Gilbert Seldes and Alice Wadhams Hall stopped by on their honeymoon, they immediately knew something was not right. Zelda's haggard face tipped off Alice that the Fitzgeralds were in trouble. "Love is a funny thing," Alice wrote later. "It says so in the advertisements, in the popular songs on the radio and in the moving pictures. Though it seldom says what do about it, it always shows what havoc is wrought."[19] Zelda had not been sleeping and was extremely agitated, and she was beginning to have abdominal pain. "For that she took Luminol, Atropine, and as a sedative, Dial, a white crystalline barbiturate in tablet form, prescribed as a sleeping aid."[20]

She was inconsolable over the loss of Jozan and becoming more erratic. She began to taunt her jailer husband, and the Halls noted that, one time, as they were driving from Velescure to Saint-Raphaël, they took a hairpin turn on a high cliff. Zelda asked Scott for a cigarette at the very moment he was turning, and as he "rummaged in his pocket with one hand, the car almost veered over the embankment. Zelda laughed hysterically and seemed to get some bizarre pleasure from this moment of control. . . . "[21] Scott had a hard time controlling his characters many times and Zelda was no exception. He later wrote Ludlow Fowler, "I feel old too this summer . . . that's the burden of this novel . . . the loss of those illusions that give such color to the world, so that you don't care whether things are true or false, as long they partake of their magical glory."[22]

The French aviator Jozan would never see Zelda again and never fully understand his impact on the Fitzgeralds. He had left the Riviera but would later recall "that one day the Fitzgeralds left and their friends scattered, each to his own destiny."[23] The writing continued as Scott beat his way toward an ending. *They were careless people, Tom and Daisy—they smashed up things and creatures and then retreated back into their money or their vast carelessness or whatever it was that kept them together, and let other people clean up the mess they had made. . . .*[24]

## CHAPTER 27

# The Death Car

## *1924*

SCOTT LISTENED OUT THE OPEN WINDOW FOR JOZAN TO RESCUE "THE princess locked in the tower"[1] that Scott had prophetically referred to many times in letters to Zelda during their courtship. The late heat of summer dampened his shirt, and his head ached from the gin, the coffee, the posture of being bent over his pad for hours, throwing pencils aside, sharpening others with a small pocketknife, hearing the surf sometimes, but mostly the lost airiness of Southern France in summer. The door thumped, and Scott looked up and stared for a moment, raising his cigarette, smoking meditatively. There was quiet, and he turned back to the page.

> *He strolled over to the garage and found George Wilson sick in his office, really sick, pale as his own hair and shaking all over. Michaelis advised him to go to bed, but Wilson refused, saying that he'd miss a lot of business if he did. While his neighbor was trying to persuade him a violent racket broke out overhead.*[2]

It had been like this for a month. Zelda not leaving her room. Scott watching the door like a centurion. Sometimes he locked it, and sometimes he didn't. She screamed sometimes. Other times, she pounded against the wall. He was turning the corner on his novel in August. On

September 10, Scott wrote Max Perkins. "Now for a promise—the novel will absolutely and definitely be mailed to you before the first of October. I've had to rewrite practically half of it and at present its stored away for a week so I can take a last look at it and see what I've left out . . . there's some intangible sequence lacking somewhere in the middle and a break in interest there inevitably means the failure of the book. It is like nothing I have ever read before."[3]

He followed this with another letter to Max Perkins. "The novel will be done next week. That doesn't mean however that it'll reach America before October 1st as Zelda and I are contemplating careful revision after a weeks complete rest."[4] It is doubtful from the state of their marriage Zelda knew about this letter. Perkins had sent him the cover of the book earlier in the summer, and in the same letter, Fitzgerald wrote, "For Christ's sake don't give anyone that cover you're saving for me. I've written it into the book."[5] The cover was a painting by Francis Cugat done for the book that showed "a woman's face over an amusement park night scene, naked irises of the eyes."[6] Scott was using everything he could for this novel, including the cover of his own book. He finished his letter with a revealing postscript: "It's been a fair summer. I've been unhappy but my work hasn't suffered from it. I am grown at last."[7]

Scott took a brief break from work in September when the Ring Lardners came to Saint-Raphaël and stayed at the Hotel Continental. Ring showed up to dinner with a bottle of Johnnie Walker Red, and the two authors got drunk. Ring later wrote an article for *Liberty* magazine about visiting the Fitzgeralds. "On the following morning we went by train to St. Raphael where who was at the statin to meet us but Mr. and Mrs. F. Scott Fitzgerald. Mr. Fitzgerald is a novelist and Mrs. Fitzgerald is a novelty. They left New York last May because New Yorkers kept mistaking their Long Island home for a real house."[8]

The Fitzgeralds must have greeted the visit with a relief. With the Lardners came glimmers of happier times in Great Neck. "We sat on the porch of the hotel all afternoon admiring the sea and then went out to the Fitzgeralds' for a home-cooked meal. I made Mr. Fitzgerald a present of some rare perfume that said Johnnie Walker on the outside which I had picked up at Marseilles."[9] Ring was Scott's old drinking partner, and he must have felt relief after the dark month. Zelda had not gotten better physically or psychologically after her failed loved affair with Jozan, and the wry, laconic humor of the journalist author was a tonic to the unhappy couple.

For Scott, it was the release of drunken abandonment with Ring with whom he would often go into Manhattan on three-day drunken sprees. He played tour guide to the Lardners during their visit. "Mr. Fitzgerald said we must see Cannes and Nice and Monte Carlo while he was in the vicinity and we set a date to make the trip to those points. Mr. Fitzgerald said he would drive us in his car, but I had often rode with him around Great Neck, Long Island, so I said how could we enjoy the scenery if had to keep watching the road and let's hire a car and a driver."[10]

The Lardners left and took with them the brief respite from their own troubles.

Several days after they left, the concussion of the affair struck. Scott was working late. It was 3:00 a.m. The strange night breeze of the Mediterranean whipped in from the patio through the open door. He had not been able to sleep. His nerves were shot. Zelda had been increasingly more erratic after it was clear the young aviator was not going to rescue her. Her husband had locked her in the bedroom during the day until mid-August, and she still felt imprisoned in her own marriage. She had cleared it in her own head. She was going to leave Scott and Scottie, leave her family for a love affair. In her head, she was leaving for love, but now she had internalized the lost love of Jozan and the realization she wasn't in love with her husband; in fact, she detested him for what he had done to her.

The physical ailments then began. "By September, Zelda's abdominal pains had worsened, accompanied by breathing paralysis she called asthma, more likely anxiety-induced panic attacks."[11] The five-week affair with Eduardo Jozan was coming for its due. Scott was almost finished. He had turned the corner, but now he needed the dramatic incident. He needed the final resolution of the denouement, and between the visits from the Ring Lardners and he and Zelda's fights, he had lost all his psychic steam. He was once again at a crossroads in his book and his marriage.

Scott lit a Chesterfield and looked toward the bedroom door. He no longer locked her in unless she seemed particularly unstable. He knew Jozan had been transferred and that Zelda could not see him even if she wanted to. The villa was quiet except for the slight swish of the Mediterranean. Moonlight fell in patches like littered glass on the patio. The long curtains twirled in long, ghostly shoots of light. Scott stared at the door and heard nothing. It was damn quiet. Too quiet.

Scott stood up and walked to the door slightly ajar. He pushed it open and saw the mound of covers with the moonlight draping the bunched sheets. Scott walked in quietly and saw Zelda face down on her pillow. He took another step and felt something crack under his foot. He picked up the glass vial. It was Zelda's Dial, the sedative she took for anxiety and to sleep. Scott had taken it before as well, but what stopped his heart was the dark glass vial was empty. It had at least ten pills in it before. Scott grabbed Zelda's shoulder. She didn't move. He turned her over and slapped her cheeks lightly, then put his hand over her mouth and put his ear to her chest. Zelda was limp. He heard nothing, and then a faint heartbeat. He put his ear to her mouth, detecting the shallowest of breathing. Scott frantically tried to get Zelda up, but it was like lifting a dead person. He needed help. Scott ran from the room and jumped into the Renault, driving furiously for the Hotel Du Cap, where the Murphys were staying. He drove down the darkened narrow streets so like the two-lane highways on Long Island. Even now, he was writing.

*A moment later she rushed out into the dusk, waving her hands and shouting . . . The death car as the newspapers called it didn't stop it came out of the gathering darkness, wavered tragically for a moment, and then disappeared around the next bend.*[12]

Scott reached the hotel and grabbed a candle in the lobby and made his way to the Murphys' room. The daughter, Honoria, answered the door. "He was green faced, holding a candle, trembling—Zelda had taken an overdose of sleeping pills. We went with him. . . . "[13] The Murphys drove back with Scott to the villa, flying through the night while wild whips of panic went over him. Scott drove as fast as he could, not knowing if they would find Zelda alive or dead, keeping his eyes on the road signs flashing by. They reached the villa and rushed up the stairs into the bedroom where Zelda was still laying in the exact same position Scott had left her. Her night gown was slightly open.

*The other car, the one going toward New York, came to rest a hundred yards beyond and its driver hurried back to where Myrtle Wilson, her life violently extinguished, knelt in the road and mingled her thick dark blood with the dust. Michaelis and this man reached her first, but when they had torn open her shirtwaist still damp with perspiration they saw that her left breast was swinging loose like a flap and there was no need to listen to her heart beneath. The mouth was wide open and ripped a little at the corners, as though she had choked a little in giving up the tremendous vitality she had stored so long.[14]*

Sarah and Gerald lifted Zelda up and shouted at her and shook her. Zelda, finally, groggily moved her head. Then they all lifted Zelda to her feet and began to walk her through the villa. "Sara walked her up and down, up and down, to keep her from going to sleep. We tried to make her drink olive oil, but Zelda murmured, 'Sara . . . don't make me take that, please. If you drink too much you turn into a Jew.'"[15] They continued walking Zelda, inducing her to vomit. She had clearly tried to commit suicide, and it was years before the Murphys would reveal the attempt to Calvin Tompkins, who then shared it with biographer Nancy Milford. It was the final evolution of the Jozan affair. The spurned lover who takes her own life out of grief, guilt, love. Neither Fitzgerald ever spoke of Zelda's attempt to end her life. Scott would only cryptically refer to it by writing, "that September 1924, I knew something had happened that could never be repaired."[16] But he never specified what that "something" was, and he was blind to his wife's unhappiness, only to record in his ledger in September "trouble clear away," and then "last sight of Jozan."[17]

But he had his ending. Scott returned to his writing while Zelda recovered the next day. His marriage was dead and his heart broken, but he kept it in a place apart from himself.

*Daisy and Tom were sitting opposite each other at the kitchen table with a plate of cold fried chicken between them and two bottles of ale. He was talking intently across the table at her, and in his earnestness his hand had fallen and covered her own. Once in a while she looked up at him and nodded. They weren't happy and neither of them had touched the chicken or the ale. And yet they weren't unhappy either.[18]*

Scott didn't know what was left of his marriage, but what he and Zelda had before was gone. He had lost everything on the Riviera and had only survived by physically blocking his wife from leaving. His muse could never leave, but love had. He had sacrificed everything to finish his book, and the world had changed forever.

*He must have felt that he had lost the old warm world, paid a high price for living too long with a single dream. He must have looked up at an unfamiliar sky though the startling leaves and shivered as he found what a grotesque thing a rose is and how raw the sunlight was upon the scarcely created grass. A new world, material without being real, where poor ghosts, breathing dreams like air, drifted fortuitously about . . . like that pale ashen figure that was gliding toward him through the amorphous trees. The chauffer, one of Wolfsheim's people, heard the shots.[19]*

In September, Scott wrote in his ledger, "hard work sets in,"[20] after completing a rough first draft. In October, he wrote, "working at high pressure to finish,"[21] and, "last sight of Jozan." Scott finished *The Great Gatsby* in late October and wrote to Max Perkins the manuscript would be coming soon and alerted him to a young writer he had heard of. "This is to tell you about a young man named Ernest Hemingway, who lives in Paris, (an American) writes for the transatlantic review and has a brilliant future. Ezra Pound published a collection of his short pieces in Paris at some place like the Egotist Press, I haven't it here now, but it's remarkable and I'd look him up right way. He's the real thing."[22]

In November, Scott recorded in his ledger, "novel off at last."[23]

# CHAPTER 28

# That Awful Thing

## *1924*

SCOTT WAS DRUNK WITH PAIN NOW. THE PAIN KNOCKED OUT THE GIN, and there were explosions of light in his head as the fists landed all over his face. The Italians hated Scott almost as much as he hated them. This self-satisfied drunk American would feel their wrath. He represented everything they despised about the Americans: their arrogance, their money, their demand that the world bend to them. They needed no pretext to beat him. He had punched a plainclothes Italian policeman in the face. They needed nothing, and they took turns beating him. No one knew he was an author who had just written a masterpiece. To them, he was an American punching bag.

Scott would never speak about the beating. He would later say "what had happened to him was so awful that nothing could make any difference."[1] But in *Tender is the Night*, he relived the moment with Dick Diver. " . . . He was clubbed down and fists and boots beat on him in a savage tattoo. He felt his nose break like a shingle and his eyes jerk as if they had snapped back on a rubber band into his head. A rib splintered under a stamping heel. Momentarily he lost consciousness, regained it as he was raised to a sitting position and his wrists jerked together with handcuffs. He struggled automatically. The plainclothes lieutenant whom he had knocked down, stood dabbing his jaw with a handkerchief and looking into it for blood; he came over to Dick, poised himself, drew back his arm and smashed him to the floor. When Doctor Diver lay still a pail of water was sloshed over him. One of his eyes opened dimly as he was being dragged along by the wrists through a bloody haze . . . choking and sobbing, over vague irregular surfaces into some small place where he was dropped upon a stone floor. The men went out, a door clanged, he was alone."[2]

The author who had just finished *The Great Gatsby* was lying in a dirty Italian cell, bloodied and unconscious. It had just been a month before that he had stood on the patio of the villa looking at the Mediterranean one last time. The Jozan affair had killed any allure the Riviera held for Scott and for Zelda. "The lush promenade under the trees, so rich and full of life and summer swept of all its content. There was nothing but a cheap café and the leaves in the gutter and a dog prowling about."[3] But more than that, Scott had finished *The Great Gatsby*. It was over. It was time to go. He had just sent off the manuscript to Max Perkins on October 27.

"Dear Max, under separate cover I am sending you my third novel, *The Great Gatsby*. I think that at last I've done something really my own, but how good my own is, is something to be seen. The book is only a little over fifty thousand words long but I believe, as you know, that Whitney Darrow has the wrong psychology about prices (and about what class constitute the book buying public now that the lowbrows go to movies) and I'm anxious to charge two dollars for it and have a full size book. Of course I want the binding to be absolutely uniform with my other books—the stamping too—and the jacket we discussed before. This time I don't want any signed blurbs on the jacket—not Mencken's for Lewis or Howards or anyone's. I'm tired of being the author of *This Side of Paradise* and I want to start over. . . . "[4]

Scott believed his third novel would be a hit financially and anticipated a big serial rights sale where the novel would run in the magazines in an abbreviated form. But he also knew because of the strong content some magazines wouldn't be interested, and he had already broken with Hearst over the short stories he failed to provide after the front-page photo of he and Zelda. Scott did not want to slow down publication for the serialization unless it was very lucrative. *This Side of Paradise* and *The Beautiful and the Damned* had both been serialized for sizeable advances, and Scott believed *Gatsby* would bring even more. "About serialization, I am bound under contract to show it to Hearst but I am asking a prohibitive price, Long hates me and it's not a very serialized book. If they should take it—they won't—it would put publication in the fall. Otherwise you can publish it in the spring. When Hearst turns it down, I' m going to offer it to Liberty for $15,000 on condition that they publish it in ten weekly installments before April 15. If they don't want it. I shan't serialize."[5]

Scott was still unsure of the title and proposed another suggestion. "I have an alternative title: *Gold hatted Gatsby.* After you've read the book, let me know what you think about the title. Naturally I won't get a night's sleep until I hear from you, but do tell me the absolute truth, your first impression of the book, and tell me anything that bothers you."[6]

They left for Rome on November 7. Scott was mentally exhausted, and the seven-thousand-dollar nest egg was gone. He would have to write some short stories while waiting for the proofs to revise in Italy. After a gloomy drive across Italy with stops in Savona and San Remo, they arrived in Rome and checked in to Hotel Quirinale on Via Nazionale. The hotel was fashionable, but "November happened to be flea season and the insects were catapulting from everywhere from the gilded filigree of the hotels chandeliers onto its draperies and tablecloths."[7] Italy was cold and gloomy as well, so they settled into the Hotel des Prince with a view of John Keats's house. "The sheets were damp and the nights were perforated by the snores of the people next door,"[8] Zelda wrote later, still suffering from abdominal distress.

Scott wired Max Perkins for a $750 advance, increasing his indebtedness to $5,000 to his publisher. They ate Bel Paese cheese and drank Corvo wine waiting for the proofs of *The Great Gatsby* that Scott would revise. The Fitzgeralds were still hot copy, and a paper in Rome covered Fitzgerald's arrival under the headline "American Writer Finds a Home in Rome." The theme of the article is their finances delivered in a jocular style, but the truth was the Fitzgeralds were broke and the article shows they are still smarting from being ripped off by their servants.

"Mr. Scott Fitzgerald the American novelist and short story writer has arrived in Rome where he intends to spend the winter. Mr. Fitzgerald is accompanied by Mrs. Fitzgerald and their little girl, Scottie . . . 'The main and avowed purpose of our European sojourn being to keep the wolf from the door,' explained Mr. Fitzgerald. 'We thought it advisable to find out her whereabouts as soon as possible. We do not expect her to return the visit.' Since after their arrival in Europe the author of *This Side of Paradise* [and] *The Beautiful and the Damned* and his family have lived in almost every country of the continent. Their experiences in cosmopolitan house getting and keeping is consequently as wide as their doctrine and the 'Thirty Six Thousand Dollars a Year with no Luxury Margin' articles . . . 'what at first seemed a secluded villa just right for us to live in quietly,' said Mrs. Fitzgerald with her brightest smile, 'had a habit of developing into a sort of charity institution, owing to the mysterious complaints by which the domestic personnel was stricken down by necessitating of their relatives, sometimes down to the third and fourth generations.'"[9]

There is an accompanying picture of Scott, Zelda, and Scottie sitting among crumbling Roman ruins by a column, with Scott in a dark suit with a cigarette clipped in his fingers, Scottie in Zelda's lap, and Zelda peering unhappily at the camera. The setting in the ruins is a fitting backdrop. Scott had to write three stories for money that exercised some of the damage from the Jozan affair. "Love in the Night," "Not in the Guidebook," and "The Adjustor" all explored his marital problems. "The Adjuster" went to the heart of the way Scott saw his wife and the reason for their unhappiness. "We make an agreement with children that they can sit in the audience without helping to make the play . . . but if they still sit in the audience after they're grown, somebody's got to work double time for them so that they can enjoy the light and glitter of the world."[10]

Clearly, this was pointed at Zelda.

Scott and Zelda had hoped by going to Italy they might save some money on the exchange rate, but this fantasy vanished with the cab ride in Rome. The cab driver had taken them back to the hotel, but Scott was not going to pay him a hundred lire for the fare. Scott had been drinking all night, and Zelda was standing on the curb. In Scott's mind, they were broke because the servants in the Riviera had ripped them off along with the tradesman, the grocers, the cafes. Scott had enough. The man got in Scott's face, swearing in Italian. Scott pushed him away, and the driver came right back. He was not backing down.

"First there was one cab driver," he wrote later in the short story, "The High Cost of Macaroni," "and I had a little of the best of it, then there were two and I was having a little the worst of it. But I didn't think I was and when the meddlesome stranger stepped between us I was in no mood to have it stop there and I pushed him impatiently out of the way. He came back, persistently, lurching in between us, talking in a stream of Italian, doing his best it seemed to me, to interrupt my offenses and to the advantage of the taximan. . . . Blind with anger I turned on him quickly and caught him under the point of the chin, whereupon, rather to my surprise, he sat down."[11]

Scott had slugged a plainclothes policeman, and this resulted in his arrest and being taken back to the police station, where he was badly beaten by the Carabinieri at the jail. Zelda would eventually have to pay $100 and enlist the aid of the US consulate and journalist Howard Coxe, a Princetonian they had met with the crew filming *Ben-Hur* in Rome. Scott later called the beating and the subsequent night in jail "just about the rottenest thing that ever happened to me in my life."[12] He later reflected in *Tender is The Night*. "What had happened to him was so awful that nothing could make any difference unless he could choke it to death, and as this was unlikely, he was hopeless. He would be a different person henceforward, and in his raw state he had bizarre feelings of what the new self would be. The matter had about it the impersonal quality of God."[13]

After being freed, Scott slowly recovered from the beating and a lingering flu in their thin-walled and damp hotel room. "The doctor washed off the rest of the blood and the oily sweat, set his nose, his fractured ribs and fingers, disinfected the smaller wounds, and put a hopeful dressing on the eye."[14] On November 18, he received a letter from Max Perkins that improved his mood.

"I think the novel is a wonder. I'm taking it home to read again and shall then write my impression in full, but it has a vitality to an extraordinary degree and glamour and a great deal of underlying thought of unusual quality. It has a kind of mystic atmosphere at times that you infused into parts of Paradise and have not since used. It is a marvelous fusion, into a unit of presentation, of the extradentary incongruities of life today. As for sheer writing, it's astonishing. Now deal with this question: various gentlemen here don't like the title, in fact none like it but me. To me, the strange incongruity of the words in it sounds the note of the book. But the objectors are more practical men than I. Consider as quickly as you can the question of a change. But if you do not change you will have to leave that note off the wrap. Its presence would injure it too much and good as the wrap always seemed, it now seems a masterpiece for the book. So judge of the value of the title where it stands alone and write or cable your decision the instant you can."[15]

Zelda preferred the title *The Great Gatsby*, and Scott let it stand. Scott did feel better, but the quarrels with Zelda along with drinking continued unabated. An operation to allow Zelda to become pregnant again, removing scar tissue from her earlier abortion, a move surely to get their marriage back on track, went badly and left her with a lingering ovarian infection along with severe attacks of what eventually would be diagnosed as colitis. Clearly, the physical ramifications of the Jozan affair were coming for their due. Max Perkins then sent another letter two days later.

"I think you have every right to be proud of the book. It is an extraordinary book, suggestive of all sorts of thoughts and moods. You adopted exactly the right method of telling it, that of employing a narrator who is more of a spectator than an actor . . . in the eyes of Dr. Eckleburg various readers will see different significances; but their presence gives a superb touch to the whole thing; great unblinking eyes, expressionless, looking down upon the human scene. It's magnificent! . . . . The presentation of Tom, his place, Daisy and Jordan, and the unfolding of their characters is unequalled so far as I know. . . . The amount of meaning you get into a sentence, the dimensions and intensity of the impressions you make a paragraph carry, are most extraordinary. The manuscript is full of phrases that make a scene blaze with life. . . . You once told me you were not a natural writer, My God! You have plainly mastered the craft, of course, but you needed far more than craftsmanship for this."[16]

Scott responded on December 1: "Your wire and your letters made me feel like a million dollars—I'm sorry I could make no better response than a telegram whining for money. But the long siege of the novel winded me a little and I've been slow on starting the stories on which I must live . . . thanks enormously for making up the $5,000. I know I don't technically deserve it . . . but since you force it on me . . . I will accept it. I hope to Christ you get ten times it back on *Gatsby* and I think perhaps you will."[17]

Money problems were never far away, but the money from Perkins gave them some relief, and Scott and Zelda killed time by mingling with the American movie crew filming *Ben-Hur* while waiting for the proofs. Scott quickly became infatuated with the film's young star, Carmel Myers, and openly flirted with her. He wrote later that she was "the most exquisite thing I have met yet . . . as nice as she is beautiful."[18] Zelda saw this and was receiving attention from journalist Howard Coxe and allowed Scott's "inconsequential but gallant gestures."[19] At a Christmas ball held by the movie company, Coxe took Zelda home when she began feeling ill. Zelda rejected Coxe's overtures and went to her hotel room alone. But Coxe later, in the bar with Scott present, bragged, "I could sleep with Zelda any time I wanted to."[20]

Scott flew into a rage, feeling the salt in the still-fresh wound from Jozan, and wrote in his ledger later for December 1924, "depression . . . row in café . . . Xmas Row . . . reconciliation."[21] On December 22, the proofs arrived for his revisions. Scott went on the wagon to give the proofs the best he had to offer. "They had a Christmas tree in their hotel room hung with silver bells . . . but they expected too much from Christmas, tried too hard, drank too much, destroyed their festivities."[22] The best Zelda and Scott could hope for was that 1925 would be better than 1924. At least *The Great Gatsby* would be coming out.

## CHAPTER 29

# Waiting for Gatsby

## *1925*

IT RAINED CONTINUALLY IN ROME, AND THE HOTEL ROOM HAD BECOME intolerably small. Scott tried to find an office to rent but was unsuccessful. The quarreling increased while he worked on the proofs for *The Great Gatsby*. Zelda was still ill with an abdominal infection. Scott wrote to his friend Bishop optimistically: " . . . the cheerfulest things in my life are first Zelda and second the hope that my book has something extraordinary about it. I want to be extravagantly admired again." But his ledger cryptically revealed more about the winter in Rome: " . . . ill feeling with Zelda."[1]

Scott worked on the proofs of *Gatsby* for two months, addressing problems that Max Perkins had pointed out. The day before Christmas, Scott wrote Perkins a long letter. "I'm a bit (not very dangerously) stewed tonight and I'll probably write you a long letter. We're living in a small unfashionable but most comfortable hotel at 525 a month, including tips, meals, etc. Rome does not particularly interest me but it's a big year here, and early in the spring we're going to Paris. There's no use telling you my plans because they're usually just about as unsuccessful as to work as religious prognosticators are as to the End of the World. . . . "[2]

The biggest problem was where the confrontation over Daisy's affair with Gatsby should take place. Fitzgerald had centered on polo grounds, a baseball game, Central Park. But it was while he was in Rome in the small damp apartment with Zelda ill in bed or recovering from their latest quarrel that he decided the confrontation would take place in New York at the Plaza Hotel. As he mulled over the changes, he also mulled over the Jozan affair with Zelda hovering nearby. "The Chapter 7 scene will never be quite up to the mark—I've worried about it too long and I can't quite place Daisy's [Zelda's] reaction. But I can improve it a lot. It isn't imaginative thinking that's lacking it's because I'm automatically prevented from thinking it out over again because I must get the characters to New York in order to have the catastrophe on the road going back and I must have it that way."[3] Scott reworked the proofs.

*"But it's so hot," insisted Daisy, on the verge of tears, "and everything's so confused. Let's all go to town."*[4]

On January 24, Scott wrote Max Perkins, explaining the problems he had addressed. Fitzgerald's revisions in the proof stage were extensive and done while the white-hot light of Zelda's betrayal was still on him. "I want Myrtle Wilsons breast ripped off—it's exactly the thing, I think, and I don't want to chop up the good scenes by too much tinkering . . . Orgastic is the adjective for orgasm and it expresses exactly the intended ecstasy It's not a bit dirty. I'm much more worried about the disappearance of Tom and Myrtle . . . I think it's alright but I'm not sure."[5] Then, on February 18, he wrote Max again after having addressed all the problems Perkins had brought up and infusing Gatsby with the miasmic flavor of a man betrayed and one facing his mortality.

*I was thirty. Before me stretched the portentous menacing road of a new decade . . . the promise of a decade of loneliness a thinning list of single men to know, a thinning briefcase of enthusiasm, thinning hair.*[6]

To Max, Scott relayed his satisfaction with the book. "After six weeks of uninterrupted work the proof is finished and the last of it goes to you this afternoon. On the whole it's been very successful labor. 1. I've brought Gatsby to life. 2. I've accounted for his money. 3. I've fixed up the two weak chapters. 4. I've improved his first party. 5. I've broken up his long narrative in Chapter VIII . . . We're moving to Capri. We hate

Rome. I'm behind financially and have to write three short stories. Then I try another play and by June, I hope, begin my new novel."[7]

An early weathervane of *Gatsby*'s reception occurred when Scott's agent, Harold Ober, reported he couldn't sell the serialization rights to the magazines. Scott had hoped to get $15,000 to $20,000 for *Gatsby* serialization, which was a great way to advertise the book before publication. Hearst magazines had first refusal rights, and editor Ray Long rejected the book because it was too strong for his female audience. Then John Wheeler of *Liberty* magazine turned it down, saying, "it's too ripe for us. Running only one serial as we do, we could not publish this story with as many mistresses and as much adultery as there is in it."[8] Only *College Humor* made an offer for $10,000, which Scott turned down, not wanting to delay publication for five months while waiting for the magazine to come out. Also, he saw it's publication in the magazine as tarnishing the novel. "Most people who saw it advertised in *College Humor* would be sure that *Gatsby* was a great halfback and that would kill it in book form."[9]

Still, the rejections rattled Scott's already-strained prepublication jitters, and he doubled down on his drinking while Zelda recovered. With an April 10 publication date looming, the Fitzgeralds left the gloomy hotel room in Rome and drove to Naples, then booked passage on a ferry for a two-hour ride to the sunny island of Capri. They booked the top-floor suite at the Tiberio Palace Hotel with a bright balcony overlooking the sea. Zelda later described it as "a high white hotel . . . scalloped about the base by the rounded roofs of Capri, cupped to catch rain which never falls."[10] Scott dug in to write some more stories while Zelda began getting injections for the lingering colitis and infection. Scott wrote his agent. "We've had a hell of a time here. My wife's been sick in bed three weeks and there isn't a typist nearer than Naples—the farmer who did this kept it for ten days at the other end of the island. I have another ready if he ever brings it back. Good stories write themselves bad ones have to be written so this took up about three weeks. And look at it. I'd rather not offer it to the *Post* because everybody sees the *Post* but I know its saleable and I need the money . . . I don't know what's the matter with me. I can't seem to keep out of debt."[11]

Scott then looked up his literary idol, Scottish novelist Compton Mackenzie. Scott had admired his work greatly while at Princeton, reading Mackenzie's novel, *Sinister Street*, and then his second, *Carnival*. Scott was deflated to find the famous novelist dull and now producing what Scott considered cheap commercial fiction to meet financial obligations. "Scott told Bishop that the author of much admired *Sinister Street* was merely polite, handsome, and pleasantly monotonous. Scott felt Mackenzie had been wounded by the war in the way Wells had."[12]

Waiting for the publication of *The Great Gatsby*, Scott hoped the book would not only put him over the top critically but financially. He feared that if *Gatsby* failed to perform, he could easily find himself in the same situation as Compton Mackenzie. Zelda's abdominal infection finally subsided after five weeks in bed, and she began daily walks up to "the scalloped . . . high white hotel, through devious dark alleys that house the island's Rembrandt butcher shops and bakeries."[13] Scott's aunt, Annabel, visited the Fitzgeralds during this time.

Scott's nerves got the best of him, worrying about the length of the book at fifty thousand words, the lack of a strong female character, the fact the novel dealt with the rich, and now the issue with the violence and sex. On March 7, Scott wired Perkins to change the title to *Gold Hatted Gatsby* or *Trimalchio*. Perkins wired back on March 9 that "title change would cause delay and bad confusion."[14] Scott then, in a fit of doubt, cabled him again on March 19. "Crazy about title UNDER THE RED WHITE AND BLUE STOP WHAT WOULD DELAY BE."[15] Max Perkins responded, saying it would delay publication. It was simply too late. Scott wasn't even sure anymore what the publication date was.

On March 31, Scott wrote his editor, "As the day approaches my nervousness increases. Tomorrow is the 1st and your wire says the 10th. I'll be here until the 25th probably later so if the book prospers I'll expect some sort of cable before I leave for Paris. All letters that you write after the 15th of April should be addressed to the Guaranty Trust Company, Paris, but if there's any dope in the first two or three days of publication. I'd love a reassuring line here, even if the success doesn't justify a cable . . . I had or rather saw a letter from my uncle who had seen a preliminary announcement of the book. He said, 'it sounded as if it were very much like his others.' This is only a vague impression of course but I wondered if we could think of some way to advertise it so that people who are perhaps weary of assertive jazz and society novels might not dismiss it as 'just another book like his others.' I confess that today the problem baffles me—all I can think of is to say in general to avoid such phrases 'a picture of New York life' or 'modern society—though as that is exactly what the book is, it's hard to avoid them.'"[16]

The Fitzgeralds did not stay in Capri very long. Scott was too nervous and wanted to be in Paris to gauge reaction, and they left on April 10, the day of publication, and he wrote Max on his way to Paris. "The book comes out today and I am overcome with fears and forebodings. Supposing women didn't like the book because it has no important woman in it, and critics don't like it because it dealt with the rich and contained no peasants borrowed out of Tess in it and set to work in Idaho? Suppose it didn't even wipe out my debt to you. Why it will have to sell 20,000 copies to even do that! In fact all my confidence is gone . . . I'm sick of the book myself . . . I wrote it over at least five times and I still feel that what should be the strong scene (in the Hotel) is hurried and ineffective."[17]

Their odyssey to Paris was a bad omen. They had planned on driving to Paris, but Zelda still was not strong, and they booked passage on the *SS President Garfield* for Marseilles. The Renaults top was damaged from being loaded on the ship, and rather than pay to have it repaired, Zelda convinced a mechanic to remove it. They then drove back to Southern France in the Renault, but torrential rains stopped them in Lyon, where a mechanic showed them that the car had been run without oil or water. They garaged the car and continued on to Paris by train. It did not bode well for publication day. Scott was a wreck. He had gone all-in. He had given everything he had, wrecked his marriage, his health, Zelda's health, been beaten by the Italian police, and now the book he had put everything into was coming out. He was terrified that his very best might not be good enough. On April 11, Scott cabled Max Perkins in the morning two words.

"ANY NEWS."[18]

# CHAPTER 30

# The Germs of Bitterness

## *1925*

THE FITZGERALDS RENTED AN APARTMENT AT 14 RUE DE TILSITT. IT was near the Arc de Triomphe, and they leased it for eight months. The fifth-floor walkup was not bright. A photograph of the Fitzgeralds taken the following Christmas shows them in front of a Christmas tree all doing a chorus line kick. Scott is in an ill-fitting wool suit that hangs on him with thick-soled black shoes one might see on a tradesman. Zelda has a long twenties dress on with a tight smile. She is holding Scottie's hand, who does the kick biting her lip. They are the supposed to be the happy, prosperous Fitzgeralds, kicking their heels at their good fortune and enjoying the good life in Paris. Nothing could be further from the truth.

Novelist Louis Bromfield picked up right away that all was not right. To him, the apartment "represented to some degree the old aspirations and yearning for stability, but somehow got only halfway and was neither one thing nor the other . . . the furniture was gilt Louis XVI but a suite from the Galleries Lafayette (department store). The wallpaper was the usual stripe stuff in dull colors that went with that sort of flat. It was all rather like a furniture shop window and I always had the impression that the Fitzgeralds were camping there between two worlds."[1]

Zelda zeroed in on the problem with their time in Paris in the apartment right away. She said the flat "smelled of a church chancery because it was impossible to ventilate . . . a perfect breeding ground for the germs of bitterness they brought from the Riviera."[2] Those germs of bitterness were compounded by the publication of *The Great Gatsby* on April 10, 1925. The dedication page read "To Zelda," and the price was $2.00, with a first printing of 20,780 copies. To Scott's wire asking for news, Max Perkins shot back a cryptic, heartbreaking reply on April 20: "Sales situation doubtful, excellent reviews."[3]

This news crushed Fitzgerald, who was hoping for a financial windfall to put his ship right. "Your telegram depressed me . . . I hope I'll find better news in Paris am writing you from Lyons. There's nothing more to say until I hear more. If the book fails commercially it will be from one of two reasons or both. The title is only fair, rather bad than good. And most important, the book contains no important women characters and women control the fiction market at present."[4]

The sales did not improve. The bookstores just did not order up. The book was thin, and the subject matter of a bootlegger trying to get the girl of his dreams didn't catch the public's attention. Scott would eventually earn $6,261, which cancelled his debt to Scribner's but did nothing to take him away from the grind of writing for the magazines. Early on, Scott could see the writing on the wall. He was still hoping for a sale of seventy-five thousand, but he wrote Perkins that he would continue writing, "if it will support me with no more intervals of trash, I'll go on as a novelist. If not, I'm going to quit, come home and learn the movie business. I can't reduce our scale of living and I can't stand this financial insecurity."[5]

Even Perkins assessment that the reviews were excellent was a bit of sugar for a bitter pill. Scott, already desperate for any good news on the book, wrote Max on April 22, "I suppose you've sent the book to Collins (British publisher). If not, please do, and let me know right away. If he won't take it because of its flop we might try Capes (another British publisher) I'm miserable at owing you all that money—if I'd taken the serial money I could have at least squared up with you. I've had enthusiastic letters from Mencken and Wilson—the latter says he's reviewing it for that *Chicago Tribune* syndicate he writes for. I think all the reviews I've seen except two have been stupid and lousy. Someday they'll eat grass by

God! This thing, both the effort and the result, have hardened me and I think now that I'm much better than any of the young Americans without exception."[6]

In fact, the reviews were not excellent but more mixed. Ruth Hale of the *Brooklyn Eagle* told Max Perkins at a party "that the new book by your enfant terrible is really terrible."[7] Perkins took a beating from the sales and advertising departments at Scribner's, who had bet heavily on Fitzgerald's book. "So many people have attacked me about *The Great Gatsby* that I feel bruised," he wrote Elisabeth Lemmon, "but they don't know. They can't see that Fitzgerald is a satirist. The fact that he throws a glamour over vice—if he didn't have it there would be none—prevents them from seeing that he lays a lash upon the vicious." Perkins knew before anyone else that Fitzgerald had outgrown his public. "His virtuosity has made a popular novelist of one who is above the heads of the multitudes."[8]

Scott had tapped his literary contacts and sent an early review copy to Edmund Wilson, who reviewed it the day after publication on April 11 and wrote to Scott, "it is undoubtedly in some ways the best thing you have done—the best planned, the best sustained, the best written." This was followed by Mencken's assessment which damned the book with faint praise. "*The Great Gatsby* fills me with pleasant sentiments. I think it is incomparably the best piece of work you have done . . . my one complaint is that the basic story is somewhat trivial, that it reduces itself to a sort of anecdote . . . but God will forgive you for that."[9]

In his published review, Menken gave Fitzgerald high marks but could not resist a final jab. "I certainly don't think much of *The Great Gatsby* as a story. It is in part too well made and in part incredible. But as a piece of writing is it sound and laudable work."[10] Menken was a good friend of Scott, but with friends like these, who needs enemies. He dismissed the plot of *The Great Gatsby* as trivial, and though Scott thanked him profusely, he must have felt the jab from a friend he admired and whose approval he sought. Gertrude Stein and Edith Wharton lauded the book but with qualifications. Gertrude Stein gave the bone to Fitzgerald: "Here we are and have read your book and it is a good book. . . . You write naturally in sentences and one can read all of them and that among other things is a comfort."[11] Edith Wharton quickly pointed out that the Gatsby character was never really clear. "My present quarrel with you is only this, that to make Gatsby really great you ought to have given us his early career instead of as short resume of it."[12]

T. S. Eliot, the author of *The Waste Land*, wrote, "it seems to be the first step that American fiction has taken since Henry James."[13] These reviews made Scott feel good about the book, but these were Fitzgerald's if not friends, his literary circle. Other critics were not so tepid. On April 12, the *New York World* ran a review under the headline "F. Scott Fitzgerald's Latest a Dud." Then Ruth Hale of the *Brooklyn Daily Eagle* took her shot with the headline, "Fitzgerald is a Strange Little Bird."[14] She then went for the jugular. "I can't make head or tale of him. I did not read *This Side of Paradise* until I had my head talked off about it so that it fell a little short of what I had been led to expect . . . in order to set myself straight about him, I read all his other books the moment they came out and they did seem to me to be terrible. Now I have just read *The Great Gatsby* . . . with a note on the jacket to the effect it is a magical living book, blended of irony, romance and mysticism . . . find me one chemical trace of magic, life, irony, romance or mysticism in all of *The Great Gatsby*. . . . Why he should be called an author, or why any of us should behave as if he were, has never been explained satisfactorily to me."[15]

Ruth Snyder let go with a sidewinder in *The New York Evening*, with a plot summary that ended with, "We are quite convinced that after reading *The Great Gatsby* that Mr. Fitzgerald is not one of the great American writers today."[16] Scott's literary mentor from Princeton and close friend John Peale Bishop didn't like the brevity of the book (at 218 pages) and "the vagueness of Gatsby." *The Herald Tribune* postulated that "though Scott had managed the exact tone and shade of contemporary life, he had not yet gone below that glittering surface, except by a kind of happy accident."[17] Even Ring Lardner, who had read the book in proofs, concerned himself with errors in the book and gave little praise at all to the book's merits: "Perhaps it's not perfect!" Max wrote Scott on April 25, 1912: "It's one thing to ride a sleepy cob of talent to perfection and quite another to master a wild young thoroughbred of talent."[18]

These Gatling gun of reviews rained down on Scott, who was still hoping that sales might pick up on the book, but this was not to be. "There's no use for indignation against the long suffering public when even a critic who likes the book fails to be fundamentally held . . . most of the reviews floundered around in a piece of work that obviously they failed to understand and tried to give it reviews that committed them neither pro or con until someone of culture had spoken. . . . We have taken an apartment here from May 12th to January 12th, eight months where I shall do my best. What six months in Italy! Christ! I'm hoping that by some miracle the book will go up to 23,000 and wipe off my debt to you. I haven't been out of debt now for three years and with the years it grows heavy on my aging back."[19]

It was painfully clear to Scott that even with the sale of the movie rights of *The Great Gatsby*, his fundamental situation had remained unchanged. While the movie sale gave him enough money to clear the board, he would still have to continue to write for the magazines. He had taken his shot to write to the very top of his ability, but in letters to friends, he referred to his book as *Gatsby's Flop*. He was right. The book, by the fall of 1925, was dead and not in the bookstores. The only way to get a copy of *The Great Gatsby* for Christmas, even for F. Scott Fitzgerald, was to order it directly from Scribner's.

The next year, the novel was finally serialized in *Famous Story Magazine* in five issues from April to August, and for a quarter, people could read the chopped-up novel. A British edition was published in 1926 in England by Chatto & Windus and quickly died off into the remaindered dust. A French translation in 1926 went nowhere as well, along with a German translation. A play was produced that opened at the New York Ambassador Theatre on February 2, 1926. It ran for 113 performances with mixed reviews and closed in May of 1926. The silent movie of *Gatsby* was released in November 1926 with a line of Busby Berkley Dancing girls and quickly fell into obscurity with no print surviving of the nitrate film that probably disintegrated in some dusty vault and then was pitched. *The Great Gatsby* then, incredibly, fell into literary obscurity and essentially disappeared.

From the publication of *The Great Gatsby*, movie and serial sales, and the play, Scott received $25,000 in 1925, which was very good money, but of course, it didn't last. Scott lost himself in drinking again while Zelda tried to carve out a life with painting and writing, but the rift deepened between them. They hooked up with the Murpheys once again and met them for dinner at the St. Paul de Vence in the mountains above Nice. They dined on a terrace two hundred feet above the valley with stone steps leading down the side of the mountain. Isadora Duncan sat nearby. "Scott didn't know who she was, so I told him," Gerald Murphy recalled. "He immediately went to her table and sat at her feet. She ran his fingers through his hair and called him her centurion." Zelda suddenly jumped up from her chair and leaped across the table in front of Gerald and hurled herself down the stairs. "I was sure she was dead. We were all stunned and motionless."[20] Zelda then reappeared at the top of the stairs while Sarah wiped blood from her knees. It was a foreshadowing of the destruction of a character that happened to be F. Scott Fitzgerald's wife.

Two weeks after the publication of *The Great Gatsby*, Scott went to the Dingo bar in Paris with Donald Ogden Stuart and met a dark-haired, heavy-set young man whom he had heard of from Edmund Wilson. He had recommended to his editor, Max Perkins, that he look him up, as he was "the real thing." The real thing greeted Scott with a wide smile and an easy handshake. He had one self-published collection of short stories to his name. He had been wounded in World War I by a trench mortar while giving out candy and cigarettes and could drink just about anyone under the table. He had been living on his first wife's trust fund in Paris, and his next wife would finance safaris, Florida homes, anything the big-ticket writer desired. He would come to dominate the twentieth century in a way no writer could ever duplicate again. But at this stage, nobody knew who he was, just one of the multitudes who had come to postwar Paris to find art and leave their mark on the world. Scott was already in awe of this man whom he would promote to Max Perkins and then suffer when he turned on him. It was hard to believe that the literary torch would pass to this quivering mass of sensitivity that was Ernest Hemingway.

## CHAPTER 31

# Finding Gatsby

## *1940*

IN 1940, IN A DUSTY CORNER OF THE SCRIBNER WAREHOUSE, SAT A PAL-
let of books that was buried back behind the bestsellers of the day. The
books had sat there waiting patiently since 1925 to come back to life.
After the publication of *The Great Gatsby*, there had been several attempts
to resurrect the moribund novel. In 1932, the Modern Library brought
out an edition of *Gatsby* with an introduction from Fitzgerald that he
was paid $50 for. The edition was priced at ninety-five cents, but it did
not sell. In fact, it became the worst-selling edition in Modern Library
history and was discontinued in 1939. The book was once more serialized
in Sunday supplements of the *Philadelphia Inquirer* and *Chicago Herald
Examiner* along with a pulp serialization in the British pulp magazine
*Argosy* in 1937. None of these brief appearances kick-started sales of the
book.

Famously, Scott himself went looking for his books in local bookstores with his girlfriend, Hollywood columnist Sheila Graham, in 1939
and could find no store with any of his titles. F. Scott Fitzgerald's last
royalty check from Scribner's was for $13.13. On May 20, 1940, he wrote
his editor Max Perkins. "I wish I was in print. It will be an odd year or
so from now when Scottie assures her friends I was an author and finds
that no book is procurable. It is certainly no fault of yours. You (and one
other man, Gerald Murphy) have been a friend through every dark time

in these five years . . . professionally I know, the next move must come from me. Would the 25 cent press keep *Gatsby* in the public eye—or is the book unpopular? Has it had its chance? Would a popular reissue in that series with a preface not by me but one of its admirers—I can maybe pick one—make it a favorite with classrooms, profs, lovers of English prose—anybody? But to die so completely and unjustly after having given so much! Even now there is little published in American fiction that doesn't slightly bear my stamp—in a small way I was an original."[1]

When F. Scott Fitzgerald died on December 21, 1940, the dusty copies in the Scribner warehouses of *The Great Gatsby* still sat and waited. They had been through a Great Depression and seen the beginnings of a Second World War. They were not discarded because a few thousand books did not take up much space at all. The books would have been moved, they would have been cataloged, they would have been sought after if someone somewhere in the United States or the world requested a copy of the book. But no one did.

When F. Scott Fitzgerald died, *The New York Times* obituary set the tone. "Mr. Fitzgerald in his life and writings epitomized 'all the sad young men' of the post-war generation . . . roughly his own career began and ended with the nineteen twenties . . . the promise of a brilliant career was never fulfilled."[2] *The Great Gatsby* was not evaluated in many of the Fitzgerald obituaries; worse, it was not mentioned in most of them. Columnist Westbrook Pegler of the Hearst papers took a final swipe, "The death of Scott Fitzgerald recalls memories of a queer brand of undisciplined and self-indulgent brats who were determined not to pull their weight in the boat and wanted the world to drop everything and sit down and bawl with them."[3]

Many summed up Fitzgerald as a drunk of the 1920s who spurned his talent on the jazz age doing hack work for the magazines. A few mentioned the books in the Scribner warehouse, but not many. Few attended his funeral, not even Zelda, who was in a sanitarium. Even in death, Scott had managed to use his own life for Gatsby.

*As we started through the gate into the cemetery I heard a car stop and then the sound of some one splashing after us over the soggy ground.*

*I looked around. It was the man with the owl-eyed glasses whom I had found marveling over Gatsby's books in the library three months before. I'd never seen him since then. I don't know how he knew about the funeral, or even his name. The rain poured down his thick glasses and he took them off and wiped them to see the protecting canvas unrolled from Gatsby's grave. I tried to think about Gatsby then for a moment, but he was already too far away, and I could only remember, without resentment, that Daisy hadn't sent a message or a flower. Dimly I heard someone murmur, "Blessed are the dead that the rain falls on," and then the owl-eyed man said, "Amen to that," in a brave voice.*

*We struggled down quickly through the rain to the cars. Owl Eyes spoke to me.*

*"I couldn't get to the house," he remarked.*

*"Neither could anybody else."*

*"Go on!" He stared "Why by God, they used to go there by the hundreds."*

*He took off his glasses and wiped them again, outside and in.*

*"The poor son of a bitch."*[4]

And then the author and his books in the warehouse were simply forgotten. Life went on. But then . . . then, World War II changed everything. There was a war to be fought, and the soldiers needed reading material. ASEs were born. Armed Services Editions. "The ASE program is often referred to as 'the biggest book giveaway in history.' Between the time it was launched in 1943 to its end in 1947, nearly 123 million books were distributed to US troops overseas. . . . "[5] They were to be disposable, read six times, passed around, printed on cheap, flimsy paper, and then disposed of. Maybe those books in the corner of the Scribner warehouse might be used after all. You couldn't send those dusty, old books, but you might send that book in a green-and-yellow cover printed on the cheapest paper you could get your hands on. So they did. *The Great Gatsby* went to war, and when the war ended, hundreds of thousands of soldiers had read the strange little tale of a bootlegger and his American dream of becoming wealthy and getting the golden girl.

The discovery of *The Great Gatsby* on Okinawa by thousands of soldiers probably happened like this: A GI hit the sand and raised up his Thompson machine gun, firing the .45 caliber APC slugs into the trees. The returning fire kicked up the sand and blinded him. The Japanese were everywhere and, worse, they kept jumping up out of caves and tunnels. He motioned the marine forward with the two tanks of jellied gasoline. Burn them out. That was the only way. The flamethrower leapt into the far trees and shot down the tunnel where the Japanese had just retreated. The GI sucked on the cigarette, raising his Thompson, feeling the kick in his shoulder letting go with fifty bullets and then falling back down and pivoting around, breathing like a man who had just run a fifty-yard dash.

He threw his cigarette and saw the marine with the flamethrower fall forward and onto his stomach. His helmet rolled forward and out came a small, green book, an Armed Services Edition paperback. An ASE. He stared at the book with yellow lettering. The guy was a reader. Hell, they were all readers now. Troops needed to read. Between using jellied gasoline and Thompson machine guns on the Japanese dug into caves tunnels, hanging in trees, mountain sides, there were lulls. Sometimes, the lulls went on for days or months, and the trick was to keep up morale. Books. Send them books. *Millions of books.* But they had to fit in pockets. They had to be cheap to print and would only last for seven readings. They were 5.5 inches by 3.78 inches. Some were condensed, and some weren't. No margins and the text was printed in side-by-side columns. One hundred and twenty-three million copies printed for six cents a copy would be given away to GIs, who were given the books as they headed for Normandy, Okinawa, Iwo Jima. The authors received a half-cent per copy, but the exposure they received was priceless. A lot of the GIs carried the books in their helmets, and after cutting down some Germans or Japanese, they would flop down into a foxhole and pull down their book that went through the war as a literary halo.

A lot of the books were ones the GIs had never heard of. What did they care . . . it was something to escape the hell they found themselves in. The most popular of these flimsy paperbacks was *A Tree Grows in Brooklyn*. General Eisenhower himself had approved an ASE for each solider boarding a transport for the invasion of Normandy. One solider had Carl Sandburg's *Storm Over the Land* in his helmet. He had been carrying the book since Guam, Guadalcanal, and now he was on Okinawa, and this looked like it was going to be a long, hard slog. He had read it over three times and, forty years later, he told a reporter, "During the lull in the battle I would read what he wrote about another war and found a great deal of comfort and reassurance. You looked for any escape from this madness and guys would give up a lot of things in their packs but kept their ASEs."[6]

The solider stood up and walked over the marine lying face down with the flamethrower in the sand. It happened like that. A medic came up alongside him and shook his head. "He's gone." The GI picked up the flimsy paperback laying in the sand. It was well-worn. Hell, the books were so flimsy they practically fell apart in your hands. He cupped a cigarette, flared his Zippo, and muttered the title, "*The Great Gatsby*." The medic glanced at him then the book with the cheesy green cover with the title in bright yellow; "a red band running across the bottom of the ASE assures readers that 'This Is the Complete Book—Not a Digest.' Inside the full text of *Gatsby* is printed on double columns with the thinnest of margins."[7] He flipped the book over, cradling his machine gun, reading the back cover of yellow print against the dye of green.

"Just as F. Scott Fitzgerald's *This Side of Paradise* immortalized college life in America in the 1920s, so *The Great Gatsby* presented a deathless figure in the person of Jay Gatsby, one of the first, and certainly one of the greatest of the racketeers in American fiction. Gatsby is a great and mysterious figure. The story of his life among the Long Island bootleggers and society people of well remembered years is unequalled."[8]

He flipped the book around again. The cover was severely creased, and the pages were greasy and thumbed. Yeah. This guy had been holding onto this one. He had found an escape from the madness and wasn't giving it up. The GI mouthed his cigarette and put *The Great Gatsby* in his helmet and picked up his Thompson. He looked at the dead marine one more time, then began moving forward, cocking his machine gun, breathing the scent of charred human flesh. The GI felt the book in his helmet and puffed on his cigarette.

They were soldiers in the worst conditions of their young lives reading to escape the hell they found themselves in. But the ones that survived would go back to civilian life and become lawyers, plumbers, mechanics, doctors, and some would become teachers, and some would become professors. And those teachers and professors would tell their students about a book they read called *The Great Gatsby* by unknown author F. Scott Fitzgerald. Critical assessments would follow, literary revisionism, new compendiums of F. Scott Fitzgerald's life. A movement would begin. But the way the world rediscovered *The Great Gatsby* was really in the mud and the blood and the unspeakable human tragedy that is war. In this way, a novel of infinite hope came back to life during the worst moment in human history.

# CHAPTER 32

# Writing Gatsby

FOR GOOD OR FOR BAD, *THE GREAT GATSBY* IS A YOUNG MAN'S DREAM. IT was written by a young man running after the American Dream that promises wealth, happiness, nothing short of a fountain of youth where no one gets old, no one dies, no one fails. The promise of that American Dream is baked into the writing of *The Great Gatsby*, and the furnace of that struggle to find this nirvana is a history really written in braille, so anyone can follow it and see the brilliance and the shortfalls promised by the young continent that Dutch sailors *"held their breath for one enchanted moment face to face with something for the last time that was commensurate with mans capacity to dream."*[1]

One cannot assess *The Great Gatsby* without understanding the author's place in time. F. Scott Fitzgerald was born in the nineteenth century with more knowledge of the Civil War than 99 percent of the people alive today. That was because he was born thirty-one years after the Great Conflagration that was a dividing line between the urban-based world America would become and her rural antecedents. In truth, *The Great Gatsby* is the first test tube of a modern urban landscape that emerged in the twentieth century and was frozen in place after World War I. Scott and Zelda stumbled onto the first modern metropolis of New York at the same time America was discovering the changed values and rapid pace of life that the modern world presented. *The Great Gatsby* was simply the first take on what this changed world meant for the America of small towns and farms. Those quaint Victorians would never quite recover from the schism produced after the rapid industrialization and mass buildup that World War I required that produced mass culture and that little novel written in the hot attic spaces in St. Paul (*This Side of Paradise*), which inadvertently summed up the youth who had come of age into this strange urban world that "found all Gods dead, all wars fought, all faiths in man shaken."[2] *The Great Gatsby* took *This Side of Paradise* one step further and reflected back what America had become thirty years after the frontier was declared closed and Oswald Spengler's thesis in *The Decline of the West* (which Fitzgerald read on the Riviera) pointed to a secular, urban-based world without the moral and religious underpinnings of the vanishing rural, small-town tapestry.

In another sense, Scott Fitzgerald's dream intersected with the dream of a vast republic, and in the furnace of creation, he set it down for all to read. It was created from his own life, and unknowingly, Scott, along with Zelda, fired up that furnace, lived it, tried for the dream, and found all its shortcomings, heartache, pathos, and deadly consequences. But it is the dream that millions aspire to, and by living it and having the ability to transmute his experience into a mystical dream of literary magic, he left behind in that Scribner warehouse a testament to his own heartbreak, his own dreams, and then, with the flourish of a magician, flipped it up as only a great writer can and gave back it to all of us as the American Dream. We just didn't know it for thirty years.

Scott and Zelda paid the price. Fitzgerald could only fuel his furnace with what he saw and experienced, and he and Zelda were pioneers in that modern twentieth-century dream of becoming rich and famous. *They lived it*. And Scott knew he and Zelda had to go down the road to find the tarnished nickels on the road to success. He did encourage Zelda. She was his experimental character that would people *This Side of Paradise*, *The Beautiful and the Damned*, *The Great Gatsby*, *Tender is the Night*, and many of his short stories, including all the Gatsby cluster stories, "Winter Dreams," "The Sensible Thing," and "The Ice Palace." She was his heroine, his femme fatale, his modern creation that coincided with the advent of a modern urban culture that produced the flapper, who was transmuted into Zelda. And she was one of his main characters and influences in the writing of his greatest creation, *The Great Gatsby*.

The writing of *Gatsby* is the life lived by F. Scott Fitzgerald. The story became a living parable from the moment he saw Zelda in Montgomery, Alabama, to the heartbreaking years in New York when he lost her, and to the moment he wrote *This Side of Paradise* and became immensely famous, wealthy, won her back, and did "repeat the past" on Long Island, with all its tragic consequences. And then, like Gatsby, he was betrayed again with the devastating effect of losing his raison d'être, his dream, and like all dreams that are lost, all that is left is destruction. Zelda's affair and suicide attempt ended Scott's marriage as he had dreamed it and "*lost the old warm world.*" Scott's destruction was assured as his very being was tied up in the dream of getting the golden girl, and when he lost her, he saw "*what a horrible thing a rose was.*"[3] Gatsby's death and Scott's eventual destruction at that point was preordained.

Eduardo Jozan never understood what an impact his summer fling had on Fitzgerald's masterpiece: "Creating the emotional triangle between its main characters. What began as Gatsby's quest for vanished love evolved into something deeper, the wonderment Daisy had inspired and disillusionment over its demise. Scott's recollection of his broken engagement with Zelda merged with her betrayal and the confrontation that never took place between himself and the French pilot got dramatized at the Plaza Hotel."[4]

In a more terrestrial sense, the affair altered the plot course of the novel, giving a new way to end Daisy's failed marriage with the confrontation in the Plaza Hotel and finally the destruction of Gatsby. "When one compares Scott's first draft of *The Great Gatsby* with its final version, the influence of the Jozan affair becomes evident. Both have nine chapters with the first two almost identical. The differences occur in chapters 6 and 7 where Scott deleted two conversations, the first between Gatsby and Nick Carraway, in which the bewildered hero rejects any notion of running away with Daisy. 'I'm very sad old sport . . . Daisy wants us to run off together . . . but we mustn't just run away . . . that won't do at all . . . it's all so sad because I can't make her understand.' The second deleted conversation, also involving Nick, occurs between Nick and Daisy . . . 'Do you think I'm making a mistake . . . I just want to go and not tell Tom anything.'"[5]

It is the confrontation that destroys Gatsby's dream of the golden girl, which happened to Scott as well on the Riviera. But to find this American parable, Scott had to put it all on the line. He took his money, his soul, his talent, his guts, and went to the Riviera to get a view of his own country. He took the celebratory years on Long Island, where he had the golden girl, and he had the money the fame, and he led the Gatsby life, and he took that lighthouse across the bay and planted his flag in the green beacon of American aspiration. And incredibly, he allowed, or he even pushed, Zelda into an affair, and he sat back and cataloged the tragedy that unfolded and stumbled across the story of America. "Though hurt by Zelda's involvement with Jozan, Fitzgerald quickly grasped its impressionistic possibilities for his new novel, letting it haunt *The Great Gatsby* as it haunted him. The extent to which the relationship made its way into Fitzgerald's writing can only be guessed at, yet just as fragments of Zelda's journals appeared in *The Beautiful and the Damned* and pieces of her medical record would later materialize in *Tender is the Night*— something of that summers twilight mood crept into *Gatsby*."[6]

*She was his muse. She was his character.* And Scott had to find out what the result of an affair might be with that character. Cruel as it may seem, but writers are ruthless creatures about their art; no one is more cold-blooded than the artist bent on their singular vision.

It was the intangible genius of F. Scott Fitzgerald's prose that took this fodder and forged a diamond. Ultimately, though, this diamond would not be appreciated, and like Gatsby . . . Scott failed in his time. It is very American that his book should be appreciated by some, mis-understood by many, and then, committing that most egregious of all American sins, by not selling commercially. It was fitting this masterpiece should be dismissed in Scott's time. People were still drinking too much gin, too self-absorbed in that overheated party that was America in the twenties. And then they were too busy surviving the Great Depression and then a second World War. But between the breaks in the battle in foxholes and on beaches, behind the lines, young men read of another young man's story, and they saw themselves. Many of them died, but the thousands that came home told their wives, their sons, their daughters, about a book called *The Great Gatsby*.

And then slowly, the slumbering books began to disappear in the corner of the Scribner warehouse. Maybe it was Malcom Cowley's reassessment of Fitzgerald's work. Maybe it was the future college professors who read the strange green-and-yellow book while waiting to jump out of an airplane or getting into a tank, who then began to assign it to their students. But by the middle of the 1950s, the stack in the corner of the Scribner warehouse, those copies from 1925 that meant so much to Scott and Zelda, had vanished. Bookstores wanted copies of this *Gatsby* book because people were asking for it. And *The Great Gatsby* and its author continued to grow through the sixties and the seventies, and a Hollywood film was made, and then another. Word had gone out: this author, F. Scott Fitzgerald, he was very good, and his book, *The Great Gatsby*, was nothing short of amazing.

So under the Hemingway juggernaut that Scott had begun by telling Max Perkins about the unknown writer in Paris and then orchestrated getting him to Scribner's, came this little bauble rolling out from the Christmas tree of literary expectations and suddenly people understood that this story of just fifty thousand words stood for more than just the 1920s and "Ain't We Got Fun." Maybe it was that last paragraph that summed up the American character, that "willingness of the heart" so hard to define, when Scott wrote:

> *I became aware of the old island here that flowered once for Dutch sailors eyes, a fresh green breast of the new world. Its vanished trees, the trees that had made way for Gatsby house, had once pandered in whispers to the last and greatest of all human dreams; for a transitory enchanted moment man must have held his breath in the presence of this continent, compelled into an aesthetic contemplation he neither understood nor desired, face to face for the last time in history with something commensurate to his capacity for wonder.*[7]

And after people fell out of their chairs after reading those lines, they must have known . . . *That is me*. Scott's dream. *Our dream*. Gatsby's dream. It is all one in the same, and sacrificing all for that dream is very, very American. And that is what the writing of *Gatsby* is all about in the end. Not content to just go along writing and making very good money, F. Scott Fitzgerald reached beyond himself for something more, and in the process, it defined us. And so, in the end, he did win, but just like Gatsby, "his romantic readiness" was his Achilles' heel. The great irony of the American Dream could only be summed up with the lines written by a writer who is at the height of his powers, able to see over the walls of our terrestrial existence for a moment, and then to bring it all home for the ages and for himself. The summation of *The Great Gatsby* is the summation of F. Scott Fitzgerald's life.

> *And as I sat there brooding on the old unknown world, I thought of Gatsby's wonder when he first picked out the green light at the end of Daisy's dock. He had come a long way to this blue lawn, and his dream must have seemed so close that he could hardly fail to grasp it. He did not know that it was already behind him, somewhere back in that vast obscurity beyond the city, where the dark fields of the republic rolled on under the night.[8]*

It was like Scott's journey in "The Rolling Junk" where he saw America as it had been and was unsure of where it was going, causing Zelda to burst into tears when they reached her hometown of Montgomery. "It was for her faithlessness that she wept and for the faithlessness of time." Scott understood how conflicted the American Dream was between that pastoral nirvana of small towns that had evolved into the faithless and empty urbanity that was twentieth-century America. And those two conflicting forces forged twentieth-century America and the modern American Dream: conflicted, deathless, doomed. And so, Scott wrote the lines that summed up a country on the cusp of a brimming dawn, looking back to its own storied past.

> *Gatsby believed in the green light, the orgastic future that year by year recedes before us. It eluded us then, but that's no matter—tomorrow we will run faster, stretch out our arms farther . . . And one fine morning—*

*So we beat on, boats against the current, borne back ceaselessly into the past.*[9]

There is nothing more to be said, except that what Scott knew, the world discovered later, and that after fifty million copies have sold of the book written in the heat of a blistering summer on the Riviera with a half-million sold every year, *The Great Gatsby* is now recognized the world over as an American Masterpiece on the American Dream.

# EPILOGUE

They had been sleeping for some time in the stalled Renault when the peasant saw them. The couple with the trolley bearing down. The engineer blew his horn several times, but they were drunk and almost unconscious. The train was headed right for them. The peasant who was walking to work saw them and wondered why they did not wake. He grabbed the author by the hand and shook him awake, speaking in French. The author knew little French, but the horn now blasted in his ears, and he woke up. The peasant was dragging his wife out of the car and the author helped. They got out just in time as the trolley smashed their car to bits. It was a close call. But they would not be so lucky later on.

The Fitzgeralds never recovered from the Jozan affair, and Scott never stopped drinking until the last year of his life. In 1926, they tried to have another child but without success. Zelda lashed out at Scott. "Comparing Scott unfavorably with Jozan, she began to complain that his penis was too small to give her sexual satisfaction."[1] This was an ongoing theme in the Fitzgerald marriage that led to Scott confessing to Ernest Hemingway, of all people, that he thought his penis was too small and then Ernest writing a story in *A Moveable Feast* where they go to the bathroom and Ernest assures Scott he is fine. The real reason Zelda could not become pregnant was complications from her previous abortion, but their sex life never recovered, and she began to accuse Scott of homosexuality. The real cause of the sexual problems was probably Scott's incessant drinking, which often leads to impotence.

Things between the couple were further complicated when Scott allegedly had an affair with the movie actress Lois Moran. He told Zelda's psychiatrist in 1934 that "her affair with Edouard Jozan in 1925 (and mine with Lois Moran in 1927, which was sort of revenge) shook something out of us." Zelda told the same psychiatrist, "When I knew my husband had another woman in California I was upset."[2] His stalled fourth novel, *Tender is the Night*, set in the Riviera, would not come out until 1933, and to earn money, he continued writing for the magazines until that dried up and he went to Hollywood to work on screenplays. Zelda became obsessed with becoming a world-class ballerina, but she was now thirty and experienced her first nervous breakdown in 1930. This was followed by a stay at Malmaison Hospital where she was treated. "She entered in a state of acute anxiety, unable to stay put, repeating continually, 'it's frightful, it's horrible, what's going to become of me, I must work and I no longer can. I must die and yet I have to work. . . . '"[3] For the next ten years, through the hospitalizations and breakdowns, Scott remained with her and used her madness for his unfinished novel, *Tender is The Night*, where the main character becomes mentally ill. Scott continued using Zelda as his muse and as a character even as she descended into insanity.

There were several suicide attempts, and Zelda confessed she thought "she is in love with her dance teacher as she had already thought in the past of being in love with another woman."[4] She was treated in Switzerland, and Scott moved there to be close. Nine years after *The Great Gatsby*, *Tender is the Night* was finally published in 1934; the reviews were positive, but the one person whose opinion mattered to Scott, Ernest Hemingway, didn't care for the book and stood for the general reception of the public and critics to the novel of life on the Riviera. Hemingway, in a letter to Max Perkins, wrote that *Tender* was unsound because "Scott can't invent true characters because he doesn't know anything about people . . . he has so lousy much talent and he has suffered so without knowing why, has destroyed himself and destroyed Zelda, though never as much as she has tried to destroy him, that out of this little children's immature, misunderstood, whining for lost youth death dance that they have been dragging into and out of insanity. . . . "[5]

America was in the grips of The Great Depression, and stories about rich people on the Riviera did not strike a chord. Still, *Tender is the Night* sold 7,600 copies along with two more printings of 5,075 and 2,520. The royalties of $5,104.65 did not pay off Fitzgerald's debts. In a direct letter to Fitzgerald, Hemingway went further. "I liked it and didn't like it. It started off with that marvelous description of Sarah and Gerald . . . then you started fooling with them, making them come from things they didn't come from, changing them into other people and you can't do that . . . for God's sake write and write truly no matter who or what it hurts but do not make those silly compromises."[6] This was from the most famous writer in the world who by now eclipsed Fitzgerald in the literary world and was the equivalent of a rock star today.

Scott would never complete another novel. In 1933, he began checking himself into The John Hopkins Hospital to come off benders and for lingering fevers related to his tuberculosis. He would check himself into John Hopkins no less than eight times for alcoholism between 1933 and 1937. He continued to write for the magazines, but in the Depression-era thirties, his stories became harder to place and his price fell. He tried to secure other sources of income, including pitching Clark Gable on a sound version of *The Great Gatsby* and approaching the Dean of Princeton to give a seminar on writing fiction. Gable and Dean Gauss both declined. His last entry in his ledger is foreboding: "Zelda breaks, the novel finished, hard times begin for me, slow, but sure, ill health throughout."[7] In 1934, he earned $58.35 from all of his books.

In the prologue to the 1934 ninety-five-cent Modern Library edition, Scott wrote, "reading it over one can see how it could have been improved, yet without feeling guilty of any discrepancy from the truth, the attempt at honesty and imagination . . . I had recently been kidded half haywire by critics who felt that my material was such as to preclude all dealing with mature persons in a mature world. But My God! It was my material and it was all I had to deal with."[8]

Fitzgerald's agent, Harold Ober, in 1934, wrote that Scott was destroying his magazine market with unreliability and drunken calls to editors. "Lately when you wired me that a story would be sent on a certain date I have no faith at all that it will come . . . I do think it would be better if you would make it a rule not to call up or write editors and while I am on the subject I think it would be better if you did not call up or write to moving picture executives. . . . "[9] In 1935, Zelda attempted suicide several times at Sheppard Pratt Institution, and one time, with

Scott, she tried to throw herself under a train when they were taking a walk. In 1935, Scott wrote *The Crack-Up* for *Esquire*, a series of articles about his emotional bankruptcy. A brutal *New York Post* article in 1936 titled "The Other Side of Paradise" cataloged his fall and alcoholism. The interview took place at The Rock View Inn, where Scott had holed up with his nurse in North Carolina.

"Physically he was suffering the aftermath of an accident eight weeks ago, when he broke his right shoulder in a dive from a fifteen-foot springboard. But whatever pain the fracture might still cause him, it did not account for his jittery jumping off and on to his bed, his restless pacing, his trembling hands, his twitching face with its pitiful expression of a cruelly beaten child. Nor could it be held responsible for his frequent trips to a highboy, in a drawer of which lay a bottle. Each time he poured a drink into the measuring glass on his bedside table, he would look appealingly at the nurse and ask, 'Just one ounce?' Each time the nurse cast down her eyes without replying. Fitzgerald, for that matter, did not attempt to make his injury an excuse for his thirst."[10]

In 1937, Scott headed to Hollywood in severe debt and began the final phase of his literary career. Writing to Harold Ober's wife after his first week in Hollywood, he gushed that he had "talked with Taylor, dined with March, danced with Ginger Rogers, been in Rosalind Russel's dressing room, drunk ginger ale with Zukor and Lasky, lunched alone with Maureen Sullivan, watched Crawford act and lost my heart to a beautiful half caste Chinese girl. . . . "[11]

The studio days were hard, where Scott drank Coca-Cola all day to stay on the wagon and had to take choral and Nembutal to sleep and Benzedrine to get him started in the morning. He began to experience heart trouble and had forty-eight drops of Digitalin added to his nightly medication. He tried to build a Hollywood career but felt outside of the new industry where writers were low in rank. The problem was his elegant prose did not transfer to the rule by committee that produced stamped-out screenplays required by the studio system of the late 1930s. In 1940, he expressed his true feelings in a letter to a friend, "Isn't Hollywood a dump? In the human sense of the word. A hideous town pointed up the insulting gardens of its rich, full of the human spirit at a new low of debasement."[12] He was allowed to work on the script of *Gone with the Wind* and then put on other films, never earning a screen credit and losing jobs as his drinking increased.

He began a relationship with Hollywood columnist Sheila Graham, who endured his alcoholic tirades and would eventually publish a book on her years with Fitzgerald called *Beloved Infidel*, which would be made into a movie starring Gregory Peck. Scott was fired from different studios for drinking, and finally, he went on the wagon and began a new novel, *The Last Tycoon*, based on the life of Hollywood boy genius Irving Thalberg. He never finished it.

While buying cigarettes at Schwab's Pharmacy, Scott experienced a crushing pain in the center of his chest and shortness of breath. His doctor gave him nitroglycerin under his tongue and an EKG, suspecting a mild heart attack, and ordered him to bed rest. There were no bypasses, and the "rest cure" was standard advice for heart patients. On Saturday, December 21, 1940, Scott sat in Sheila's living room and ate a chocolate bar and read the *Princeton Alumni Weekly*, while waiting for a doctor to arrive after suffering from dizziness the night before at a theatre. At 3 p.m., he stood up suddenly, grabbed the fireplace mantle, then fell forward. F. Scott Fitzgerald was dead at forty-four from a massive heart attack. The cause of death was diagnosed as occlusive coronary arteriosclerosis, common among alcoholics, where the walls of the heart are weakened over time.

The author of *The Great Gatsby* was taken to the Wordsworth Room of Pierce Brothers Mortuary at 720 West Washington Boulevard. The funeral home was in a seedy part of town, and few came to the visitation. One visitor recalled, "Except for one bouquet of flowers and a few empty chairs, there was nothing to keep him company except his casket . . . I never saw a sadder scene than the end of the father of all the young men. He was laid out to look like a cross between a floor walker and a wax dummy . . . but in technicolor . . . his hands were horribly wrinkled and thin, the only proof left after death that for all the props of youth, he had actually suffered and died an old man."[13] When Dorothy Parker came to the funeral home, she delivered the line that was the final comment on Gatsby, "the poor son of a bitch."[14]

Scott's funeral was attended by twenty people. Zelda, who by now was severely schizophrenic, did not attend but wrote a letter to Scott's agent Harold Ober and the Murpheys. "He was as spiritually generous a soul as ever was . . . in retrospect it seems as if he was always planning happinesses for Scottie and me. Books to read—places to go. Life seemed so promissory always when he was around and I always believed that he could take care of anything. I grieve for his brilliant talent, his faithful effort to keep me under the best of very expensive care and Scottie in school; his devotion to those that he felt were contributing to the aesthetic and spiritual purposes of life—and for his generous and vibrant soul that never spared itself, and never found anything too much trouble save the fundamentals of life itself."[15]

The Catholic church refused to let him be buried next to his parents in the St. Mary's Church in Rockville because he was not a practicing Catholic. An Episcopal service was held in the Pumphrey Funeral Home in Bethesda. The Max Perkins, the Gerald Murphys, and the Harold Obers attended, along with Scottie and Ludlow Fowler (the best man at Scott's wedding). Scott left behind a life insurance policy that provided the bulk of his estate since he had no assets or royalties coming in from any of his books. After his debts were subtracted, F. Scott Fitzgerald left behind $32,000.

Zelda Fitzgerald remained institutionalized the rest of her life and died in a fire at the Highland Institution on March 10, 1948. The fire began in the kitchen and spread up through the dumbwaiter to the top floor, where Zelda was sleeping. *The New York Herald Tribune* reported that she couldn't escape because she had been locked in. "Six patients were trapped on the fourth floor. Chains and padlocks prevented the windows from being opened far enough for patients to escape."[16] She and eight other women died, and Zelda was only identified by a charred slipper. She was buried next to Scott in Rockville Union Cemetery after the Catholic church relented and they were disinterred.

But now . . . now . . . it is 1920 again, and a young couple just married has burst out of St. Patrick's Church in Manhattan and are walking down Fifth Avenue in the early spring sunshine. They walk in the dewy Sunday quiet of New York with the world before them. They approach the Scribner building and stare at a new novel behind the glass. Their reflections stare back at them. A Southern belle with an orchid pinned to her shoulder and a young man with a carnation who just published his first novel. The couple, who shared what Scott called "a once in a century love affair" and would have their rendezvous with the Great America Century, were finally put to rest together under a headstone engraved with the final line of *The Great Gatsby*.

*So we beat on, boats against the current, borne back ceaselessly into the past.*[17]

# NOTES

## PREFACE

1 Sarah Churchwell, *Careless People: Murder Mayhem, and the Invention of* The Great Gatsby (New York: Arcade Publishing, 2003), 335.

2 Sheila Graham, *Beloved Infidel* (New York: Bantam, 1959), 212.

3 Ibid., 152.

4 Ibid.

5 Ibid., 141.

6 Ibid.

## CHAPTER 2

1 Albert Joseph Guérard, *The Personal Voice: A Contemporary Prose Reader*, Philadelphia: J. B. Lippincott & Co. 1964, 172.

2 Ibid.

3 Anon, "What a Flapper Novelist Thinks of His Wife," *Louisville Courier-Journal*, September 30, 1923, 112. In *Conversations with F. Scott Fitzgerald*, edited by Matthew Bruccoli and Judith Baughman (Jackson, MS: University Press of Mississippi, 2004), 47.

4 Ibid.

5 Ibid.

6 Ibid.

7 F. Scott Fitzgerald, *Ledger: 1919–1938. Digital Collections* (Columbia, SC: University of South Carolina), transcription, 70.

8 Phillip Lopate, *Writing New York: A Literary Anthology* (New York: Washington Square Press, 2000), 573.

9 Sarah Churchwell, *Careless People: Murder Mayhem, and the Invention of* The Great Gatsby (New York: Penguin Books, 2015), 76.

10 F. Scott Fitzgerald, *F. Scott Fitzgerald: A Life in Letters*, edited by Matthew J. Bruccoli (New York: Touchstone, 2010), 63.

11 F. Scott Fitzgerald, "How to Live on $36,000 a Year," *Saturday Evening Post*, April 5, 1924.

12 F. Scott Fitzgerald, *Ledger: 1919–1938. Digital Collections* (Columbia, SC: University of South Carolina), transcription, 73

13 Horst Kruse, *F. Scott Fitzgerald at Work: The Making of* The Great Gatsby (Tuscaloosa, AL: University of Alabama Press, 2014), 17.

14 F. Scott Fitzgerald, *The Great Gatsby* (New York: Wordsworth, 2001), 81.

15 Horst Kruse, *F. Scott Fitzgerald at Work: The Making of* The Great Gatsby (Tuscaloosa, AL: University of Alabama Press, 2014), 41.

16 Matthew Bruccoli, *F. Scott Fitzgerald's* The Great Gatsby: *A Literary Reference* (New York: Gale Carnegie, 2000), 24.

17 Ibid., 22.

18 F. Scott Fitzgerald, *The Great Gatsby* (New York: Grossett & Dunlap, 1925), 118.

19 Matthew Bruccoli, *F. Scott Fitzgerald's* The Great Gatsby: *A Literary Reference* (New York: Gale Carnegie, 2000), 24.

20 F. Scott Fitzgerald, *The Great Gatsby* (New York: Grossett & Dunlap, 1925), 118.

21 Nelson W. Aldrich Jr., *Old Money: The Mythology of America's Upper Class* (New York: Vintage Books, 1989), 182.

22 F. Scott Fitzgerald, *The Great Gatsby* (New York: Grossett & Dunlap, 1925), 47

23 Koula Svokos Hartnett, *Zelda Fitzgerald and the Failure of the American Dream for Women* (Ann Arbor, MI: University of Michigan Press, 2008), 67.

24 David Brown, *Paradise Lost: A Life of F. Scott Fitzgerald* (Boston, MA: Belknap Press Harvard, 2017), 50.

25 F. Scott Fitzgerald, *Tender is the Night* (New York: Wordsworth, 1994), 88.

26 Richard Morris, *Perspectives in Abnormal Behavior* (New York: Elsevier Science, 2013), 289.

27 Matthew Bruccoli, *Some Sort of Epic Grandeur: The Life of F. Scott Fitzgerald* (Columbia, SC: University of South Carolina Press, 2002), 213.

28 Anon, "What a Flapper Novelist Thinks of His Wife," *Louisville Courier-Journal*, September 30, 1923, 112. In *Conversations with F. Scott Fitzgerald*, edited by Matthew Bruccoli and Judith Baughman (Jackson, MS: University Press of Mississippi, 2004), 47.

## CHAPTER 3

1 David Brown, *Paradise Lost: A Life of F. Scott Fitzgerald* (Boston, MA: Belknap Press Harvard, 2017), 158.

2 F. Scott Fitzgerald, *The Vegetable* (Columbia, SC: University of South Carolina Press, 2003), 16.

3 F. Scott Fitzgerald, *The Letters of F. Scott Fitzgerald*, edited by Andrew Turnbull (University Park, PA: Pennsylvania State University Press, 1966), 181.

4 Matthew Bruccoli, *Some Sort of Epic Grandeur: The Life of F. Scott Fitzgerald* (Columbia, SC: University of South Carolina Press, 2002), 219.

5 Ibid.

6 John F. Irwin, *F. Scott Fitzgerald's Fiction: "An Almost Theatrical Innocence"* (Baltimore, MD: John Hopkins University Press, 2014), 45.

7 Bryant Mangum, ed., *F. Scott Fitzgerald in Context* (Cambridge: Cambridge University Press, 2013), 72.

8 F. Scott Fitzgerald, *Ledger: 1919–1938. Digital Collections* (Columbia, SC: University of South Carolina), transcription, 74.

9 F. Scott Fitzgerald, "How to Live on $36,000 a Year," *Saturday Evening Post*, April 5, 1924.

10 F. Scott Fitzgerald, *Ledger: 1919–1938. Digital Collections* (Columbia, SC: University of South Carolina), transcription, 74.

11 Matthew J. Bruccoli and Judith S. Baughman, eds., *Conversations with F. Scott Fitzgerald* (Jackson, MS: University Press of Mississippi, 2004), 39.

12 Sarah Churchwell, *Careless People: Murder, Mayhem, and the Invention of* The Great Gatsby (New York: Penguin Books, 2015), 26.

13 F. Scott Fitzgerald, *Ledger: 1919–1938. Digital Collections* (Columbia, SC: University of South Carolina), transcription, 74.

14 Unknown author, "Zelda and The Fitzgerald Legend," *Denver Quarterly* 6: 66.

15 Stephen Potts, *The Price of Paradise: The Magazine Career of F. Scott Fitzgerald* (Berkley, CA: University of California Press, 1993), 203.

16 William Fahey, *F. Scott Fitzgerald and the American Dream* (Ann Arbor, MI: University of Michigan Press, 2008), 66.

17 F. Scott Fitzgerald, *My Lost City: Personal Essays, 1920–1940 (The Cambridge Edition of the Works of F. Scott Fitzgerald)* (Cambridge: Cambridge University Press, 2005), 35.

18 F. Scott Fitzgerald, *Ledger: 1919–1938. Digital Collections* (Columbia, SC: University of South Carolina), transcription, 74.

19 Ibid.

20 F. Scott Fitzgerald, *Dear Scott, Dearest Zelda: The Love Letters of F. Scott and Zelda Fitzgerald*, edited by Jackson R. Bryer and Cathy W. Barks (Berkley, CA: University of California, 1971), p 69.

21 F. Scott Fitzgerald, *The Great Gatsby* (New York: Scribner, 1925), 16.

22 F. Scott Fitzgerald, *Ledger: 1919–1938. Digital Collections* (Columbia, SC: University of South Carolina), transcription, 74.

23 F. Scott Fitzgerald, *The Great Gatsby* (New York: Scribner, 1925), 16.

## CHAPTER 4

1 F. Scott Fitzgerald, *The Great Gatsby* (New York: Scribner, 1925), 202.

2 F. Scott Fitzgerald, *The Basil and Josephine Stories* (New York: Simon and Schuster, 1973), 78.

3 David Brown, *Paradise Lost: A Life of F. Scott Fitzgerald* (Boston, MA: Belknap Press Harvard, 2017), 22.

4 F. Scott Fitzgerald, *The Romantic Egoists: A Pictorial Autobiography from the Scrapbooks and Albums of F. Scott and Zelda Fitzgerald*, edited by Matthew J. Bruccoli, Scottie Fitzgerald Smith, and Joan P. Kerr (New York: Scribner, 1974), 10.

5 Ibid.

6 F. Scott Fitzgerald, *The Great Gatsby* (New York: Scribner, 1925), 1.

7 F. Scott Fitzgerald, *My Lost City: Personal Essays, 1920–1940 (The Cambridge Edition of the Works of F. Scott Fitzgerald)* (Cambridge: Cambridge University Press, 2005), 181.

8 Ibid., 4.

9 William Fahey, *F. Scott Fitzgerald and the American Dream* (Ann Arbor, MI: University of Michigan Press, 2008), 5.

10 F. Scott Fitzgerald, *The Basil and Josephine Stories* (New York: Simon and Schuster, 1973), 183.

11 F. Scott Fitzgerald, *The Great Gatsby* (New York: Scribner, 1925), 63.

12 John Jacob Clayton, *Gestures of Healing: Anxiety and the Modern Novel* (Amherst, MA: University of Massachusetts Press, 2008), 65.

13 F. Scott Fitzgerald, *The Short Stories of F. Scott Fitzgerald*, edited by Matthew J. Bruccoli (New York: Scribner, 1989), 263.

14 Mary Jo Tate, *Critical Companion to F. Scott Fitzgerald: A Literary Reference to His Life and Work* (New York: Facts on File, 2007), 298.

15 F. Scott Fitzgerald, *The Great Gatsby* (New York: Scribner, 1925), 177.

16 F. Scott Fitzgerald, *The Basil and Josephine Stories* (New York: Simon and Schuster, 1973), 184.

17 Ibid.

18 Ibid.

19 Ibid., 188.

20 Ibid.

21 Ibid., 201.

22 F. Scott Fitzgerald, *This Side of Paradise* (New York: Scribner, 1920), 29.

23 F. Scott Fitzgerald, *Ledger: 1919–1938. Digital Collections* (Columbia, SC: University of South Carolina), transcription, 63.

24 F. Scott Fitzgerald, *The Romantic Egoists: A Pictorial Autobiography from the Scrapbooks and Albums of F. Scott and Zelda Fitzgerald*, edited by Matthew J. Bruccoli, Scottie Fitzgerald Smith, and Joan P. Kerr (New York: Scribner, 2003), 16.

25 F. Scott Fitzgerald, *The Great Gatsby* (New York: Scribner, 1925), 94.

26 F. Scott Fitzgerald, *Ledger: 1919–1938. Digital Collections* (Columbia, SC: University of South Carolina), transcription, 66.

27 F. Scott Fitzgerald, *This Side of Paradise* (New York: Scribner, 1920), 179.

28 David Brown, *Paradise Lost: A Life of F. Scott Fitzgerald* (Boston, MA: Belknap Press Harvard, 2017), 63.

29 F. Scott Fitzgerald, *The Basil and Josephine Stories* (New York: Simon and Schuster, 1973), 86.

## CHAPTER 5

1 Sarah Churchwell, *Careless People: Murder, Mayhem, and the Invention of* The Great Gatsby (New York: Penguin Books, 2015), 1.

2 Barney Tanner, *Joycean Elements in F. Scott Fitzgerald's* The Great Gatsby: *Aspects of Burlesque, Shadowing, Dichotomies and Doubling* (Ann Arbor, MI: University of Michigan Press, 2008), 2.

3 Maxwell E. Perkins, *The Sons of Maxwell Perkins: Letters of F. Scott Fitzgerald, Ernest Hemingway, Thomas Wolfe, and Their Editor*, edited by Matthew J. Bruccoli and Judith S. Baughman (Columbia, SC: University of South Carolina Press, 2004), 20.

4 F. Scott Fitzgerald, *Tender is the Night* (New York: Scribner, 1995), 266.

5 F. Scott Fitzgerald, *My Lost City: Personal Essays, 1920–1940 (The Cambridge Edition of the Works of F. Scott Fitzgerald)* (Cambridge: Cambridge University Press, 2005), 41.

6 Horst Kruse, *F. Scott Fitzgerald at Work* (Tuscaloosa, AL: University of Alabama Press, 2014), 68.

7 Bernadine Szold, "About Town," *New York Daily News*, May 11, 1924, 6.

8 F. Scott Fitzgerald, "The Rough Crossing," in *The Stories of F. Scott Fitzgerald: A Selection of Twenty-Eight Stories with an Introduction by Malcolm Cowley* (University Park, PA: Pennsylvania State University Press, 1954), 254. Originally published in *Saturday Evening Post*, June 8, 1929.

9 Ibid., 262.

10 Ibid., 269.

11 F. Scott Fitzgerald, *The Great Gatsby* (New York: Scribner, 1925), 133.

12 Fitzgerald, "The Rough Crossing."

## CHAPTER 6

1 Nancy Milford, *Zelda: A Biography* (New York: Harper Books, 2013), 9.

2 Sally Cline, *Zelda Fitzgerald: Her Voice in Paradise* (New York: Arcade Publishing, 2003), 231.

3 Nancy Milford, *Zelda: A Biography* (New York: Harper Books, 2013), 1898.

4 Ibid., 8.

5 Ibid., 1901 (e-book location).

6 Ibid., 1900 (e-book location).

7 Ibid., 1902 (e-book location).

## CHAPTER 7

1 Sally Cline, *Zelda Fitzgerald: Her Voice in Paradise* (New York: Arcade Publishing, 2003), ii.

2 F. Scott Fitzgerald, *Dear Scott, Dearest Zelda: The Love Letters of F. Scott and Zelda Fitzgerald*, edited by Jackson R. Bryer and Cathy W. Barks (New York: Scribner, 2019), 54.

3 F. Scott Fitzgerald, *My Lost City: Personal Essays, 1920–1940 (The Cambridge Edition of the Works of F. Scott Fitzgerald)* (Cambridge: Cambridge University Press, 2005), 118.

4 Sarah Churchwell, *Careless People: Murder, Mayhem, and the Invention of* The Great Gatsby (New York: Penguin Books, 2015), 273.

5 F. Scott Fitzgerald, *My Lost City: Personal Essays, 1920–1940 (The Cambridge Edition of the Works of F. Scott Fitzgerald)* (Cambridge: Cambridge University Press, 2005), 42.

6 Sally Cline, *Zelda Fitzgerald: Her Voice in Paradise* (New York: Arcade Publishing, 2003), 143.

7 Ibid., iii.

8 Mary Ellen Haight, *Walks in Gertrude Stein's Paris* (Salt Lake City, UT: Peregrine Smith Books, 1988), 14.

9 Sally Cline, *Zelda Fitzgerald: Her Voice in Paradise* (New York: Arcade Publishing, 2003), III.

10 Ibid.
11 Ibid.
12 F. Scott Fitzgerald, *The Romantic Egoists: A Pictorial Autobiography from the Scrapbooks and Albums of F. Scott and Zelda Fitzgerald*, edited by Matthew J. Bruccoli, Scottie Fitzgerald Smith, and Joan P. Kerr (New York: Scribner, 2003), 113.

## CHAPTER 8

1 David Brown, *Paradise Lost: A Life of F. Scott Fitzgerald* (Boston, MA: Harvard University Press, 2017), 31.
2 Ibid.
3 Ibid., 32.
4 F. Scott Fitzgerald, *Ledger: 1919–1938. Digital Collections* (Columbia, SC: University of South Carolina), transcription, 167.
5 F. Scott Fitzgerald, *F. Scott Fitzgerald on Authorship*, edited by Matthew J. Bruccoli (Columbia, SC: University of South Carolina Press, 1996), 38.
6 F. Scott Fitzgerald, *The Short Stories of F. Scott Fitzgerald*, edited by Matthew J. Bruccoli (New York: Scribner, 1994), 428.
7 F. Scott Fitzgerald, *My Lost City: Personal Essays, 1920–1940 (The Cambridge Edition of the Works of F. Scott Fitzgerald)* (Cambridge: Cambridge University Press, 2005), 197.
8 F. Scott Fitzgerald, *This Side of Paradise* (New York: Scribner, 1920), 56.
9 F. Scott Fitzgerald, *The Great Gatsby* (New York: Scribner, 1925), 129.
10 F. Scott Fitzgerald, *The Romantic Egoists: A Pictorial Autobiography from the Scrapbooks and Albums of F. Scott and Zelda Fitzgerald*, edited by Matthew J. Bruccoli, Scottie Fitzgerald Smith, and Joan P. Kerr (New York: Scribner, 2003), 29.
11 Ibid.
12 James L. West III, *The Making of* This Side of Paradise (University Park, PA: University of Pennsylvania Press, 2016), 11.
13 F. Scott Fitzgerald, *The Romantic Egoists: A Pictorial Autobiography from the Scrapbooks and Albums of F. Scott and Zelda Fitzgerald*, edited by Matthew J. Bruccoli, Scottie Fitzgerald Smith, and Joan P. Kerr (New York: Scribner, 2003), 10.
14 Mary Jo Tate, *Critical Companion to F. Scott Fitzgerald: A Literary Reference to His Life and Work* (New York: Facts on File, 2007), 341.
15 David Brown, *Paradise Lost: A Life of F. Scott Fitzgerald* (Boston, MA: Harvard University Press, 2017), 35.
16 F. Scott Fitzgerald, *Afternoon of an Author* (New York: Scribner, 1958), 234.
17 F. Scott Fitzgerald, *The Basil and Josephine Stories* (New York: Scribner, 1997), 92.
18 Ibid., 101.
19 Ibid., 110.
20 Andrew Turnbull, *F. Scott Fitzgerald* (New York: Grove Press, 2001), 79.
21 Mary Jo Tate, *Critical Companion to F. Scott Fitzgerald: A Literary Reference to His Life and Work* (New York: Facts on File, 2007), 126.
22 F. Scott Fitzgerald, *The Stories of F. Scott Fitzgerald: A Selection of Twenty-Eight Stories with an Introduction by Malcolm Cowley* (New York: Scribner, 1954), 240.

23 F. Scott Fitzgerald, *The Complete Short Stories, Essays, and a Play, Volume 1* (New York: Scribner, 2004), 1084.

24 F. Scott Fitzgerald, *Ledger: 1919–1938. Digital Collections* (Columbia, SC: University of South Carolina), transcription, 25.

## CHAPTER 9

1 F. Scott Fitzgerald, *The Correspondence of F. Scott Fitzgerald*, edited by Matthew J. Bruccoli and Margaret M. Duggan (Ann Arbor, MI: University of Michigan, 1980), 141.

2 Sarah Mayfield, *Exiles from Paradise: Zelda and Scott Fitzgerald* (New York: Delacorte Press, 1971), 94.

3 F. Scott Fitzgerald, *My Lost City: Personal Essays, 1920–1940 (The Cambridge Edition of the Works of F. Scott Fitzgerald)* (Cambridge: Cambridge University Press, 2005), 44.

4 Ibid., 53.

5 E. Ray Canterbery and Thomas Birch, *F. Scott Fitzgerald: Under the Influence* (New York: Paragon House, 2006), 185.

6 Sarah Churchwell, *Careless People: Murder, Mayhem, and the Invention of* The Great Gatsby (New York: Penguin Books, 2015), 274.

7 Jackson Breyer, editor, *F Scott Fitzgerald: New Perspectives* (Athens, GA: University of Georgia Press, 2012), 257.

8 Sally Cline, *Zelda Fitzgerald: Her Voice in Paradise* (New York: Arcade Publishing, 2003), iii.

9 John F. Irwin, *F. Scott Fitzgerald's Fiction: "An Almost Theatrical Innocence"* (Baltimore, MD: John Hopkins University Press, 2014), 187.

10 F. Scott Fitzgerald, *My Lost City: Personal Essays, 1920–1940* (New York: Scribner, 2005), 44.

11 Koula Svokos Hartnett, *Zelda Fitzgerald and the Failure of the American Dream for Women* (New York: Peter Lang Publishing, Inc., 1991), 78.

12 F. Scott Fitzgerald, *My Lost City: Personal Essays, 1920–1940* (New York: Scribner, 2005), 56.

13 F. Scott Fitzgerald, *The Great Gatsby* (New York: Scribner, 1925), 217.

## CHAPTER 10

1 F. Scott Fitzgerald, *The Romantic Egoists: A Pictorial Autobiography from the Scrapbooks and Albums of F. Scott and Zelda Fitzgerald*, edited by Matthew J. Bruccoli, Scottie Fitzgerald Smith, and Joan P. Kerr (New York: Scribner, 2003), 46.

2 Ibid., p 47.

3 Nancy Milford, *Zelda: A Biography* (New York: HarperCollins, 2013), 1918 (e-book location).

4 Ibid.

5 Kendall Taylor, *The Gatsby Affair: Scott, Zelda, and the Betrayal that Shaped an American Classic* (Lanham, MD: Rowman & Littlefield, 2018), p 14.

6 Andrew Turnbull, *F. Scott Fitzgerald* (New York: Grove Press, 2001), 87.

7 F. Scott Fitzgerald, *The Great Gatsby* (New York: Scribner, 1925), 4.

8 F. Scott Fitzgerald, *The Short Stories of F. Scott Fitzgerald*, edited by Matthew J. Bruccoli (New York: Scribner, 1994), 450.

9 Howard Greenfield, *F. Scott Fitzgerald* (New York: Crown Publishers, 1974), 58.

10 F. Scott Fitzgerald, *This Side of Paradise* (New York: Scribner, 1920), 183.

11 Kendall Taylor, *The Gatsby Affair: Scott, Zelda, and the Betrayal that Shaped an American Classic* (Lanham, MD: Rowman & Littlefield, 2018), 16.

12 Ibid., 20.

13 Ibid., 16.

14 Joshua Zeitz, *Flapper: A Madcap Story of Sex, Style, Celebrity, and the Women Who Made America Modern* (New York: Crown Publishing, 2009), 18.

15 F. Scott Fitzgerald, *The Apprentice Fiction of F. Scott Fitzgerald: 1909–1917* (New Brunswick, NJ: Rutgers University Press, 1965), 136.

16 F. Scott Fitzgerald, *The Short Stories of F. Scott Fitzgerald*, edited by Matthew J. Bruccoli (New York: Scribner, 1994), 450.

17 Ibid.

18 F. Scott Fitzgerald, *This Side of Paradise* (New York: Scribner, 1920), 118.

19 F. Scott Fitzgerald, *The Great Gatsby* (Oxford: Oxford University Press, 1991), 86.

20 Ibid.

21 F. Scott Fitzgerald, *Dear Scott, Dearest Zelda: The Love Letters of F. Scott and Zelda Fitzgerald*, edited by Jackson R. Bryer and Cathy W. Barks (New York: Scribner, 2019), 24.

22 Ibid.

23 Jackson Bryer, *The Short Stories of F. Scott Fitzgerald: New Approaches in Criticism* (Madison, WI: University of Wisconsin, 1982), 124.

24 F. Scott Fitzgerald, *The Great Gatsby (Cambridge Edition)* (Cambridge: Cambridge University Press, 1991), 116.

25 Ibid., 117.

26 F. Scott Fitzgerald, *The Indispensable F. Scott Fitzgerald* (London: Book Society, 1949), 138.

## CHAPTER 11

1 Kendall Taylor, *The Gatsby Affair: Scott, Zelda, and the Betrayal that Shaped an American Classic* (Lanham, MD: Rowman & Littlefield, 2018), 55.

2 Ibid., 57.

3 Ibid., 56.

4 Sally Cline, *Zelda Fitzgerald: Her Voice in Paradise* (New York: Arcade Publishing, 2003), iii.

5 F. Scott Fitzgerald, *The Romantic Egoists: A Pictorial Autobiography from the Scrapbooks and Albums of F. Scott and Zelda Fitzgerald*, edited by Matthew J. Bruccoli, Scottie Fitzgerald Smith, and Joan P. Kerr (New York: Scribner, 2003), 118.

6 Kendall Taylor, *The Gatsby Affair: Scott, Zelda, and the Betrayal that Shaped an American Classic* (Lanham, MD: Rowman & Littlefield, 2018), 57.

7 Ibid., 56.

8 F. Scott Fitzgerald, *The Great Gatsby* (New York: Scribner, 1925), 141.

## CHAPTER 12

1 Andrew Turnbull, *F. Scott Fitzgerald* (New York: Grove Press, 2001), 92.

2 James L. West III, *The Making of* This Side of Paradise (University Park, PA: University of Pennsylvania Press, 2016), 73.

3 F. Scott Fitzgerald, *The Short Stories of F. Scott Fitzgerald*, edited by Matthew J. Bruccoli (New York: Scribner, 1994), 290.

4 David Brown, *Paradise Lost: A Life of F. Scott Fitzgerald* (Boston, MA: Harvard University Press, 2017), 73.

5 F. Scott Fitzgerald, *The Best Early Short Stories of F. Scott Fitzgerald*, edited by Bryant Mangum (New York: Modern Library, 2005), 104.

6 Kendall Taylor, *The Gatsby Affair: Scott, Zelda, and the Betrayal that Shaped an American Classic* (Lanham, MD: Rowman & Littlefield, 2018), 22.

7 Ibid., 209.

8 F. Scott Fitzgerald, *F. Scott Fitzgerald on Authorship*, edited by Matthew J. Bruccoli (Columbia, SC: University of South Carolina Press, 1996), 159.

9 F. Scott Fitzgerald, *Dear Scott, Dearest Zelda: The Love Letters of F. Scott and Zelda Fitzgerald*, edited by Jackson R. Bryer and Cathy W. Barks (New York: Scribner, 2019), 24.

10 Andrew Turnbull, *F. Scott Fitzgerald* (New York: Grove Press, 2001), 91.

11 Ibid., 94.

12 F. Scott Fitzgerald, *The Great Gatsby (Cambridge Edition)* (Cambridge: Cambridge University Press, 1991), 118.

13 F. Scott Fitzgerald, *The Short Stories of F. Scott Fitzgerald*, edited by Matthew J. Bruccoli (New York: Scribner, 1994), 290.

14 David Brown, *Paradise Lost: A Life of F. Scott Fitzgerald* (Boston, MA: Harvard University Press, 2017), 74.

15 Andrew Turnbull, *F. Scott Fitzgerald* (New York: Grove Press, 2001), 96.

16 F. Scott Fitzgerald, *The Short Stories of F. Scott Fitzgerald*, edited by Matthew J. Bruccoli (New York: Scribner, 1994), 292.

17 Nancy Milford, *Zelda: A Biography* (New York: HarperCollins, 2013), 1813 (e-book location).

18 Andrew Turnbull, *F. Scott Fitzgerald* (New York: Grove Press, 2001), 204.

19 F. Scott Fitzgerald, *The Short Stories of F. Scott Fitzgerald*, edited by Matthew J. Bruccoli (New York: Scribner, 1995), 292.

20 Ibid., 293.

21 Ibid., 294.

22 Ibid., 295.

23 Ibid., 296.

24 Ibid.

25 F. Scott Fitzgerald, *The Great Gatsby (Cambridge Edition)* (Cambridge: Cambridge University Press, 1991), 119.

26 Ibid.

27 F. Scott Fitzgerald, *The Short Stories of F. Scott Fitzgerald*, edited by Matthew J. Bruccoli (New York: Scribner, 1994), 296.
28 James E. Miller, *The Fictional Technique of F. Scott Fitzgerald* (Dordrecht, Netherlands: Springer Netherlands, 2013), 83.
29 F. Scott Fitzgerald, *The Great Gatsby* (New York: Scribner, 1925), 133.

## CHAPTER 13

1 Matthew J. Bruccoli and Judith S. Baughman, eds., *Conversations with F. Scott Fitzgerald* (Jackson, MS: University Press of Mississippi, 2004), 77.
2 Zelda Fitzgerald, *Save Me the Waltz* (New York: Scribner, 2013).
3 Sally Cline, *Zelda Fitzgerald: Her Voice in Paradise* (New York: Arcade Publishing, 2003), 427.
4 Sarah Churchwell, *Careless People: Murder, Mayhem, and the Invention of* The Great Gatsby (New York: Penguin, 2015), 279.
5 Kendall Taylor, *The Gatsby Affair: Scott, Zelda, and the Betrayal that Shaped an American Classic* (Lanham, MD: Rowman & Littlefield, 2018), 58.
6 Sally Cline, *Zelda Fitzgerald: Her Voice in Paradise* (New York: Arcade Publishing, 2003), 148.
7 Kendall Taylor, *The Gatsby Affair: Scott, Zelda, and the Betrayal that Shaped an American Classic* (Lanham, MD: Rowman & Littlefield, 2018), 59.
8 Ibid.
9 Ibid.
10 F. Scott Fitzgerald, *The Great Gatsby* (New York: Scribner, 1925), 11.

## CHAPTER 14

1 F. Scott Fitzgerald, *The Great Gatsby* (New York: Scribner, 1925), 69.
2 F. Scott Fitzgerald, *The Best Early Short Stories of F. Scott Fitzgerald*, edited by Bryant Mangum (New York: Random House, 2007), 124
3 F. Scott Fitzgerald, *My Lost City: Personal Essays, 1920–1940 (The Cambridge Edition of the Works of F. Scott Fitzgerald)* (Cambridge: Cambridge University Press, 2005), 109.
4 F. Scott Fitzgerald, *F. Scott Fitzgerald on Authorship*, edited by Matthew J. Bruccoli (Columbia, SC: University of South Carolina Press, 1996), 33.
5 F. Scott Fitzgerald, *My Lost City: Personal Essays, 1920–1940 (The Cambridge Edition of the Works of F. Scott Fitzgerald)* (Cambridge: Cambridge University Press, 2005), 185.
6 F. Scott Fitzgerald, *The Letters of F. Scott Fitzgerald*, edited by Andrew Turnbull (New York: Dell, 1966), 155.
7 David Brown, *Paradise Lost: A Life of F. Scott Fitzgerald* (Boston, MA: Belknap Press Harvard, 2017), 94.
8 Scott Berg, *Max Perkins: Editor of Genius* (New York: Scribner, 2013), II.
9 F. Scott Fitzgerald, *The Short Stories of F. Scott Fitzgerald*, edited by Matthew J. Bruccoli (New York: Scribner, 1994), 315.
10 Ibid.

11 F. Scott Fitzgerald, *The Romantic Egoists: A Pictorial Autobiography from the Scrapbooks and Albums of F. Scott and Zelda Fitzgerald*, edited by Matthew J. Bruccoli, Scottie Fitzgerald Smith, and Joan P. Kerr (New York: Scribner, 2003), 53.

12 James L. West III, *The Making of* This Side of Paradise (University Park, PA: University of Pennsylvania Press, 2016), 94.

13 Ibid., 95.

14 Kendall Taylor, *Sometimes Madness Is Wisdom: Zelda and Scott Fitzgerald: A Marriage* (New York: Ballantine Books, 2003), 62.

15 F. Scott Fitzgerald, *Dear Scott, Dearest Zelda: The Love Letters of F. Scott and Zelda Fitzgerald*, edited by Jackson R. Bryer and Cathy W. Barks (New York: Scribner, 2019), 38.

16 F. Scott Fitzgerald, *The Correspondence of F. Scott Fitzgerald*, edited by Matthew J. Bruccoli and Margaret M. Duggan (Ann Arbor, MI: University of Michigan, 1980), 48.

17 F. Scott Fitzgerald, *The Short Stories of F. Scott Fitzgerald*, edited by Matthew J. Bruccoli (New York: Scribner, 1994), 297.

18 Ibid., 298.

19 Ibid., 300.

20 F. Scott Fitzgerald, *The Great Gatsby* (New York: Scribner, 1925), 116.

21 Kenneth S. Lynn, *Hemingway* (Cambridge, MA: Harvard University Press, 1995), 284.

22 Gail Stewart, *The Importance of F. Scott Fitzgerald* (New York: Lucent Books, 1999), 76.

23 F. Scott Fitzgerald, *The Romantic Egoists: A Pictorial Autobiography from the Scrapbooks and Albums of F. Scott and Zelda Fitzgerald*, edited by Matthew J. Bruccoli, Scottie Fitzgerald Smith, and Joan P. Kerr (New York: Scribner, 2003), 66.

24 Kendall Taylor, *The Gatsby Affair: Scott, Zelda, and the Betrayal that Shaped an American Classic* (Lanham, MD: Rowman & Littlefield, 2018), 27.

25 Ibid.

26 Michael Glenday, *F. Scott Fitzgerald* (New York: Macmillan, 2011), 25.

27 Ibid., 65.

28 F. Scott Fitzgerald, *The Great Gatsby* (New York: Scribner, 1925), 133.

## CHAPTER 15

1 John Gross, *The New Oxford Book of Literary Anecdotes* (Oxford: Oxford University Press, 2008), 274.

2 Sally Cline, *Zelda Fitzgerald: Her Voice in Paradise* (New York: Arcade Publishing, 2003), iii.

3 John Gross, *The New Oxford Book of Literary Anecdotes* (Oxford: Oxford University Press, 2008), 274.

4 Andrew Turnbull, *F. Scott Fitzgerald* (New York: Grove Press, 2001), 184.

5 Kendall Taylor, *The Gatsby Affair: Scott, Zelda, and the Betrayal that Shaped an American Classic* (Lanham, MD: Rowman & Littlefield, 2018), 62.

6 Ibid.

7 Ibid.

8 Linda Wagner-Martin, *Zelda Sayre Fitzgerald: An American Woman's Life* (New York: Palgrave Macmillan, 2004), 83.

9 Sally Cline, *Zelda Fitzgerald: Her Voice in Paradise* (New York: Arcade Publishing, 2003), iii.

10 Ibid., 149.

11 Ibid., iii.

12 Warren Sloat, *1929: Before the Crash* (New York: Cooper Square Press, 2004), 343.

13 Kendall Taylor, *The Gatsby Affair: Scott, Zelda, and the Betrayal that Shaped an American Classic* (Lanham, MD: Rowman & Littlefield, 2018), 65.

14 Linda Wagner-Martin, *Zelda Sayre Fitzgerald: An American Woman's Life* (New York: Palgrave Macmillan, 2004), 85.

15 Nancy Milford, *Zelda: A Biography* (New York: HarperCollins, 2013), 108.

16 Ibid.

## CHAPTER 16

1 Matthew J. Bruccoli and Judith S. Baughman, editors, *Conversations with F. Scott Fitzgerald* (Jackson, MS: University Press of Mississippi, 2004), 77.

2 Ruth Prigozy, editor, *The Cambridge Companion to F. Scott Fitzgerald* (Cambridge: Cambridge University Press, 2001), 49.

3 F. Scott Fitzgerald, *The Romantic Egoists: A Pictorial Autobiography from the Scrapbooks and Albums of F. Scott and Zelda Fitzgerald*, edited by Matthew J. Bruccoli, Scottie Fitzgerald Smith, and Joan P. Kerr (New York: Scribner, 2003), 59.

4 John F. Irwin, *F. Scott Fitzgerald's Fiction: "An Almost Theatrical Innocence"* (Baltimore, MD: John Hopkins University Press, 2014), 114.

5 F. Scott Fitzgerald, *The Beautiful and the Damned* (New York: Penguin, 1991), 184.

6 Sarah Churchwell, *Careless People: Murder, Mayhem, and the Invention of* The Great Gatsby (New York: Penguin, 2015), 10.

7 Andrew Turnbull, *F. Scott Fitzgerald* (New York: Grove Press, 2001), 109.

8 Sarah Churchwell, *Careless People: Murder, Mayhem, and the Invention of* The Great Gatsby (New York: Penguin Books, 2015), 120.

9 Ibid., 121.

10 Ibid.

11 Sally Cline, *Zelda Fitzgerald: Her Voice in Paradise* (New York: Arcade Publishing, 2003), ii.

12 Michael Glenday, *F. Scott Fitzgerald* (New York: Macmillan, 2011), 4.

13 Ibid.

14 William Shimer, *The American Scholar* 70 (2001): 138.

15 Sally Cline, *Zelda Fitzgerald: Her Voice in Paradise* (New York: Arcade Publishing, 2003), 11.

16 Sarah Churchwell, *Careless People: Murder, Mayhem, and the Invention of* The Great Gatsby (New York: Penguin Books, 2015), 87.

17 David Brown, *Paradise Lost: A Life of F. Scott Fitzgerald* (Boston, MA: Belknap Press Harvard, 2017), 126.

18 Matthew Bruccoli, editor, *Fitzgerald/Hemingway Annual 1978* (Detroit, MI: Gale Research Press, 1979), 47.

19 Andrew Turnbull, *F. Scott Fitzgerald* (New York: Grove Press, 2001), 112.

20 Sally Cline, *Zelda Fitzgerald: Her Voice in Paradise* (New York: Arcade Publishing, 2003), ii.

21 Sarah Churchwell, *Careless People: Murder, Mayhem, and the Invention of* The Great Gatsby (New York: Penguin, 2015), 355.

22 Ibid.

23 Nancy Milford, *Zelda: A Biography* (New York: HarperCollins, 2013), 1886 (e-book location).

24 Robert Sklar, *F. Scott Fitzgerald: The Last Laocoon* (Oxford: Oxford University Press, 1967), 111.

25 F. Scott Fitzgerald, *F. Scott Fitzgerald: The Princeton Years: Selected Writings, 1914–1920*, edited by Chip Deffaa (Fort Bragg, CA: Cypress House, 1996), 116.

26 Horst Kruse, *F. Scott Fitzgerald at Work: The Making of* The Great Gatsby (Tuscaloosa, AL: University of Alabama Press, 2014), 46.

27 Milton R Stern, *Golden Moment: The Novels of F. Scott Fitzgerald* (Champaign, IL: University of Illinois Press, 1970), 110.

28 Andrew Turnbull, *F. Scott Fitzgerald* (New York: Grove Press, 2001), 122.

29 Sarah Churchwell, *Careless People: Murder, Mayhem, and the Invention of* The Great Gatsby (New York: Penguin Books, 2015), 154.

30 F. Scott Fitzgerald, *The Great Gatsby* (New York: Scribner, 1925), 48.

# CHAPTER 17

1 Kendall Taylor, *The Gatsby Affair: Scott, Zelda, and the Betrayal that Shaped an American Classic* (Lanham, MD: Rowman & Littlefield, 2018), 68.

2 Ibid., 71.

3 Ibid., 66.

4 Ibid., 67.

5 Ibid.

6 Kendall Taylor, *The Gatsby Affair: Scott, Zelda, and the Betrayal that Shaped an American Classic* (Lanham, MD: Rowman & Littlefield, 2018), 70.

7 Ibid., 71.

8 F. Scott Fitzgerald, *My Lost City: Personal Essays, 1920–1940 (The Cambridge Edition of the Works of F. Scott Fitzgerald)* (Cambridge: Cambridge University Press, 2005), 56.

9 Kendall Taylor, *The Gatsby Affair: Scott, Zelda, and the Betrayal that Shaped an American Classic* (Lanham, MD: Rowman & Littlefield, 2018), 60.

10 Ibid., 62.

11 Stavola, Thomas J., *Scott Fitzgerald: Crisis in American Identity* (London: Vision Press Ltd. 1979), 55.

12 Sally Cline, *Zelda Fitzgerald: Her Voice in Paradise* (New York: Arcade Publishing, 2003), III.

13 Kendall Taylor, *The Gatsby Affair: Scott, Zelda, and the Betrayal that Shaped an American Classic* (Lanham, MD: Rowman & Littlefield, 2018), 63.

14 Zelda Fitzgerald, *Save Me the Waltz* (New York: Scribner, 2013).

15 Kendall Taylor, *The Gatsby Affair: Scott, Zelda, and the Betrayal that Shaped an American Classic* (Lanham, MD: Rowman & Littlefield, 2018), 64.

16 Nicolas Tredell, editor, *F. Scott Fitzgerald: The Great Gatsby: Essays, Articles, Reviews* (New York: Columbia University Press, 1999), 131.

17 Kendall Taylor, *The Gatsby Affair: Scott, Zelda, and the Betrayal that Shaped an American Classic* (Lanham, MD: Rowman & Littlefield, 2018), 71.

18 Ibid., 70.

19 Ibid.

20 F. Scott Fitzgerald, *The Great Gatsby* (New York: Scribner, 1925), 156.

## CHAPTER 18

1 Andrew Turnbull, *F. Scott Fitzgerald* (New York: Grove Press, 2001), 112.

2 F. Scott Fitzgerald, *This Side of Paradise followed by The Beautiful and Damned* (Morrisville, NC: Lulu Press, 2017), 337.

3 Sally Cline, *Zelda Fitzgerald: Her Voice in Paradise* (New York: Arcade Publishing, 2003), 11.

4 Ibid.

5 Andrew Turnbull, *F. Scott Fitzgerald* (New York: Grove Press, 2001), 112.

6 F. Scott Fitzgerald, *The Great Gatsby* (New York: Scribner, 1925), 4.

7 F. Scott Fitzgerald, *Cruise of the Rolling Junk* (London: Hesperus Press, 2011), 56.

8 Ibid., 57.

9 Ibid., 58.

10 Ibid.

11 Ibid., 59.

12 Ibid.

13 Ibid.

14 Ibid., 75.

15 Ibid.

16 Ibid., 85.

17 Eleanor Lanahan, Scottie the Daughter Of . . . : The Life of Frances Scott Fitzgerald Lanahan Smith (New York: HarperCollins, 1995), 410.

18 F. Scott Fitzgerald, *This Side of Paradise followed by The Beautiful and Damned* (Morrisville, NC: Lulu Press, 2017), 343.

19 Jackson Bryer, editor, *F. Scott Fitzgerald: Novels & Stories 1920–1922* (New York: Library of America, 2000), 540.

20 F. Scott Fitzgerald, *Cruise of the Rolling Junk* (London: Hesperus Press, 2011), 88.

21 *Atlantic Monthly* 187: 65.

22 Andrew Turnbull, *F. Scott Fitzgerald* (New York: Grove Press, 2001), 112.

23 Ibid., 113.

24 F. Scott Fitzgerald, *Ledger: 1919–1938. Digital Collections* (Columbia, SC: University of South Carolina), transcription, 15.

25 Matthew Bruccoli, editor. *Fitzgerald/Hemingway Annual 1978* (Detroit, MI: Gale Research Press, 1979), 46.

26 Milton R Stern, *Golden Moment: The Novels of F. Scott Fitzgerald* (Champaign, IL: University of Illinois Press, 1970), 110.

27 Linda Wagner-Martin, *Zelda Sayre Fitzgerald: An American Woman's Life* (New York: Palgrave Macmillan, 2004), 44.

28 Kendall Taylor, *The Gatsby Affair: Scott, Zelda, and the Betrayal that Shaped an American Classic* (Lanham, MD: Rowman & Littlefield, 2018), 41.

29 Sally Cline, *Zelda Fitzgerald: Her Voice in Paradise* (New York: Arcade Publishing, 2003), 107.

30 Ibid.

31 Ibid.

32 Ibid., 108.

33 Sally Cline, *Zelda Fitzgerald: Her Voice in Paradise* (New York: Arcade Publishing, 2003), 108.

34 F. Scott Fitzgerald, *The Romantic Egoists: A Pictorial Autobiography from the Scrapbooks and Albums of F. Scott and Zelda Fitzgerald*, edited by Matthew J. Bruccoli, Scottie Fitzgerald Smith, and Joan P. Kerr (Columbia, SC: University of South Carolina Press, 2003), 67.

35 Matthew Bruccoli, editor. *Fitzgerald/Hemingway Annual 1978* (Detroit, MI: Gale Research Press, 1979), 44.

36 Ibid., 48.

37 Ibid.

38 Ibid.

39 Ibid.

40 Ibid.

41 Sarah Mayfield, *Exiles from Paradise: Zelda and Scott Fitzgerald* (New York: Delacorte Press, 1971), 62.

42 Sarah Churchwell, *Careless People: Murder, Mayhem, and the Invention of* The Great Gatsby (New York: Penguin Books, 2015), 19.

43 Joshua Zeitz, *Flapper: A Madcap Story of Sex, Style, Celebrity, and the Women Who Made America Modern* (New York: Crown Publishing, 2009), 268.

44 Kendall Taylor, *The Gatsby Affair: Scott, Zelda, and the Betrayal that Shaped an American Classic* (Lanham, MD: Rowman & Littlefield, 2018), 31.

45 Ibid., 192.

46 F. Scott Fitzgerald, *The Great Gatsby* (New York: Scribner, 1925), 43.

## CHAPTER 19

1 F. Scott Fitzgerald, *My Lost City: Personal Essays, 1920–1940 (The Cambridge Edition of the Works of F. Scott Fitzgerald)* (Cambridge: Cambridge University Press, 2005), 41.

2 Ibid., 55.

3 Ibid.

4 Kendall Taylor, *The Gatsby Affair: Scott, Zelda, and the Betrayal that Shaped an American Classic* (Lanham, MD: Rowman & Littlefield, 2018), 216.

5 F. Scott Fitzgerald, *The Great Gatsby* (New York: Scribner, 1925), 142.

6 Gail Stewart, *The Importance of F. Scott Fitzgerald* (New York: Lucent Books, 1999), 79.

## CHAPTER 20

1 Howard Greenfield, *F. Scott Fitzgerald* (New York: Crown Publishers, 1974), 67.

2 Andrew Hook, *F. Scott Fitzgerald: A Literary Life* (New York: Palgrave Macmillan, 2002), 46.

3 Andrew Turnbull, *F. Scott Fitzgerald* (New York: Grove Press, 2014), 111.

4 Kendall Taylor, *The Gatsby Affair: Scott, Zelda, and the Betrayal that Shaped an American Classic* (Lanham, MD: Rowman & Littlefield, 2018), 43.

5 Sally Cline, *Zelda Fitzgerald: Her Voice in Paradise* (New York: Arcade Publishing, 2003), 111.

6 F. Scott Fitzgerald, *Ledger: 1919–1938. Digital Collections* (Columbia, SC: University of South Carolina), transcription, 65.

7 F. Scott Fitzgerald, *My Lost City: Personal Essays, 1920–1940 (The Cambridge Edition of the Works of F. Scott Fitzgerald)* (Cambridge: Cambridge University Press, 2005), 117.

8 F. Scott Fitzgerald, *The Short Stories of F. Scott Fitzgerald*, edited by Matthew J. Bruccoli (New York: Scribner, 1994), 56.

9 Sally Cline, *Zelda Fitzgerald: Her Voice in Paradise* (New York: Arcade Publishing, 2003), 115.

10 Ibid.

11 Allen Churchill, *The Literary Decade* (Hoboken, NJ: Prentice Hall, 1971), 119.

12 F. Scott Fitzgerald, *Ledger: 1919–1938*. Digital Collections (Columbia, SC: University of South Carolina), transcription.

13 Zelda Fitzgerald, *The Collected Writings of Zelda Fitzgerald* (New York: Scribner, 2013), 113.

14 Matthew J. Bruccoli and Judith S. Baughman, eds., *Conversations with F. Scott Fitzgerald* (Jackson, MS: University Press of Mississippi, 2004), 8.

15 Sally Cline, *Zelda Fitzgerald: Her Voice in Paradise* (New York: Arcade Publishing, 2003), 116.

16 Ibid.

17 F. Scott Fitzgerald, *The Great Gatsby* (New York: Scribner, 1925), 21.

18 Kendall Taylor, *The Gatsby Affair: Scott, Zelda, and the Betrayal that Shaped an American Classic* (Lanham, MD: Rowman & Littlefield, 2018), 44.

19 Howard Greenfield, *F. Scott Fitzgerald* (New York: Crown Publishers, 1974), 68.

20 F. Scott Fitzgerald, *F. Scott Fitzgerald: A Life in Letters*, edited by Matthew J. Bruccoli (New York: Scribner, 1995), 191.

21 F. Scott Fitzgerald, *The Short Stories of F. Scott Fitzgerald*, edited by Matthew J. Bruccoli (New York: Scribner, 1994), 64.

22 Ibid.

23 Sally Cline, *Zelda Fitzgerald: Her Voice in Paradise* (New York: Arcade Publishing, 2003), 117.

24 Ibid.

25 Kendall Taylor, *The Gatsby Affair: Scott, Zelda, and the Betrayal that Shaped an American Classic* (Lanham, MD: Rowman & Littlefield, 2018), 44.

26 F. Scott Fitzgerald, *The Short Stories of F. Scott Fitzgerald*, edited by Matthew J. Bruccoli (New York: Scribner, 1994), 67.

## CHAPTER 21

1 Kendall Taylor, *The Gatsby Affair: Scott, Zelda, and the Betrayal that Shaped an American Classic* (Lanham, MD: Rowman & Littlefield, 2018), 71.

2 Zelda Fitzgerald, *Save Me the Waltz* (New York: Scribner, 2013), 58.

3 Ibid.

4 F. Scott Fitzgerald, *The Great Gatsby* (New York: Scribner, 1925), 145.

5 Ibid.

6 Sally Cline, *Zelda Fitzgerald: Her Voice in Paradise* (New York: Arcade Publishing, 2003), 107.

7 F. Scott Fitzgerald, *The Best Early Short Stories of F. Scott Fitzgerald*, edited by Bryant Mangum (New York: Modern Library, 2005), 288.

8 Ibid., 286.

## CHAPTER 22

1 Sally Cline, *Zelda Fitzgerald: Her Voice in Paradise* (New York: Arcade Publishing, 2003), 126.

2 F. Scott Fitzgerald, *Ledger: 1919–1938. Digital Collections* (Columbia, SC: University of South Carolina), transcription.

3 Sally Cline, *Zelda Fitzgerald: Her Voice in Paradise* (New York: Arcade Publishing, 2003), 118.

4 Kendall Taylor, *The Gatsby Affair: Scott, Zelda, and the Betrayal that Shaped an American Classic* (Lanham, MD: Rowman & Littlefield, 2018), 44.

5 Joshua Zeitz, *Flapper: A Madcap Story of Sex, Style, Celebrity, and the Women Who Made America Modern* (New York: Crown Publishing, 2009), 63.

6 Michael Glenday, *F. Scott Fitzgerald* (New York: Macmillan, 2011), 37.

7 Sally Cline, *Zelda Fitzgerald: Her Voice in Paradise* (New York: Arcade Publishing, 2003), 121.

8 Ibid., 120.

9 F. Scott Fitzgerald, *Dear Scott, Dearest Zelda: The Love Letters of F. Scott and Zelda Fitzgerald*, edited by Jackson R. Bryer and Cathy W. Barks (New York: Scribner, 2019), 28.

10 F. Scott Fitzgerald, *The Romantic Egoists: A Pictorial Autobiography from the Scrapbooks and Albums of F. Scott and Zelda Fitzgerald*, edited by Matthew J. Bruccoli, Scottie Fitzgerald Smith, and Joan P. Kerr (Columbia, SC: University of South Carolina Press, 2003), 98.

11 Ibid., 84.

12 F. Scott Fitzgerald, *The Beautiful and the Damned* (New York: Scribner, 1922), 203.

13 F. Scott Fitzgerald, *The Best Early Short Stories of F. Scott Fitzgerald*, edited by Bryant Mangum (New York: Modern Library, 2005), 288.

14 Matthew J. Bruccoli and Judith S. Baughman, eds., *Conversations with F. Scott Fitzgerald* (Jackson, MS: University Press of Mississippi, 2004), 29.

15 Milton R Stern, *Golden Moment: The Novels of F. Scott Fitzgerald* (Champaign, IL: University of Illinois Press, 1970), 126.

16 F. Scott Fitzgerald, *The Correspondence of F. Scott Fitzgerald*, edited by Matthew J. Bruccoli and Margaret M. Duggan (Ann Arbor, MI: University of Michigan, 1980), 89.

17 James E. Miller, *The Fictional Technique of F. Scott Fitzgerald* (Dordrecht, Netherlands: Springer Netherlands, 2013), 59.

18 Rick Shefchik, *From Fields to Fairways: Classic Golf Clubs of Minnesota* (Minneapolis, MN: University of Minnesota Press, 2012), 104.

19 Nancy Milford, *Zelda: A Biography* (New York: Harper Books, 2013), 93.

20 Linda Wagner-Martin, *Zelda Sayre Fitzgerald: An American Woman's Life* (New York: Palgrave Macmillan, 2004), 75.

21 F. Scott Fitzgerald, *The Great Gatsby* (New York: Scribner, 1925), 6.

## CHAPTER 23

1 Zelda Fitzgerald, *Save Me the Waltz* (New York: Scribner, 2013), 78.

2 Kendall Taylor, *The Gatsby Affair: Scott, Zelda, and the Betrayal that Shaped an American Classic* (Lanham, MD: Rowman & Littlefield, 2018), 59.

3 Ibid., 71.

4 Ibid., 72.

5 Ibid., 73.

6 Ibid.

7 Ibid., 216.

8 Ibid., 70.

9 Ibid.

10 Ibid.

11 Ibid.

12 Ibid.

13 F. Scott Fitzgerald, *Beautiful and the Damned* (New York: Dover, 2019), 120.

14 Ibid., 75.

15 Ibid.

16 Ibid.

17 Sally Cline, *Zelda Fitzgerald: Her Voice in Paradise* (New York: Arcade Publishing, 2003), 154.

18 F. Scott Fitzgerald, *The Beautiful and the Damned* (New York: Scribner, 1922), 97

19 Kendall Taylor, *The Gatsby Affair: Scott, Zelda, and the Betrayal that Shaped an American Classic* (Lanham, MD: Rowman & Littlefield, 2018), 75.

20 F. Scott Fitzgerald, *The Great Gatsby* (New York: Scribner, 1925), 158.

## CHAPTER 24

1 Sarah Churchwell, *Careless People: Murder, Mayhem, and the Invention of* The Great Gatsby (New York: Penguin Books, 2015), 224.

2 F. Scott Fitzgerald, *Ledger: 1919–1938. Digital Collections* (Columbia, SC: University of South Carolina), transcription.

3 Sally Cline, *Zelda Fitzgerald: Her Voice in Paradise* (New York: Arcade Publishing, 2003), 135.

4 F. Scott Fitzgerald, *F. Scott Fitzgerald on Authorship*, edited by Matthew J. Bruccoli (Columbia, SC: University of South Carolina Press, 1996), 93.

5 Matthew Bruccoli, editor. *Fitzgerald/Hemingway Annual 1978* (Detroit, MI: Gale Research Press, 1979), 216.

6 F. Scott Fitzgerald, *The Short Stories of F. Scott Fitzgerald*, edited by Matthew J. Bruccoli (New York: Scribner, 1994), 259.

7 Ibid., 263.

8 F. Scott Fitzgerald, *The Great Gatsby* (New York: Scribner, 1925), 63.

9 F. Scott Fitzgerald, *The Best Early Short Stories of F. Scott Fitzgerald*, edited by Bryant Mangum (New York: Random, 2007), 266.

10 Ibid.

11 Ibid.

12 F. Scott Fitzgerald, *The Great Gatsby* (New York: Scribner, 1925), 99.

13 Jonathan Yardley, *Ring: A Biography of Ring Lardner* (Lanham, MD: Rowman & Littlefield, 2001), 58.

14 Kendall Taylor, *The Gatsby Affair: Scott, Zelda, and the Betrayal that Shaped an American Classic* (Lanham, MD: Rowman & Littlefield, 2018), 49.

15 Ibid.

16 Sally Cline, *Zelda Fitzgerald: Her Voice in Paradise* (New York: Arcade Publishing, 2003), 136.

17 Sarah Churchwell, *Careless People: Murder, Mayhem, and the Invention of* The Great Gatsby (New York: Penguin Books, 2015), 228.

18 Ibid., 228.

19 Kendall Taylor, *The Gatsby Affair: Scott, Zelda, and the Betrayal that Shaped an American Classic* (Lanham, MD: Rowman & Littlefield, 2018), 47.

20 Linda Wagner-Martin, *Zelda Sayre Fitzgerald: An American Woman's Life* (New York: Palgrave Macmillan, 2004), 75.

21 F. Scott Fitzgerald, *Ledger: 1919–1938. Digital Collections* (Columbia, SC: University of South Carolina), transcription.

22 F. Scott Fitzgerald, *The Great Gatsby* (New York: Scribner, 1925), 6.

23 Ibid., 8.

24 Ibid., 155.

25 Henry Piper, *F. Scott Fitzgerald: A Critical Portrait* (New York: Holt, Rinehart & Winston, 1966), 116.

26 F. Scott Fitzgerald, *The Great Gatsby* (New York: Scribner, 1925), 88.

27 Ibid., 85.

28 Ibid., 152.

29 Ibid., 118.
30 Ibid., 27.
31 F. Scott Fitzgerald, *Ledger: 1919–1938. Digital Collections* (Columbia, SC: University of South Carolina), transcription.
32 Ibid.
33 F. Scott Fitzgerald, *The Beautiful and the Damned* (New York: Random House, 2002), 191.
34 F. Scott Fitzgerald, *The Great Gatsby* (New York: Scribner, 1925), 82.
35 Kendall Taylor, *The Gatsby Affair: Scott, Zelda, and the Betrayal that Shaped an American Classic* (Lanham, MD: Rowman & Littlefield, 2018).
36 Ibid., 73.
37 Zelda Fitzgerald, *Save Me the Waltz* (New York: Scribner, 2013), p 89
38 F. Scott Fitzgerald, *The Great Gatsby* (New York: Scribner, 1925), 44.
39 Sarah Churchwell, *Careless People: Murder, Mayhem, and the Invention of* The Great Gatsby (New York: Penguin Books, 2015), 117.
40 F. Scott Fitzgerald, *My Lost City: Personal Essays, 1920–1940 (The Cambridge Edition of the Works of F. Scott Fitzgerald)* (Cambridge: Cambridge University Press, 2005), 112.
41 F. Scott Fitzgerald, *The Great Gatsby* (New York: Scribner, 1925), 26.
42 Alice Hall Petry, *Fitzgerald's Craft of Short Fiction: The Collected Stories, 1920–1935* (Tuscaloosa, AL: University Alabama Press, 1991), 191.
43 F. Scott Fitzgerald, *The Great Gatsby* (New York: Scribner, 1925), 3.

## CHAPTER 25

1 F. Scott Fitzgerald, *The Great Gatsby* (New York: Scribner, 1925), 137.
2 F. Scott Fitzgerald, *The Letters of F. Scott Fitzgerald*, edited by Andrew Turnbull (New York: Dell, 1966), 185.
3 Zelda Fitzgerald, *Save Me the Waltz* (New York: Scribner, 2013).
4 Ibid.
5 Sally Cline, *Zelda Fitzgerald: Her Voice in Paradise* (New York: Arcade Publishing, 2003), 148.
6 David Brown, *Paradise Lost: A Life of F. Scott Fitzgerald* (Boston, MA: Belknap Press Harvard, 2017), 184.
7 F. Scott Fitzgerald, *The Great Gatsby* (New York: Scribner, 1925), 156.
8 Kendall Taylor, *The Gatsby Affair: Scott, Zelda, and the Betrayal that Shaped an American Classic* (Lanham, MD: Rowman & Littlefield, 2018), 75.
9 Ibid., 157.
10 Ibid., 75.
11 Ibid., 159.
12 Kendall Taylor, *The Gatsby Affair: Scott, Zelda, and the Betrayal that Shaped an American Classic* (Lanham, MD: Rowman & Littlefield, 2018), 75.
13 F. Scott Fitzgerald, *The Great Gatsby* (New York: Scribner, 1925), 158.
14 Kendall Taylor, *The Gatsby Affair: Scott, Zelda, and the Betrayal that Shaped an American Classic* (Lanham, MD: Rowman & Littlefield, 2018), 75.

15 F. Scott Fitzgerald, *The Great Gatsby* (New York: Scribner, 1925), 160.
16 Kendall Taylor, *The Gatsby Affair: Scott, Zelda, and the Betrayal that Shaped an American Classic* (Lanham, MD: Rowman & Littlefield, 2018), 75.
17 Ibid., 76.
18 F. Scott Fitzgerald, *The Great Gatsby* (New York: Scribner, 1925), 176.
19 Ibid., 165.
20 Kendall Taylor, *The Gatsby Affair: Scott, Zelda, and the Betrayal that Shaped an American Classic* (Lanham, MD: Rowman & Littlefield, 2018), 76.
21 Sarah Churchwell, *Careless People: Murder, Mayhem, and the Invention of* The Great Gatsby (New York: Penguin Books, 2015), 280.
22 F. Scott Fitzgerald, *The Great Gatsby* (New York: Scribner, 1925), 162.
23 Ibid., 158.

## CHAPTER 26

1 F. Scott Fitzgerald, *The Great Gatsby* (New York: Scribner, 1925), 156.
2 Ibid., 144.
3 Ibid., 159.
4 F. Scott Fitzgerald, *Ledger: 1919–1938. Digital Collections* (Columbia, SC: University of South Carolina), transcription, 55.
5 Kirk Curnutt, *A Historical Guide to F. Scott Fitzgerald* (Oxford: Oxford University, 2004), 33.
6 F. Scott Fitzgerald, *The Great Gatsby* (New York: Scribner, 1925), 163.
7 Kendall Taylor, *The Gatsby Affair: Scott, Zelda, and the Betrayal that Shaped an American Classic* (Lanham, MD: Rowman & Littlefield, 2018), 76.
8 Ibid.
9 Ibid., 77.
10 Ibid., 77.
11 Ibid., 217.
12 Ibid., 77.
13 Ibid., 76.
14 Scott Donaldson, *Fool For Love: A Biography of F. Scott Fitzgerald* (Minneapolis, MN: University of Minnesota Press, 2012).
15 Sally Cline, *Zelda Fitzgerald: Her Voice in Paradise* (New York: Arcade Publishing, 2003), 151.
16 Kendall Taylor, *The Gatsby Affair: Scott, Zelda, and the Betrayal that Shaped an American Classic* (Lanham, MD: Rowman & Littlefield, 2018), 216.
17 Sally Cline, *Zelda Fitzgerald: Her Voice in Paradise* (New York: Arcade Publishing, 2003), 150.
18 F. Scott Fitzgerald, *The Great Gatsby* (New York: Scribner, 1925), 92.
19 Kendall Taylor, *The Gatsby Affair: Scott, Zelda, and the Betrayal that Shaped an American Classic* (Lanham, MD: Rowman & Littlefield, 2018), 78.
20 Ibid.
21 Ibid.
22 Ibid., 79.

23 Ibid., 77.
24 F. Scott Fitzgerald, *The Great Gatsby* (New York: Scribner, 1925), 216.

## CHAPTER 27
1 Andrew Turnbull, *F. Scott Fitzgerald* (New York: Grove Press, 2001), 93.
2 F. Scott Fitzgerald, *The Great Gatsby* (New York: Scribner, 1925), 164.
3 Matthew J. Bruccoli, *F. Scott Fitzgerald's* The Great Gatsby: *A Documentary Volume* (New York: Gale Group, 2000), 54.
4 Ibid., 135.
5 Maxwell E. Perkins, *The Sons of Maxwell Perkins: Letters of F. Scott Fitzgerald, Ernest Hemingway, Thomas Wolfe, and Their Editor*, edited by Matthew J. Bruccoli and Judith S. Baughman (Columbia, SC: University of South Carolina Press, 2004), 27.
6 F. Scott Fitzgerald, *The Great Gatsby* (Oxford: Oxford University Press, 1991), 209.
7 Scott Berg, *Max Perkins: Editor of Genius* (New York: Scribner, 2013), v.
8 F. Scott Fitzgerald, *The Romantic Egoists: A Pictorial Autobiography from the Scrapbooks and Albums of F. Scott and Zelda Fitzgerald*, edited by Matthew J. Bruccoli, Scottie Fitzgerald Smith, and Joan P. Kerr (New York: Scribner, 2003), 118.
9 Ibid.
10 Ibid.
11 Kendall Taylor, *The Gatsby Affair: Scott, Zelda, and the Betrayal that Shaped an American Classic* (Lanham, MD: Rowman & Littlefield, 2018), 79.
12 F. Scott Fitzgerald, *The Great Gatsby* (New York: Scribner, 1925), 165.
13 Judith Mackrell, *Flappers: Six Women of a Dangerous Generation* (New York: Farrar, Straus & Giroux, 2014), 314.
14 F. Scott Fitzgerald, *The Great Gatsby* (New York: Scribner, 1925), 165.
15 Judith Mackrell, *Flappers: Six Women of a Dangerous Generation* (New York: Farrar, Straus & Giroux, 2014), 314.
16 Sarah Churchwell, *Careless People: Murder, Mayhem, and the Invention of* The Great Gatsby (New York: Penguin Books, 2015), 24.
17 F. Scott Fitzgerald, *Ledger: 1919–1938. Digital Collections* (Columbia, SC: University of South Carolina), transcription.
18 F. Scott Fitzgerald, *The Great Gatsby* (New York: Scribner, 1925), 175.
19 Ibid., 194.
20 F. Scott Fitzgerald, *Ledger: 1919–1938. Digital Collections* (Columbia, SC: University of South Carolina), transcription.
21 Ibid.
22 John Cohassey, *Hemingway and Pound: A Most Unlikely Friendship* (Jefferson, NC: McFarland & Company, 2014), 73.
23 F. Scott Fitzgerald, *Ledger: 1919–1938. Digital Collections* (Columbia, SC: University of South Carolina), transcription.

## CHAPTER 28

1 John F. Irwin, *F. Scott Fitzgerald's Fiction: "An Almost Theatrical Innocence"* (Baltimore, MD: John Hopkins University Press, 2014), 24.

2 F. Scott Fitzgerald, *Tender is the Night* (New York: Scribner, 2003), 256.

3 Kendall Taylor, *The Gatsby Affair: Scott, Zelda, and the Betrayal that Shaped an American Classic* (Lanham, MD: Rowman & Littlefield, 2018), 77.

4 F. Scott Fitzgerald, *Dear Scott, Dear Max: The Fitzgerald-Perkins Correspondence*, edited by John Kuehl and Jackson Bryer (New York: Cassell, 1973), 80.

5 F. Scott Fitzgerald, *The Letters of F. Scott Fitzgerald*, edited by Andrew Turnbull (New York: Dell, 1966), 188.

6 Arthur T. Vanderbilt II, *The Making of a Bestseller: From Author to Reader* (New York: McFarland Publishing, 1999), 96.

7 Kendall Taylor, *The Gatsby Affair: Scott, Zelda, and the Betrayal that Shaped an American Classic* (Lanham, MD: Rowman & Littlefield, 2018), 83.

8 Sarah Mayfield, *Exiles from Paradise: Zelda and Scott Fitzgerald* (New York: Delacorte Press, 1971), 100.

9 F. Scott Fitzgerald, *The Romantic Egoists: A Pictorial Autobiography from the Scrapbooks and Albums of F. Scott and Zelda Fitzgerald*, edited by Matthew J. Bruccoli, Scottie Fitzgerald Smith, and Joan P. Kerr (New York: Scribner, 2003), 120.

10 Sally Cline, *Zelda Fitzgerald: Her Voice in Paradise* (New York: Arcade Publishing, 2003), 158.

11 F. Scott Fitzgerald, *The High Cost of Macaroni*, Interim IV 1954, 6.

12 John F. Irwin, *F. Scott Fitzgerald's Fiction: "An Almost Theatrical Innocence"* (Baltimore, MD: John Hopkins University Press, 2014), 123.

13 Ibid., 24.

14 F. Scott Fitzgerald, *The High Cost of Macaroni*, Interim IV 1954, 6.

15 Scott Berg, *Max Perkins: Editor of Genius* (New York: Scribner, 2013), v.

16 Ibid.

17 Ibid.

18 Kendall Taylor, *Sometimes Madness Is Wisdom: Zelda and Scott Fitzgerald: A Marriage* (New York: Ballantine Books, 2003), 142.

19 Sally Cline, *Zelda Fitzgerald: Her Voice in Paradise* (New York: Arcade Publishing, 2003), 159.

20 Ibid.

21 F. Scott Fitzgerald, *Ledger: 1919–1938. Digital Collections* (Columbia, SC: University of South Carolina), transcription.

22 Sally Cline, *Zelda Fitzgerald: Her Voice in Paradise* (New York: Arcade Publishing, 2003), 159.

## CHAPTER 29

1 Koula Svokos Hartnett, *Zelda Fitzgerald and the Failure of the American Dream for Women* (Ann Arbor, MI: University of Michigan Press, 2008), 70.

2 F. Scott Fitzgerald, *The Romantic Egoists: A Pictorial Autobiography from the Scrapbooks and Albums of F. Scott and Zelda Fitzgerald*, edited by Matthew J. Bruccoli, Scottie Fitzgerald Smith, and Joan P. Kerr (New York: Scribner, 2003), 121.

3 F. Scott Fitzgerald, *The Letters of F. Scott Fitzgerald*, edited by Andrew Turnbull (New York: Dell, 1966), 192.

4 F. Scott Fitzgerald, *The Great Gatsby* (New York: Scribner, 1925), 142.

5 Matthew Bruccoli, editor, *New Essays on The Great Gatsby* (Cambridge: Cambridge University Press, 1985), 94.

6 F. Scott Fitzgerald, *The Great Gatsby* (New York: Scribner, 1925), 163.

7 Andrew Hook, *F. Scott Fitzgerald: A Literary Life* (New York: Palgrave Macmillan, 2002), 68.

8 Mary Jo Tate, *Critical Companion to F. Scott Fitzgerald: A Literary Reference to His Life and Work* (New York: Facts on File, 2007), 336.

9 Andrew Hook, *F. Scott Fitzgerald: A Literary Life* (New York: Palgrave Macmillan, 2002), 64.

10 Kendall Taylor, *The Gatsby Affair: Scott, Zelda, and the Betrayal that Shaped an American Classic* (Lanham, MD: Rowman & Littlefield, 2018), 218.

11 Ibid.

12 Sally Cline, *Zelda Fitzgerald: Her Voice in Paradise* (New York: Arcade Publishing, 2003), 161.

13 Ibid.

14 F. Scott Fitzgerald, *Dear Scott, Dear Max: The Fitzgerald-Perkins Correspondence*, edited by John Kuehl and Jackson Bryer (New York: Cassell, 1973), 272.

15 Andrew Hook, *F. Scott Fitzgerald: A Literary Life* (New York: Palgrave Macmillan, 2002), 68.

16 Ibid., 69.

17 Matthew J. Bruccoli, F. *Scott Fitzgerald's* The Great Gatsby: *A Documentary Volume* (New York: Gale Group, 2000), 156.

18 Matthew Bruccoli, *Some Sort of Epic Grandeur: The Life of F. Scott Fitzgerald* (Columbia, SC: University of South Carolina Press, 2002), 255.

## CHAPTER 30

1 David Brown, *Paradise Lost: A Life of F. Scott Fitzgerald* (Boston, MA: Belknap Press Harvard, 2017), 187.

2 Jeannette Weber and Joan Grumman, *Woman as Writer* (New York: Houghton Mifflin, 1978), 217.

3 Andrew Turnbull, *F. Scott Fitzgerald* (New York: Grove Press, 2001), 149.

4 Andrew Hook, *F. Scott Fitzgerald: A Literary Life* (New York: Palgrave Macmillan, 2002), 70.

5 F. Scott Fitzgerald, *F. Scott Fitzgerald on Authorship*, edited by Matthew J. Bruccoli (Columbia, SC: University of South Carolina Press, 1996), 17.

6 F. Scott Fitzgerald, *The Letters of F. Scott Fitzgerald*, edited by Andrew Turnbull (New York: Dell, 1966), 199.

7 Rodger L. Tarr, *As Ever Yours: The Letters of Max Perkins and Elizabeth Lemmon* (University Park, PA: Penn State University Press, 2003), 36.

8 Ibid.

9 Scott Donaldson, *Critical Essays on F. Scott Fitzgerald's* The Great Gatsby (Boston, MA: G. K. Hall & Company, 1984), 264.

10 F. Scott Fitzgerald, *The Romantic Egoists: A Pictorial Autobiography from the Scrapbooks and Albums of F. Scott and Zelda Fitzgerald*, edited by Matthew J. Bruccoli, Scottie Fitzgerald Smith, and Joan P. Kerr (New York: Scribner, 2003), 124.

11 Ibid., 135.

12 F. Scott Fitzgerald, *The Crack-Up*, edited by Edmund Wilson (New York: New Directions Books, 2009), 309.

13 Peter Conn, *Literature in America: An Illustrated History* (Cambridge: Cambridge University Press, 1989), 389.

14 F. Scott Fitzgerald, *The Romantic Egoists: A Pictorial Autobiography from the Scrapbooks and Albums of F. Scott and Zelda Fitzgerald*, edited by Matthew J. Bruccoli, Scottie Fitzgerald Smith, and Joan P. Kerr (New York: Scribner, 2003), 125.

15 Ibid.

16 Catherine Morley, *Modern American Literature* (Edinburgh Critical Guides to Literature) (Edinburgh: Edinburgh University Press, 2012), 171.

17 Sally Cline, *Zelda Fitzgerald: Her Voice in Paradise* (New York: Arcade Publishing, 2003), 165.

18 F. Scott Fitzgerald, *Dear Scott, Dear Max: The Fitzgerald-Perkins Correspondence*, edited by John Kuehl and Jackson Bryer (New York: Cassell, 1973), 103.

19 Ibid.

20 Michael Nelson, *Americans and the Making of the Riviera* (New York: McFarland, 2007), 87.

## CHAPTER 31

1 Michael Glenday, *F. Scott Fitzgerald* (New York: Macmillan, 2011), 1.

2 Sarah Churchwell, *Careless People: Murder, Mayhem, and the Invention of* The Great Gatsby (New York: Penguin, 2015), 334.

3 F. Scott Fitzgerald, *The Crack-Up*, edited by Edmund Wilson (New York: New Directions Books, 2009), 332.

4 F. Scott Fitzgerald, *The Great Gatsby* (New York: Scribner, 1925), 211.

5 Maureen Corrigan, *So We Read On: How* The Great Gatsby *Came to Be and Why It Endures* (New York: Little, Brown and Company, 2014), 230.

6 Ibid.

7 Maureen Corrigan, *So We Read On: How The Great Gatsby Came to Be and Why It Endures* (New York: Little, Brown and Company, 2014), 74.

8 Ibid., 230.

## CHAPTER 32

1 F. Scott Fitzgerald, *The Great Gatsby* (New York: Scribner, 1925), 217.

2 F. Scott Fitzgerald, *This Side of Paradise* (New York: Fall Rivers Press, 2012), 205.

3 F. Scott Fitzgerald, *The Great Gatsby* (New York: Scribner, 1925), 194.

4 Kendall Taylor, *The Gatsby Affair: Scott, Zelda, and the Betrayal that Shaped an American Classic* (Lanham, MD: Rowman & Littlefield, 2018), 79.

5 Ibid., 80.

6 David Brown, *Paradise Lost: A Life of F. Scott Fitzgerald* (Boston, MA: Belknap Press Harvard, 2017), 184.

7 F. Scott Fitzgerald, *The Great Gatsby* (New York: Scribner, 1925), 217.

8 Ibid., 218.

9 Ibid.

## EPILOGUE

1 Kendall Taylor, *The Gatsby Affair: Scott, Zelda, and the Betrayal that Shaped an American Classic* (Lanham, MD: Rowman & Littlefield, 2018).

2 Richard Buller, *A Beautiful Fairy Tale: The Life of Actress Lois Moran* (Pompton Plains, NJ: Limelight Editions, 2005), 136.

3 Andrew Turnbull, *F. Scott Fitzgerald* (New York: Grove Press, 2001), 192.

4 Sally Cline, *Zelda Fitzgerald: Her Voice in Paradise* (New York: Arcade Publishing, 2003), 5.

5 Maxwell E. Perkins, *The Sons of Maxwell Perkins: Letters of F. Scott Fitzgerald, Ernest Hemingway, Thomas Wolfe, and Their Editor,* edited by Matthew J. Bruccoli and Judith S. Baughman (Columbia, SC: University of South Carolina Press, 2004), 177.

6 Ibid.

7 F. Scott Fitzgerald, *Ledger: 1919–1938. Digital Collections* (Columbia, SC: University of South Carolina), transcription, 52.

8 Matthew Bruccoli, *The Composition of* Tender is The Night (Pittsburgh, PA: University of Pittsburgh Press, 1963), 9.

9 Andrew Hook, *F. Scott Fitzgerald: A Literary Life* (New York: Palgrave Macmillan, 2002), 119.

10 Andrew Turnbull, *F. Scott Fitzgerald* (New York: Grove Press, 2001), 279.

11 F. Scott Fitzgerald, *F. Scott Fitzgerald: A Life in Letters,* edited by Matthew J. Bruccoli (New York: Scribner, 1995), 334.

12 Mary Jo Tate, *Critical Companion to F. Scott Fitzgerald: A Literary Reference to His Life And Work* (New York: Facts on File, 2007), 321.

13 Sarah Churchwell, *Careless People: Murder, Mayhem, and the Invention of* The Great Gatsby (New York: Penguin, 2015), 333.

14 Ibid.

15 Bryant Mangum, editor, *F. Scott Fitzgerald in Context* (Cambridge: Cambridge University Press, 2013), 33.

16 "Zelda Fitzgerald Dies," *New York Herald Tribune,* May 10, 1948.

17 F. Scott Fitzgerald, *The Great Gatsby* (New York: Scribner, 1925), 218.

# BIBLIOGRAPHY

Aldrich Jr., Nelson W. *Old Money: The Mythology of America's Upper Class*. New York: Vintage Books, 1989.

Anon. "What a Flapper Novelist Thinks of His Wife." *Louisville Courier-Journal*. September 30, 1923, 112. In *Conversations with F. Scott Fitzgerald*. Edited by Matthew Bruccoli and Judith Baughman. Jackson, MS: University Press of Mississippi, 2004.

Berg, Scott. *Max Perkins: Editor of Genius*. New York: New American Library, 2016.

Breyer, Jackson, ed. *F. Scott Fitzgerald: New Perspectives*. Athens, GA: University of Georgia Press, 2012.

Brown, David S. *Paradise Lost: A Life of F. Scott Fitzgerald*. Boston, MA: Harvard, 2017.

Bruccoli, Matthew. *The Composition of* Tender is The Night. Pittsburgh, PA: University of Pittsburgh Press, 1963.

Bruccoli, Matthew, ed. *Fitzgerald/Hemingway Annual 1978*. Detroit, MI: Gale Research Press, 1979.

Bruccoli, Matthew, ed. *New Essays on The Great Gatsby*. Cambridge: Cambridge University Press, 1985.

Bruccoli, Matthew J. *F. Scott Fitzgerald's* The Great Gatsby*: A Documentary Volume*. New York: Gale Group, 2000.

Bruccoli, Matthew. *Some Sort of Epic Grandeur: The Life of F. Scott Fitzgerald*. Columbia, SC: University of South Carolina Press, 2002.

Bruccoli, Matthew J., and Judith S. Baughman, eds. *Conversations with F. Scott Fitzgerald*. Jackson, MS: University Press of Mississippi, 2004.

Bryer, Jackson. *The Short Stories of F. Scott Fitzgerald: New Approaches in Criticism*. Madison, WI: University of Wisconsin, 1982.

Bryer, Jackson, editor. *F. Scott Fitzgerald: Novels & Stories 1920–1922*. New York: Library of America, 2000.

Buller, Richard. *A Beautiful Fairy Tale: The Life of Actress Lois Moran*. Pompton Plains, NJ: Limelight Editions, 2005).

Curnutt, Kirk. *A Historical Guide to F. Scott Fitzgerald*. Oxford: Oxford University, 2004.

Canterbery, E. Ray, and Thomas Birch. *F. Scott Fitzgerald: Under the Influence*. New York: Paragon House, 2006.

Churchill, Allen. *The Literary Decade*. Hoboken, NJ: Prentice Hall, 1971.

Churchwell, Sarah. *Careless People: Murder, Mayhem, and the Invention of the Great Gatsby*. New York: Penguin, 2015.

Claridge, Henry. "F. Scott Fitzgerald." University of Michigan 1 (2011): 377.

Clayton, John Jacob. *Gestures of Healing: Anxiety and the Modern Novel*. Amherst, MA: University of Massachusetts Press, 2008.

Cline, Sally. *Zelda Fitzgerald: Her Voice in Paradise*. New York: Arcade Publishing, 2003.

Cohassey, John. *Hemingway and Pound: A Most Unlikely Friendship*. Jefferson, NC: McFarland & Company, 2014.

Conn, Peter. *Literature in America: An Illustrated History*. Cambridge: Cambridge University Press, 1989.

Corrigan, Maureen. *So We Read On: How* The Great Gatsby *Came to Be and Why It Endures*. New York: Little, Brown and Company, 2014.

Donaldson, Scott. *Critical Essays on F. Scott Fitzgerald's* The Great Gatsby. Boston, MA: G. K. Hall & Company, 1984.

Donaldson, Scott. *Fool For Love: A Biography of F. Scott Fitzgerald*. Minneapolis, MN: University of Minnesota Press, 2012.

Dyer, Geoff. *Working the Room: Essays and Reviews, 1999–2010*. Edinburgh, UK: Canongate Books, 2011.

Fahey, William. *F. Scott Fitzgerald and the American Dream*. Ann Arbor, MI: University of Michigan Press, 1973.

Fitzgerald, F. Scott. *Afternoon of an Author*. New York: Scribner, 1958.

Fitzgerald, F. Scott. *The Apprentice Fiction of F. Scott Fitzgerald: 1909–1917*. New Brunswick, NJ: Rutgers University Press, 1965.

Fitzgerald, F. Scott. *The Basil and Josephine Stories*. New York: Simon and Schuster, 1973.

Fitzgerald, F. Scott. *The Basil and Josephine Stories*. New York: Scribner, 1997.

Fitzgerald, F. Scott. *The Beautiful and the Damned*. New York: Scribner, 1922.

Fitzgerald, F. Scott. *The Beautiful and the Damned*. New York: Penguin, 1991.

Fitzgerald, F. Scott. *The Beautiful and the Damned*. New York: Random House, 2002.

Fitzgerald, F. Scott. *The Beautiful and the Damned*. New York: Dover, 2019.

Fitzgerald, F. Scott. *The Best Early Short Stories of F. Scott Fitzgerald*. Edited by Bryant Mangum. New York: Modern Library, 2005.

Fitzgerald, F. Scott. *The Best Early Short Stories of F. Scott Fitzgerald*. Edited by Bryant Mangum. New York: Random, 2007.

Fitzgerald, F. Scott. *The Bodley Head*. Columbus, OH: Ohio University Press, 1958.

Fitzgerald, F. Scott. *The Complete Short Stories, Essays, and a Play, Volume 1*. New York: Scribner, 2004.

Fitzgerald, F. Scott. *The Complete Short Stories, Essays, and a Play, Volume 2*. New York: Scribner, 2004.

Fitzgerald, F. Scott. *The Correspondence of F. Scott Fitzgerald*. Edited by Matthew J. Bruccoli and Margaret M. Duggan. Ann Arbor, MI: University of Michigan, 1980.

Fitzgerald, F. Scott. *The Crack-Up*. Edited by Edmund Wilson. New York: New Directions Books, 2009.

Fitzgerald, F. Scott. *Cruise of the Rolling Junk*. London: Hesperus Press, 2011.

Fitzgerald, F. Scott. *Dear Scott, Dear Max: The Fitzgerald-Perkins Correspondence*. Edited by John Kuehl and Jackson Bryer. New York: Cassell, 1973.

Fitzgerald, F. Scott. *Dear Scott, Dearest Zelda: The Love Letters of F. Scott and Zelda Fitzgerald.* Edited by Jackson R. Bryer and Cathy W. Barks. Berkeley, CA: University of California Press, 1971.

Fitzgerald, F. Scott. *Dear Scott, Dearest Zelda: The Love Letters of F. Scott and Zelda Fitzgerald.* Edited by Jackson R. Bryer and Cathy W. Barks. New York: Scribner, 2019.

Fitzgerald, F. Scott. *F. Scott Fitzgerald on Authorship.* Edited by Matthew J. Bruccoli. Columbia, SC: University of South Carolina Press, 1996.

Fitzgerald, F. Scott. *F. Scott Fitzgerald: A Life in Letters.* Edited by Matthew J. Bruccoli. New York: Scribner, 1995.

Fitzgerald, F. Scott. *F. Scott Fitzgerald: A Life in Letters.* Edited by Matthew J. Bruccoli. New York: Touchstone, 2010.

Fitzgerald, F. Scott. *F. Scott Fitzgerald: The Princeton Years: Selected Writings, 1914–1920.* Edited by Chip Deffaa. Fort Bragg, CA: Cypress House, 1996.

Fitzgerald, F. Scott. *The Great Gatsby.* New York: Grosset & Dunlap, 1925.

Fitzgerald, F. Scott. *The Great Gatsby.* New York: Scribner, 1925.

Fitzgerald, F. Scott. *The Great Gatsby (Cambridge Edition).* Cambridge: Cambridge University Press, 1991.

Fitzgerald, F. Scott. *The Great Gatsby.* Oxford: Oxford University Press, 1991.

Fitzgerald, F. Scott. *The Great Gatsby.* New York: Wordsworth, 2001.

Fitzgerald, F. Scott. "How To Live on $36,000 a Year." *Saturday Evening Post.* April 5, 1924.

Fitzgerald, F. Scott. *The Indispensable F. Scott Fitzgerald.* London: Book Society, 1949.

Fitzgerald, F. Scott. *Ledger: 1919–1938.* Digital Collections. Columbia, SC: University of South Carolina, transcription.

Fitzgerald, F. Scott. *The Letters of F. Scott Fitzgerald.* Edited by Andrew Turnbull. New York: Dell, 1966.

Fitzgerald, F. Scott. *The Letters of F. Scott Fitzgerald.* Edited by Andrew Turnbull. University Park, PA: Pennsylvania State University Press, 1966.

Fitzgerald, F. Scott. *My Lost City: Personal Essays 1920–1940.* New York: Scribner, 2005.

Fitzgerald, F. Scott. *My Lost City: Personal Essays, 1920–1940 (The Cambridge Edition of the Works of F. Scott Fitzgerald).* Cambridge: Cambridge University Press, 2005.

Fitzgerald, F. Scott. *The Romantic Egoists: A Pictorial Autobiography from the Scrapbooks and Albums of F. Scott and Zelda Fitzgerald.* Edited by Matthew J. Bruccoli, Scottie Fitzgerald Smith, and Joan P. Kerr. New York: Scribner, 1974.

Fitzgerald, F. Scott. *The Romantic Egoists: A Pictorial Autobiography from the Scrapbooks and Albums of F. Scott and Zelda Fitzgerald.* Edited by Matthew J. Bruccoli, Scottie Fitzgerald Smith, and Joan P. Kerr. New York: Scribner, 2003.

Fitzgerald, F. Scott. *The Romantic Egoists: A Pictorial Autobiography from the Scrapbooks and Albums of F. Scott and Zelda Fitzgerald.* Edited by Matthew J. Bruccoli, Scottie Fitzgerald Smith, and Joan P. Kerr. Columbia, SC: University of South Carolina Press, 2003.

Fitzgerald, F. Scott. *The Short Stories of F. Scott Fitzgerald.* Edited by Matthew J. Bruccoli. New York: Scribner, 1989.

Fitzgerald, F. Scott. *The Short Stories of F. Scott Fitzgerald*. Edited by Matthew J. Bruccoli. New York: Scribner, 1994. Fitzgerald, F. Scott. *The Short Stories of F. Scott Fitzgerald*. Edited by Matthew J. Bruccoli. New York: Scribner, 1995.

Fitzgerald, F. Scott. *The Stories of F. Scott Fitzgerald: A Selection of Twenty-Eight Stories with an Introduction by Malcolm Cowley*. New York: Scribner, 1951

Fitzgerald, F. Scott. *The Stories of F. Scott Fitzgerald: A Selection of Twenty-Eight Stories with an Introduction by Malcolm Cowley*. University Park, PA: Pennsylvania State University Press, 1954.

Fitzgerald, F. Scott. *The Stories of F. Scott Fitzgerald: A Selection of Twenty-Eight Stories with an Introduction by Malcolm Cowley*. New York: Scribner, 1954.

Fitzgerald, F. Scott. *Tender is the Night*. New York: Wordsworth, 1994.Fitzgerald, F. Scott. *Tender is the Night*. New York: Scribner, 2003.

Fitzgerald, F. Scott. *This Side of Paradise*. New York: Scribner, 1920.Fitzgerald, F. Scott. *This Side of Paradise followed by The Beautiful and Damned*. Morrisville, NC: Lulu Press, 2017.

Fitzgerald, F. Scott. *The Vegetable*. Columbia, SC: University of South Carolina Press, 2003.

Fitzgerald, Zelda. *Save Me the Waltz*. New York: Scribner, 2013.

Fitzgerald, Zelda. *The Collected Writings of Zelda Fitzgerald*. New York: Scribner, 2013.

Glenday, Michael. *F. Scott Fitzgerald*. New York: Palgrave Macmillan, 2011.

Graham, Sheila. *Beloved Infidel*. New York: Bantam, 1959.

Greenfield, Howard. *F. Scott Fitzgerald*. New York: Crown Publishers, 1974.

Gross, John. *The New Oxford Book of Literary Anecdotes*. Oxford: Oxford University Press, 2008.

Guérard, Albert Joseph. *The Personal Voice: A Contemporary Prose Reader*. Philadelphia: J. B. Lippincott & Co., 1964.

Haight, Mary Ellen. *Walks in Gertrude Stein's Paris*. Salt Lake City, UT: Peregrine Smith Books, 1988.

Hartnett, Koula Svokos. *Zelda Fitzgerald and the Failure of the American Dream for Women*. New York: Peter Lang Publishing, Inc., 1991.

Hartnett, Koula Svokos. *Zelda Fitzgerald and the Failure of the American Dream for Women*. Ann Arbor, MI: University of Michigan Press, 2008.

Hook, Andrew. *F. Scott Fitzgerald: A Literary Life*. New York: Palgrave Macmillan, 2002.

Irwin, John. *F. Scott Fitzgerald's Fiction: "An Almost Theatrical Innocence."* Baltimore, MD: John Hopkins University Press, 2014.

Kruse, Horst. *F. Scott Fitzgerald at Work: The Making of The Great Gatsby*. Tuscaloosa, AL: University of Alabama Press, 2014.

Lanahan, Eleanor. *Scottie the Daughter Of . . . : The Life of Frances Scott Fitzgerald Lanahan Smith*. New York: HarperCollins, 1995.

*London Magazine* 32, nos. 7–12.

Lopate, Phillip. *Writing New York: A Literary Anthology*. New York: Washington Square Press, 2000.

Lynn, Kenneth S. *Hemingway*. Cambridge, MA: Harvard University Press, 1995.

Mackrell, Judith. *Flappers: Six Women of a Dangerous Generation*. New York: Farrar, Straus & Giroux, 2014.

Mangum, Bryant, ed. *F. Scott Fitzgerald in Context*. Cambridge: Cambridge University Press, 2013.

Mayfield, Sarah. *Exiles from Paradise: Zelda and Scott Fitzgerald*. New York: Delacorte Press, 1971.

Milford, Nancy. *Zelda: A Biography*. New York: Harper Books, 2013.

Miller, James E. *The Fictional Technique of F. Scott Fitzgerald*. Dordrecht, Netherlands: Springer Netherlands, 2013.

Morley, Catherine. *Modern American Literature (Edinburgh Critical Guides to Literature)*. Edinburgh: Edinburgh University Press, 2012.

Morris, Richard. *Perspectives in Abnormal Behavior*. New York: Elsevier Science, 2013.

Nelson, Michael. *Americans and the Making of the Riviera*. New York: McFarland, 2007.

Perkins, Maxwell E. *The Sons of Maxwell Perkins: Letters of F. Scott Fitzgerald, Ernest Hemingway, Thomas Wolfe, and Their Editor*. Edited by Matthew J. Bruccoli and Judith S. Baughman. Columbia, SC: University of South Carolina Press, 2004.

Petry, Alice Hall. *Fitzgerald's Craft of Short Fiction: The Collected Stories, 1920–1935*. Tuscaloosa, AL: University Alabama Press, 1991.

Piper, Henry. *F. Scott Fitzgerald: A Critical Portrait*. New York: Holt, Rinehart & Winston, 1966.

Potts, Stephen. *The Price of Paradise: The Magazine Career of F. Scott Fitzgerald*. Berkley, CA: University of California, 1993.

Prigozy, Ruth, ed. *The Cambridge Companion to F. Scott Fitzgerald*. Cambridge: Cambridge University Press, 2001.

*Princeton University Chronicle* 50–51 (1988).

Shimer, William. *The American Scholar* 70 (2001): 138.

Shefchik, Rick. *From Fields to Fairways: Classic Golf Clubs of Minnesota*. Minneapolis, MN: University of Minnesota Press, 2012.

Sklar, Robert. *F. Scott Fitzgerald: The Last Laocoon*. Oxford: Oxford University Press, 1967.

Sloat, Warren. *1929: Before the Crash*. New York: Cooper Square Press, 2004.

Stavola, Thomas J. *Scott Fitzgerald: Crisis in American Identity*. London: Vision Press Ltd. 1979.

Stern, Milton R. *Golden Moment: The Novels of F. Scott Fitzgerald*. Champaign, IL: University of Illinois Press, 1970.

Stewart, Gail. The Importance of F. Scott Fitzgerald. New York: Lucent Books, 1999.

Tanner, Barney. *Joycean Elements in F. Scott Fitzgerald's* The Great Gatsby: *Aspects of Burlesque, Shadowing, Dichotomies and Doubling*. (Ann Arbor, MI: University of Michigan Press, 2008).

Tarr, Rodger L. *As Ever Yours: The Letters of Max Perkins and Elizabeth Lemmon*. University Park, PA: Penn State University Press, 2003.

Tate, Mary Jo. *Critical Companion to F. Scott Fitzgerald: A Literary Reference to His Life And Work*. New York: Facts on File, 2007.

Taylor, Kendall. *Sometimes Madness Is Wisdom: Zelda and Scott Fitzgerald: A Marriage.*
New York: Ballantine Books, 2003.

Taylor, Kendall. *The Gatsby Affair: Scott, Zelda, and the Betrayal that Shaped an American Classic.* Lanham, MD: Rowman & Littlefield, 2018.

*The Atlantic Monthly* 187.

Tredell, Nicolas, ed. *F. Scott Fitzgerald: The Great Gatsby: Essays, Articles, Reviews.* New York: Columbia University Press, 1999.

Turnbull, Andrew. *F. Scott Fitzgerald.* New York: Grove Press, 2001.

Unknown author. "Zelda and The Fitzgerald Legend." *Denver Quarterly* 6: 66.

Vanderbilt II, Arthur T. *The Making of a Bestseller: From Author to Reader.* New York: McFarland Publishing, 1999.

Wagner-Martin, Linda. *Zelda Sayre Fitzgerald: An American Woman's Life.* New York: Palgrave Macmillan, 2004.

Weber, Jeannette and Joan Grumman. *Woman as Writer.* New York: Houghton Mifflin, 1978.

West III, James L. *The Making of* This Side of Paradise. University Page, PA: University of Pennsylvania Press, 1983 (2016 edition).

Yardley, Jonathan. *Ring: A Biography of Ring Lardner.* Lanham, MD: Rowman & Littlefield, 2001.

Zeitz, Joshua. *Flapper: A Madcap Story of Sex, Style, Celebrity, and the Women Who Made America Modern.* New York: Crown Publishing, 2009.

# Index